UNMASKED

UNMASKED

My Life
Solving America's
Cold Cases

PAUL HOLES

WITH ROBIN GABY FISHER

CELADON
BOOKS

NEW YORK

UNMASKED. Copyright © 2022 by Paul Holes. All rights reserved. Printed in the United States of America. For information, address Celadon Books, a Division of Macmillan Publishers, 120 Broadway, New York, NY 10271.

www.celadonbooks.com

Library of Congress Cataloging-in-Publication Data

Names: Holes, Paul, author. | Fisher, Robin Gaby, author.
Title: Unmasked : my life solving America's cold cases / Paul Holes with Robin Gaby Fisher.
Description: First U.S. edition. | New York : Celadon Books, 2022.
Identifiers: LCCN 2021059410 | ISBN 9781250622792 (hardcover) | ISBN 9781250859648 (signed) | ISBN 9781250865960 (Canadian) | ISBN 9781250622822 (ebook)
Subjects: LCSH: Cold cases (Criminal investigation)—United States. | Criminal investigation—United States.
Classification: LCC HV8073 .H599 2022 | DDC 363.250973—dc23/eng/20220131
LC record available at https://lccn.loc.gov/2021059410

Our books may be purchased in bulk for promotional, educational, or business use. Please contact your local bookseller or the Macmillan Corporate and Premium Sales Department at 1-800-221-7945, extension 5442, or by email at MacmillanSpecialMarkets@macmillan.com.

First U.S. Edition: 2022
First Canadian Edition: 2022

10 9 8 7 6 5 4 3 2 1

For the victims and their families. And for the law enforcement professionals who have sacrificed so much in the name of justice.

Contents

Prologue   1

1. The End of the Road   6

2. Last Act   14

3. Beginnings   25

4. Lab Rat   34

5. Moving Up   40

6. EAR   44

7. CSI   51

8. Abernathy   57

9. Connecting the Dots   73

10. The End of a Marriage   87

11. Antioch   96

12. Conaty and Giacomelli   102

13. Bodfish   114

14. Serial Killers   128

15. EAR Breakthrough   148

16. Postmortem   156

17. Changes   165

18. Small Victories   174

19. Hurricane Holes   180

20. EAR Revisited   188

21. Him   197

22. Roller Coaster   206

23. Michelle   218

24. The Murders   236

25. Joseph James DeAngelo   241

26. Operation Golden State Killer   255

27. Is It Him?   260

28. A Sense of Purpose   263

Acknowledgments   271

UNMASKED

Prologue

I order another bourbon, neat. This is the drink that will flip the switch. I don't even know how I got here, to this place, to this *point*. One minute I was having dinner and drinks with friends, discussing my latest cold case—the rape and strangulation of a young girl after her high school Valentine's Day dance—and the next thing I knew we were all piling into an Uber going, where? I had no idea. Something is happening to me lately. I'm drinking too much. My sheets are soaking wet when I wake up from nightmares of decaying corpses. I've looked at a woman, and rather than seeing the beauty of the female body, I've dissected it, layer by layer, as if she were on the autopsy table. I have visualized dead women during intimate moments, and I shut down.

People always ask how I am able to detach from the horrors of my work. Part of it is an innate capacity to compartmentalize, to put my thoughts in mental boxes and only access what I need, when I need it. The rest is experience and exposure, and I've had plenty of both. The macabre becomes familiar enough that I can dissociate from even the grisliest details of the job. I file the gore in my brain under "science." I suppose anyone can become desensitized to anything if they see enough of it, even dead bodies, and I've been looking at them since college when I spent hours studying death scenes in pathology books.

But real life, of course, isn't black and white like those textbook photographs. On one hand, I am fortunate to have been born with a good, analytical brain. On the other, my heart bleeds when it comes to innocent victims. Crime solving for me is more complex than the challenge of the hunt, or the process of piecing together a scientific puzzle. The thought of good people suffering drives me, for better or worse, to the point of obsession. But I have always taken pride in the fact that I can keep my feelings locked up to get the job done.

It's only been recently that it feels like all that suppressed darkness is beginning to seep out. The dam is breaking. I'm cratering fast. So I end up in a place like this, a bar on Hollywood Boulevard called Jumbo's Clown Room. Yes, it's a real place. Entirely red inside. Red walls. Red floors. Red bar. Red lights. I order another drink and swig it, trying to forget about the latest case I can't shake.

CARLA WALKER WAS A TEENAGER WHO was full of life and spunk, four feet, eleven inches tall and twinkly eyed, with everything to look forward to. Looking at her picture, I would have guessed she was nine years old, not seventeen. In the crime scene photos, she's lying in a desolate cow culvert. Her head is tilted toward me, and her eyes are closed. She has a tiny little nose. Her face contradicts the savagery she endured during the final moments of her life. She looks serene, like a sleeping doll. She's dressed in the same blue dotted swiss party dress with lace trim that she was wearing when she kissed her parents good night and headed out to a Valentine's

Day dance at her high school, only the dress has been torn off and placed carefully over her bare chest, leaving her naked lower body exposed. Two blue barrettes are still intact, but her pretty strawberry blond hair is muddy and disheveled. Thin swipes of blue on her eyelids, which, I was told, she worked so hard to match to her dress, are smudged. Semen stains, dark purple bruises around her neck, and contusions on her arms and legs tell the story of a horrific death. I study her injuries and envision what happened. Young Carla was violently beaten, raped, and strangled, and her body dragged through a barbed wire fence and ditched like garbage in the middle of nowhere, where it lay for nearly four days.

Carla's murder is no closer to being solved today than it was when it happened in 1974. But forty-five years later, the collateral damage continues to fester. Her younger brother, Jim Walker, was twelve when Carla was killed. Now he's a little older than me. When I decided to look into the cold case recently, I met with Jim in a suburb of Fort Worth. He told me that after he got his driver's license, he used to steal away to the crime scene and spend nights in the culvert, waiting for Carla's killer to show. There was something about Jim that broke my heart, and I found myself choking back tears talking to him. All this time later, the pain on his face is as fresh as if he'd lost his sister yesterday. It was even worse for his parents, he said. They suffered in silence until their deaths. His mother kept a portrait of Carla and touched it every morning when she woke up. It was her way of saying "Good morning" to her daughter. That's the thing about these tragedies. There are so many victims. So many shattered lives. So many families torn apart. Healing is subjective, but the scars never fade, and the pain is always a breath away. It's a terrible way to spend your life.

I promised Carla's family that I'd do everything in my power to solve her murder. The only peace they'll get will come with knowing who killed her, and why. And when I went to the culvert, I promised Carla, too, that I'd work tirelessly to catch her killer. I'm committed to Carla. People think I'm strictly analytical, and that's how I present myself, but there is something very spiritual for me when I'm at a crime scene. I don't just put myself in the minds of the offender and the victim, which is critical to my crime-solving process. I make my peace with the victim.

As it was in Carla's case.

The culvert where Carla was dumped is a lonely place, a tunnel under a road in rural Texas about ten miles from her high school and the Walker family home.

Standing in the exact spot where her body had lain, it was as if I was witnessing the whole terrible attack. I see the offender looming over Carla, his eyes wild with excitement as he pulls off her underwear and yanks her bra up over her breasts, ripping her party dress in his frenzy. I see her, eyes dilated, heart pounding, breath fast and shallow. Adrenaline courses through her body, and she is in full-on fear mode—fight, flight, or freeze—but she's too small and not nearly powerful enough to compete with her attacker. He grimaces as he places his hands around her neck. He starts to squeeze, and she grabs at his hands and arms, trying to loosen his hold. She gouges her own skin with her fingernails as she claws futilely at his death grip. Carla has to know this is the end of her life. There's nothing she can do to save herself. Her body is shutting down. The outer jugular veins begin to collapse, but her heart continues to push blood to her brain through the carotids, causing an intense buildup of pressure in her head. Research suggests that at this point, victims lose consciousness within six to ten seconds, but offenders have reported it can take much longer— several minutes—for a victim to die.

I can almost feel Carla as she takes her last breath. I kneel down and touch the spot where her head would have been. "I'm here for you," I say. "I don't know if I can solve your case, but I promise I will do my best."

It is a promise I know I can keep.

. . .

JUMBO'S CLOWN ROOM IS GETTING LOUDER. The music blasts, and women in skimpy bikinis climb onstage. Some swing on poles placed around the bar. Others slither seductively on the floor, scooping up dollar bills that people, both men and women, are tossing onstage. I'm sure the patrons mean well, but it feels wrong, disrespectful. I can't even watch the dancers. I wonder what kind of lives they have. I worry that they're putting themselves in danger. I know I shouldn't be here—*what am I doing?*—and I signal to the others that I'm headed out. As I pull on my jacket, a dancer catches my eye. She's maybe twenty, younger than my oldest daughter, and she's making her way toward me, slinking across the stage. I look at her and envision her broken body sprawled in a muddy ditch. I shudder, then pull out a hundred-dollar bill, wrap it in a single, and hold it out to her. "Please," I say, as she bends down to take the cash. "Be careful." The sultry expression drops from her face, and I see the little girl.

Getting up from the bar, I walk unsteadily out onto Hollywood Boulevard and hail a cab.

"Where are you going, buddy?" the driver asks as I slide into the back seat.

Crazy, I think, wiping away tears. *I'm going fucking crazy.*

1

The End of the Road

MARCH 2018

My ex-wife used to say my job was my mistress, and I chose my mistress over everyone. Those charged conversations from long ago rang in my ears as I stood in my office, boxing up the last of my belongings. *Paul, you've lost your way. . . . We need you. . . . Even when you're here you're not really here.* Lori was right about a lot of things. I wasn't there for my family—not then and not now—not in the way they wanted me to be. Not in the way I wanted to be. My work was never a job. It was a calling, my purpose, as vital to me as air and water. For nearly thirty years, I'd chosen my cases over everything. There was always a crime scene to attend, always a predator to chase down. I was happiest when I was digging into a cold case. The challenge of trying to figure out what no one else could was irresistible to me. Now I was facing down the end of a career that had consumed my entire adult life. The time had passed in a blink.

Looking around my office, at the empty shelves, at the bare desktop,

I took a deep breath. What was I feeling? Was it uncertainty? Had I been kidding myself when I decided that retirement wouldn't be so bad? That I'd finally have the time to take guitar lessons and pedal my mountain bike on rocky trails? That I'd find some other way to matter?

My office was in the county complex in the industrial city of Martinez in California's East Bay. The sun was just peeking up over the horizon when I climbed the stairs to the third floor of the criminal justice building. I had come in especially early to gather my things before my colleagues got there. I've always been quietly sentimental, especially about endings and the past. Just the other day, I drove to the first house I owned and parked on the street. The house had been brand-new when I bought it with my first wife in 1992. It was where I'd learned how to take care of a home. I built the deck on the back and planted the saplings that now tower over the rooftop. Sitting in my car, I could almost imagine myself back there, in the family room, playing with my firstborn, Renee, still too young to sit, all toothless grin and happy babble as I prop up pillows to keep her upright. Now she has a little girl of her own.

I've never been a crier, but lately the tears were coming without warning, as they did that day, driving away from my old house. Yet another reason to gather my things and get out of town before my colleagues began arriving. Was I becoming a sentimental old man at the age of fifty? My dad got softer in his older years, slowly changing from the detached career-military guy who raised me to the playful grandfather who made funny faces with my kids. I was determined to be stoic on my last day, but this place had been my life. I wasn't sure I would have chosen to leave the job if California's pension system hadn't made it financially irresponsible to stay. I'd spent nearly every day since I was twenty-two years old living and working under the dome of Contra Costa County government. The most relevant chapters of my story had played out here. Every career move. All of the ups and downs of my first marriage. The births of my first two kids.

Meeting my second wife, Sherrie. The births of our son and daughter. Dozens of homicides solved. Others still unresolved, but never forgotten, and now headed home with me on a hard drive.

Tomorrow, my office, historically reserved for whoever was chosen to oversee homicides for the district attorney, would be turned over to my successor. They would fill the empty shelves where my collection of books on forensics, sexual homicide, and serial killers had grown. They would sit behind the computer monitor I'd kept at an angle so passersby couldn't see the gruesome crime scene images that were so often on the screen. Maybe they'd make the time to wipe the years' worth of grunge off the window overlooking the Sacramento River delta. The shimmer of the water was hypnotic, but I'd barely noticed. I was always too immersed in my work.

MY JURISDICTION STRETCHED OVER HUNDREDS OF square miles of San Francisco's Bay Area. With a population of more than a million people, we had our share of crime. Four of our cities were on the FBI's list of California's one hundred most dangerous places. I'd worked on hundreds of homicides, but I'd spent the last few years almost exclusively mining cold case files. Every casualty comes with collateral damage, those who are left to pick up their lives in the agonizing aftermath of murder, and nothing motivated me more than the idea of a killer having the freedom to live a normal life after he'd destroyed so many others.

There was never a shortage of bad guys in our slice of the world, and for whatever reason, some of the most sensational crimes in contemporary history occurred in Contra Costa County. In 2003, the bodies of Laci Peterson and her unborn son, Conner, washed up a day apart on our shores, four months after Laci's husband, Scott, dumped her body into the freezing cold waters of the San Francisco Bay. I met mother and child in the morgue, and even with all of my experience with evil, it's something

I'll never forget. Conner was less than a month from birth when Laci was murdered. What kind of monster kills his eight-and-a-half-months-pregnant wife and goes about his life knowing she and his unborn son are anchored to the cold ocean floor with concrete blocks?

Six years after that, Jaycee Dugard, who'd been famously grabbed at her school bus stop in South Lake Tahoe in 1991, when she was eleven, was discovered 170 miles from home, living in a run of tents and lean-tos in the fenced backyard of her captors, sex offender Phillip Garrido and his wife, Nancy, in our jurisdiction. By then, she was twenty-nine and had given birth to two of Garrido's children. For eighteen years, she had been right under our noses. My detective buddy John Conaty was at the scene with me shortly after Jaycee and her young children were rescued. "How the hell did we miss this?" he asked, looking around at the cruel, filthy environment that she'd been forced to live in for eighteen years. I just shook my head. I had no words.

I'd caught so many strange cases over the years. Even when a case wasn't mine, if I thought I could contribute, whether with my forensics expertise or investigative doggedness, I always found a way to insert myself. I always thought maybe I could see something that the last guy had missed. It wasn't arrogance; it was just that I wouldn't take no for an answer. Both my wife and my ex-wife have ribbed me about being overly confident in myself and my abilities. I'd say that's about half-right. I can put on a good show when I have to, but I'm an introvert by nature and painfully reluctant when it comes to personal interactions. Put me face-to-face with a neighbor at a cocktail party, and my insides are twisting in knots. Sitting with a group at a restaurant, I shrink from the conversation. I am Paul the wallflower. And speaking in front of large groups? When I first started, it was paralyzing. It's better now that I've had so much experience talking about the high-profile cases I've been involved with, but it still requires a shot of bourbon before I take the stage.

I've always been most at home when I'm working on a case, my head buried in a file. I know I'm good at what I do and that I have a fighting chance at solving even the toughest cases that may have stumped others. Before I ever earned the right, I never trusted anyone else's hunches about a homicide. "I'll think about it," I'd say skeptically. My instincts were made for this kind of work, and I almost always follow them. It takes a lot of time before I feel comfortable accepting someone else's impulses and ideas. I can see how that could be construed as egotistical, and there were times, especially when I was starting out, that I wasn't always popular. The veteran criminalists never hesitated to let the rookie know when they thought I was overstepping my boundaries. I regularly heard, "That's not your job," then shrugged as I dove headfirst into an investigation.

So many cases, now reduced to files on a hard drive the size of a pack of cigarettes. It was kind of funny when I thought about it: the last vestiges of my long and distinguished law enforcement career fit into a single fifteen-by-twelve-by-ten-inch storage box. I tossed in the drive, along with the book on serial predators my parents gave me as a birthday gift twenty-five years ago when I first started, the bowl, fork, and spoon I'd kept for all the meals I ate at my desk, and the tan leather coaster with the logo of a lab equipment company that came in handy for those long days that ended with a nightcap at my desk.

Ripping a piece of packing tape from the roll, I prepared to seal the box when something caught my eye. The morning sun reflected off the glass of a picture frame, drawing my attention to the small cluster of family photographs on the credenza beside me. I almost forgot them. They were happy memories, long ago faded into the background of administrative paperwork and homicide case files. My favorite had been taken a decade earlier, when my youngest son, Ben, was a toddler. It was shot from behind as the two of us walked away from a formal ceremony called Inspection of the Troops, me in my Sheriff's Office dress uniform—Smokey

Bear hat, green jacket, and khaki trousers—my boy in a striped polo shirt and shorts, his little arms swinging as he tried to keep up with me.

I paused to study the image, now faded with time. My oldest son, Nathan, from my first marriage, had recently turned twenty-three, and I'd only just begun trying to get to know him. I was learning how hard it was to foster a relationship, even when it was with my own kid, during weekly phone calls that began and ended with stories about video games. How could I expect my son to talk to me about things that mattered when I wasn't around for the things that mattered? Nathan once told me that he didn't even remember me living in the house, he was so young when I left. Ben was from my second marriage, but I feared I had been just as emotionally absent with him and his sister, Juliette, as I had with my first set of kids. Did I have regrets about not being there when they were learning to ride a bike or awakening from a bad dream? On my last day on the job, I was just beginning to realize the consequences of putting my career before everything else. I knew more now with the children I had with Sherrie than I did when Nathan and Renee were growing up, the kind of knowledge that comes with age and maturity, but in many ways, I had not changed at all. My second wife, Sherrie, had some of the same grievances that my first wife, Lori, did twenty-five years ago. Like Lori, Sherrie interprets my reticence as not caring, which couldn't be further from the truth. She's told me she never knows what I'm thinking. Even when I'm home, I'm not "present," she says. I'm always "in my head." Why can't I take some time in the evenings to join her and our kids playing board games? I've tried, but within minutes of sitting down, I'm squirming in my seat. I move the little pawn around or toss the dice a few times, and my mind drifts to one of my cases. I can't even hide it. My lips move with my thoughts. "You're gone again," Sherrie said the other night when she and the kids were talking at dinner, and I was pretending to hear. "You're not listening," she said. "You look like a crazy old man with your lips moving."

The only way I knew how to bond with my younger kids was the same as it was with my older two. Take them outside and throw the ball. It's like "Cat's in the Cradle," that Harry Chapin song, the one where the father is too busy making something of himself to pay much attention to his son. The kid grows up, and the father retires. He calls his son to say he'd like to see him. The son responds, *I'd love to, Dad, if I can find the time.* . . . And the father realizes, *He'd grown up just like me. My boy was just like me.* I choke up whenever I hear it. It hits too close to home. My older daughter Renee and I were hiking recently, and she asked me questions about my marriage to her mom, Lori. "Why did you leave us?" she asked. "Where did it go wrong?" I tried to reassure her, telling her that I would always love her mother, but we'd simply been too young to get married and eventually grew apart. It had nothing to do with her or Nathan, I said. I hoped they knew how much I loved them. "But Dad," she said, "you were just never there." Tucking the framed photo of Ben and me into the side of the box, I took a last look around my office. Fighting back all of the feelings that come with endings, I flipped off the light and closed the door behind me. *This has been my whole life*, I thought. With my box under my arm and a lump in my throat, I walked down the hallway to the stairs and onto Ward Street in the government district of the city. It was now part of my past. The Sheriff's Office, where I'd gotten my start. The forensics library, where I'd slept on the floor after working a long night at a crime scene or reading case files into the wee hours of the morning. The courthouse, where I'd testified dozens of times. The jail, where I'd lifted weights during lunch hours. The district attorney's office, where I'd spent the last few years. Every law enforcement position I'd ever held was in Martinez, the birthplace of hometown hero Joe DiMaggio. The city was a little rough around the edges, and night and day from where I lived in rural Vacaville, but it was home.

Tomorrow I'd fill out a bunch of paperwork and be debriefed by the

FBI about what I could and couldn't do as a private citizen. *You cannot divulge "top secret" information. You must protect your sources.* I'd turn in my gun and my county car and officially retire from law enforcement. After that, there'd be time to think about the next chapter in my life. But there was still one thing I had to do before I closed this one.

2

Last Act

It was nearly noon when I finally snaked my way out of Martinez, my cardboard box of a career on the seat beside me. A veil of smog obscured the brilliant afternoon sun, just as it had in the spring of 1990 when I arrived after college for my first job interview with the county. I remembered thinking then that I was descending into hell after I drove across the mile-long truss bridge, over the sparkling swells of the Sacramento River Delta, and dropped down into the industrial landscape of oil refineries and spewing smokestacks that led to downtown. The landscape hadn't changed much since then.

Winding my way through the Shell oil refinery and up over the Benicia bridge, I headed north toward Interstate 80. On a good day, traffic should have been light in the early afternoon, but there is never a good day on California's clogged freeways. It was a long stretch of highway to get to where I was going. The news stations were prattling about Stormy Daniels and some study about Americans getting fatter. I'm not much of a talk radio kind of guy, and it's safe to say I'm probably what you'd call apolitical, so the playlist on the iPod was my go-to. Music was my therapy. Which kind depended on my mood. When I was pissed, after an argument at home, or a run-in at work, I punched in heavy metal. Last week, it was Metallica, after a witness in a cold homicide blew up at me for bothering her at home. I don't do conflict well. Being raised in a military family, and strict Catholics to boot, you learn to keep your emotions locked up (which is not so good for maintaining relationships, I've learned), so I usually released mine in the gym or, in the case of that angry witness, by blasting headbanger music and drumming my fingers on the steering wheel. On most days, though, I turned to '70s ballads to relax—you know, Billy Joel, Jim Croce, Neil Diamond kind of stuff. I didn't like feeling out of control, and my whole life was about to veer into a direction of unknowns. My house in Vacaville was on the market, and as soon as it sold, I was moving the family out of state to Colorado to enjoy the mountains. At the time, I wasn't sure what I would do for work. I'd thought about starting my own business, Paul Holes Investigates, and because I'd had a fair amount of media exposure from my high-profile cases, I'd been approached by TV producers about possibly consulting on one of those crime channels or news magazine shows. But nothing was certain, and the uncertainty made me nervous. I'd suffered from panic attacks since I was a kid, and the music helped to keep my anxiety in check.

As my car inched along the highway, my left leg jackhammered into the car floor, and I tried to unwind to Elton John's "Tiny Dancer," my all-time favorite song. *Pretty eyed, pirate smile . . . you must have seen her dancing in the sand. And now she's in me . . . tiny dancer in my hand.* Cranking up the volume, I sang along, which I often did when I was alone and restless. After four or five replays, and a break in the traffic, my anxiety began to subside.

As often happened in quieter moments, my mind took a turn to the inevitable, the Golden State Killer, the masked madman who had raped and murdered his way up and down our state and had never been caught.

Cold cases were my passion; this one was an obsession. It had stumped every investigator who had looked into it—and believe me, there had been hundreds. Over forty years, more resources had been pumped into trying to solve it than any other case in California history, and it had still remained in the cold case files. I had revisited it repeatedly since the day in 1994 when, as a curious neophyte criminalist, I stumbled across it in an abandoned file cabinet in our forensics library. There were other cases I hadn't been able to crack, and I took each one personally, but that one weighed on me more than the others—mostly because the offender had outwitted some of the best criminal investigative minds in the business. And I believed he was still out there. For ten years in the '70s and '80s, he'd cut a wide swath of psychological terror across the state with his meticulously planned attacks, breaking into homes in the middle of the night, tying up his terrified victims, viciously attacking both men and women, sometimes in front of their young kids, before eventually graduating to murder—his preferred method bludgeoning. The guy was a psychological sadist. "If you cause any problems, I'll chop up the kids. I'll bring you one of their ears," he told one of his victims before taking the man's wife into another room and repeatedly raping her. Before the attacks suddenly stopped in 1986, he'd killed at least a dozen people and savagely raped more than fifty women.

Some people thought he was dead, but not me. I imagined him living an obscure life in some middle-class neighborhood in suburbia, a place where no one would ever suspect that a serial killer was among them. He was either one lucky SOB or as cunning as a fox, and probably both. Most people believe the myth that serial killers can't stop, but they can, and they do. Some have long, dormant stretches, and some stop altogether, usually either because they come close to being caught or they substitute something else for their killing habit—a hobby, a new marriage, starting a family. Sometimes they just get too old. Crazy, right? It had always nagged at me that he was probably somewhere out there living his life—driving his car, taking trips to the hardware store, enjoying family dinners—after wrecking so many other lives. And probably laughing at all of us who weren't able to catch him.

Before he was called the Golden State Killer in a 2013 magazine story by Michelle McNamara, who would become my friend and confidant, he was known as the Original Nightstalker, and before that, the East Area Rapist, or EAR. The titles evolved as his crimes progressed, from fetish burglaries, to vicious sexual assaults in the middle of the night, to murder. He adopted the nicknames, using them to taunt us. I remember getting hold of an old recording of a call made during the EAR phase to Sacramento Dispatch from a man claiming to be him.

"This is the East Area Rapist, you dumb fuckers," he says. "I'm gonna fuck again tonight. Careful."

The voice was menacing. Cocky. Taunting. Brash.

I played it over and over.

"You know about this recording?" I asked Ken Clark, a detective with Sacramento Sheriff's Homicide who'd put plenty of time in on the investigation.

"Oh yeah," he said.

"You think it's him?"

"Likely."

"It really pisses me off," I said.

"Absolutely," Clark said. "That's what he wanted."

Two years after that call in 1977, his cat and mouse game escalated to murder.

OVER THE TWO-PLUS DECADES THAT I'D been looking into the cold case, I'd witnessed the suffering of the mothers and fathers and sons and daughters and brothers and sisters of some of his victims. I'd studied the crime scene photos of his sadistic handiwork. I'd spent hours listening to the stories of men and women who, either by the grace of God or their own raw courage, had somehow survived his merciless attacks, only to be haunted still decades later by what he had done to them.

Not long ago, my cell phone rang. The woman on the other end sounded like she was about to fall apart. "I know he's coming back to get me, so I'm moving to Mexico," she said. It had been thirty years since he broke into her home in the middle of the night and terrorized her family. Those were the people that drove me relentlessly to pursue the case, and they had been counting on me to get him. "We know you'll be the one to do it." I'd heard that so many times.

I hated disappointing her. I hated disappointing all of them. After working the case in between other open cases, usually on my own time, I'd spent the last few years of my career making the Golden State Killer, or GSK, my top priority. I'd scrutinized thousands of police documents and witness statements and interviewed everyone I could who was associated with the case and still alive. The obsession ran over into weekends, while I was mowing the lawn or playing with the kids. Even on Christmas Day, when the rest of the family opened presents, it was GSK who was on my mind. And through the long nights, when I searched computer databases for clues and drew geographic profiles of his crimes to try to determine his home base, the case played like an endless movie in my head. His victims haunted my dreams.

People like Mary, one of the youngest. She was headed into eighth grade when he forced his way into her life in 1979. Barely thirteen, she still had a playhouse in the back of her home, and her hobby was hopscotch. That summer, he broke into her Walnut Creek home at four in the morning through the sliding glass doors. As her father and sister slept in adjoining rooms, he slipped into hers. She awoke to him straddling her, a knife to her throat. "I hope you're good," he said in a menacing whisper. She didn't know what he meant. He pulled off her covers and savagely raped her in her pretty pink bedroom with unicorns painted on the walls. Mary waited nearly an hour after he was finally gone to free herself from her leg ties. He'd threatened to kill her family if she told, so she'd waited to be certain he was gone. Still shackled at the wrists, she ran to wake up her father. All these years later, she lived with the echo of her father's voice screaming to her sister, "Get those things off her!" Soon after, Mary had asked a friend's older sister, "Am I still a virgin?"

Three years after the attack, she found her father dead in his bed. She was certain he died of a broken heart. I didn't doubt it. I have two daughters. I'm not sure I could survive the grief and regret of not being able to protect my children. Mary was robbed of her innocence and her peace of mind. She'd spent her life looking over her shoulder, wondering if he was still out there somewhere, watching.

The monster had stolen so much from so many. Surely there had to be a reckoning for him. I worried that, after I retired, no one else would take up where I had left off. The investigation would, once again, get tossed into a file cabinet and be all but forgotten—the way I'd found it—and the people who had counted on me to solve it would never forgive me. What would happen to them, those whose lives had been ruined? How would they ever get the little bit of peace that comes with knowing?

So many times over the years I thought I was close to solving the case, only to be bitterly disappointed when I was proven wrong by DNA. The last time had been just a couple of weeks earlier, and it was gut crushing. I'd recently discovered something within genetic genealogy called DNA segment triangulation, a process that could determine biological relationships by combining DNA profiling—which we had for GSK—with genealogical research from paid private ancestry websites. It had gotten my attention when I'd heard it was successful in identifying a woman who was abandoned as a small child. We didn't know who the little girl was or where she came from, and she had been too young to remember much that could help us. For years, we'd tried to identify her using traditional methods, and we'd always failed. Then, during a conference call about another case, I'd heard that she had finally been identified using DNA segment triangulation. I started to wonder, could that same tool lead us to the Golden State Killer?

For several months I had been working with a small task force of investigators, crime analysts, and the same skilled genealogist who'd assisted in the other case; we were comparing DNA profiles and dissecting family trees to come up with a handful of leads for GSK. Through a process of elimination, we'd whittled down the list to a small group of men who were roughly the right age and had been living in California during the time of the attacks. From there, we'd narrowed the search even further using physical descriptions from some of the victims.

I'd zeroed in on one suspect that looked the most promising to me and spent the last few weeks before my retirement investigating him. He was a Colorado construction worker whose personal and geographical profiles closely corresponded with those of the Golden State Killer. "I think we've got our guy," I told my FBI buddy Steve Kramer. "His piece of shit uncle was a rapist. There's a family thing going on here." I was so sure we had a fit, and I was ready to tie up the case and my career with a big bow. Until I got the call from Kramer telling me that the DNA results from the construction worker's sister showed she was not the sister of GSK, which eliminated him as a suspect. I hung up the phone and dropped my head on the desk. I was devastated. It was at that moment that I resigned myself to the fact that my last real shot at getting the Golden State Killer was gone.

There was this other guy, though. This match was someone who in forty years had never appeared on the radar screen in any of the previous investigations. His name popped up, like the guy's in Colorado, because the DNA profiles of a second and third cousin triangulated back to him through their family trees. The distant cousins who'd signed up with the private ancestry website had no idea their profiles were used to try to track a notorious serial killer. I'd done some preliminary research in the days after the latest disappointment, and he matched some of the criteria. He was around the right height at five feet eleven. He was seventy-two years old, a little older than I'd thought the killer would be now, but that didn't eliminate him. He lived in a suburb of Sacramento in the general area where I'd predicted the killer lived. His name was Joseph DeAngelo, and, an interesting little detail: he was a former cop. Still, I wasn't expecting much. I'd had suspects with more circumstantial evidence suggesting they should be looked at, and they were all eliminated with DNA. What was the likelihood that this guy would be any different? Based on my theories about GSK, the Colorado suspect had been a much better fit.

IT WAS RIGHT AROUND 2:30 P.M. when I turned off of I-80 onto Antelope Road, the main artery connecting strip malls, chain restaurants, and neighborhoods across Citrus Heights. Home was an hour in the rearview mirror. It was almost like I was on automatic pilot when I passed my exit. I hadn't even slowed down. I knew I had more digging to do into Joseph DeAngelo, but with this being my last day, I told myself I would use the time for a stop. I did that in all of my cases—checked out where a suspect lived and worked in order to get some sense of who they were.

Citrus Heights sits on fourteen square miles of Sacramento County countryside. It's a nice place to live. It's clean and safe, with parks and ballfields, plenty of retail and food chains to accommodate the booming real estate market, and small-town traditions like free movies in the square on Saturday nights. DeAngelo owned a house in a '70s subdivision surrounded by more subdivisions, most with the misleading word "Estates" in the name. It's an area of cookie-cutter homes, smooshed together with wooden privacy fences offering only the flimsiest sense of separation. I swung off of Antelope and navigated a tangle of intersecting streets, with cul-de-sacs and concrete sidewalks and yellow signs cautioning drivers to watch for CHILDREN AT PLAY, until I saw Canyon Oak Drive. Counting down to number 8316, I pulled alongside the curb opposite the house, a nondescript tan ranch. The garage doors were closed. A Volvo sedan and a fishing boat on a trailer were parked in the driveway. The landscaping grabbed my attention. Even in this tidy neighborhood, with plenty of pride of ownership, his yard stood out. It was meticulous, right down to the edging along the property. Not a blade of grass out of place. For some reason he'd set three large boulders purposefully but seemingly randomly on the front lawn, I guess for decorative purposes. I backed up a bit, trying to get a view of the backyard, then pulled forward again, put the car in park, and cut the engine. The blinds were closed, but I knew he was home. After so many years of sitting in front of suspects' houses, you just know those things. It's a feeling you learn to trust.

The yearning to go to the door was overwhelming. *I should just go and introduce myself.* My mind raced and my anxiety was ratcheting up again. Sitting there, I contemplated possible scenarios.

In the first one, I walk up to the front door and knock. Joe answers.

I introduce myself: "Hi, I'm Paul Holes, Contra Costa County cold case investigator. I've been looking into this series of unsolved cases and . . ."

He looks curious but not suspicious. We immediately establish a rapport, bonded by the uniform. He invites me in.

"How about some coffee?" he asks.

"No thanks. Never drink it."

"How about a beer?"

After a few sips of beer and a little bit of small talk about police work and how different it is now than when he was on the force, I tell him that his name came up in the investigation. He seems bemused but not concerned.

"I guess it's your lucky day," I say. "One of your distant relatives uploaded DNA into a genealogy website, and that person is related to the person I'm looking for. You are likely distantly related to my offender, too."

He nods. "Ahh. What can I do to help you out?"

"Well, I just need a DNA sample." I feel a little awkward asking another cop for proof he's not a malicious serial predator. On the other hand, with the sample, I can officially eliminate him as a suspect, and he'll never be bothered again.

"Hey, I get it," he says. "Of course."

We both chuckle over the absurdity of the situation. I get the sample, tell him I'm sorry for the bother, and leave.

It will be my final act in the case.

But there's another possibility, the one that considers DeAngelo is the Golden State Killer. In that scenario, I've already made a foolish mistake. I've sat there for several minutes in front of his house in my official car. Any cop or former cop would recognize it as unmarked law enforcement. If he is the killer, I know what he's capable of. There's no telling what he'll do if he feels trapped. He knows I'm here. He's a cunning serial predator. He knew what his victims watched on TV, where they went to work and school, whose husband was out of town, whose parents were out for the evening, when people were asleep.

In this scenario, there's no doubt he's already seen the car sitting there through the blinds. When I walk toward his house, he recognizes me from the media interviews I've done on the case over the years. By the time I get to the front door, he's already armed himself. He may open up and shoot me before I have a chance to say a word. Or he'll invite me in to keep me confined, excuse himself, then sneak up behind me and bash my head in.

No one would know. No one knows where I am. I didn't radio in. I didn't call home. I just left the office and ended up here.

I take a deep breath to clear my head. What am I doing, thinking about approaching this guy? If he is GSK, and he becomes aware that we're on to him, it will risk the investigation. If he feels cornered, he'll kill me.

I just need to drive away, I tell myself, putting the car in gear. *It's too early. I don't want to blow this. I don't know enough about this DeAngelo guy.*

I start the car and will myself to put it in gear. I'm not even a block away when I begin doubting my decision. *Maybe I'm blowing it. I should have gotten the DNA. I would have at least had another genealogy data point for my team. And what if DeAngelo was the killer? I was right there. Why hadn't I gone to the front door?*

The drive home to Vacaville seemed to take forever. I was filled with regret. I had just failed to wrap up my final suspect in a case that continued to elude me. If the Golden State Killer case was ever to be solved, I would not be a part of it. I felt defeated. The survivors had counted on me as their last chance for justice, and I'd let them down. My career would end with a blemished footnote.

It felt like an anticlimactic finish to what had been an otherwise pretty good run.

3

Beginnings

1968–1989

Most people would call me a loner. Few get close enough to see past the guy who solves crimes. It's not that I don't want to reveal myself, to allow people a deeper look into who I am. It's hard for me to open up. I don't seem to know how *not* to pull inward. It's a trait I learned as a kid—don't get too close or too comfortable—because whenever I did, I was uprooted and had to start all over again. My dad was in the air force, and we never stayed put for very long. From the time I was born in 1968 at MacDill Air Force Base in Tampa, to my graduation in 1986 from Vanden High School in Fairfield, California, we moved around at least a dozen times. The bits and pieces I remember from my childhood often involve saying goodbye to teachers and friends I'd barely had the chance to know. I began to develop a protective shell in the seventh grade after experiencing the anguish of losing my first best friend when Dad was transferred again, this time from San Antonio to Travis Air Force Base in California.

That same year, spending most of my free time at home as I struggled to adjust to my new surroundings at Travis, I discovered the TV series *Quincy*. In the show, Jack Klugman played the lead role of a crusty Los Angeles medical examiner who was always getting into trouble for sticking his nose into homicide investigations but inevitably solved every case. I remember the first time I saw it. I'd finished my homework and was sitting on the living room floor turning the channels on our first color TV, an RCA console, when the image of a stern-looking man in a medical coat standing over the body of a young girl appeared on the screen. The girl had been murdered and thrown in a dumpster. I watched, wide-eyed, as Quincy went from the morgue to the lab to the murder scene, tangling with the lead investigator and finding evidence the cops had missed. By the end of the hour, this guy Quincy had single-handedly pieced the puzzle together, nabbed the killer, and saved the life of the dead girl's sister. After that, I made sure to finish my homework early on Wednesday nights. Having an aptitude for science, I thought, *I can do that. I'll go to medical school and be the real-life Quincy*.

But as I became increasingly lonely, I began trying to fit in at school, molding myself into who I thought people wanted me to be. My ability to quickly size people up and then adjust my behavior allowed me to connect with all the different cliques. I could integrate with the popular girls, the smart kids, the athletes, the nerds, and the stoners, but none of my associations had any depth or meaning. I was just blending in. It was a survival mechanism, but I was also losing sight of who I really was. That left me feeling unmoored and anxious, and this led to my first panic attack. I was fifteen years old and at the Officers' Club pool on base. Two girls walked toward me, and out of nowhere a surge of heat shot through my body. I couldn't catch a breath. It all happened so fast. My face flushed and my skin turned damp. The world blurred. The girls passed as I dropped to the pavement, my heart hammering in my ears, and curled into a ball. After a few very long minutes, the symptoms subsided, but I was drained and afraid. What had happened to me?

I kept the incident to myself at first. I didn't want to worry my mom or disappoint my dad. When I finally told them, they took me to a psychologist, who treated my stress with deep breathing exercises. Generalized anxiety disorder was a novel medical diagnosis in the early '80s. I later learned that psychological disorders run in my family. My mother has struggled with anorexia nervosa for most of her life, and my brother suffers from symptoms of obsessive-compulsive disorder. For me, it is social anxiety that I struggle with the most. I never have felt comfortable in social situations. I think my brain sees them as threatening, because they provoke deep fears of being embarrassed or rejected. This has followed me throughout my life, and now I can anticipate moments that might instigate an attack—making small talk with a stranger is a sure trigger—and try to talk myself down before it happens. I need a moment to brace myself. I've learned this about myself, but it's been a journey that's taken time and work. It is how I cope. If only I'd known back then what I've learned since, I might have been able to avoid a lot of heartache. I couldn't be a carefree kid because I was always anticipating the next dreadful panic attack.

I TRIED TO DEAL WITH THE FEAR on my own, but as the years passed, there seemed to be no controlling it. When I was in high school in 1983, I started dating a cheerleader named Kim. She was two years older than me, and it was my first serious relationship. I fell hard. Kim made it clear that she wanted her boyfriend to be a football player, so I joined the team. I didn't know anything about playing football—swimming was my sport— but I wanted to be with her, so I adjusted. Falling back on my old coping mechanism, I tried to meet her expectations by molding myself into the jock I thought she wanted.

Kim and I were opposites. I was raised in a strict Catholic family and was shy. I didn't have experience with girls. Kim was a free spirit and outgoing. Her folks were liberal with their parenting and had few rules and plenty of trust. Kim would say we were going "parking," and her mom didn't bat an eye. We were teenagers, and I was infatuated. But I was an introvert pretending to be someone else for a girl, hiding the parts of me that I thought would bring rejection. Keeping up this facade was difficult and painful, and my panic attacks escalated. The symptoms usually took over before I could remember to breathe. Trying to hide what I considered my weakness made me even more uncomfortable, leaving me vulnerable to attacks. It was a vicious cycle.

Eventually, like most first loves, the relationship played itself out. When it did, I thankfully quit the football team, and Kim started dating another football player. Soon after, a friend invited me to a Super Bowl party at a house in a wealthy section of the base we called Snob Hill. The girl who was hosting the party was someone I recognized from school. I didn't know much more about her than her name, Lori. She was beautiful—with a round face and shiny brown hair that fell to the middle of her back. Super Bowl XIX was a big deal. "The Battle of the Quarterbacks" pitted the rival Miami Dolphins' Dan Marino against Joe Montana and the home team, the San Francisco 49ers. On that same day in 1985, California's former governor, Ronald Reagan, was inaugurated for his second term as president of the United States. President Reagan did the coin toss to start the game via satellite from the White House. It was such an exciting time, even for someone who had given up on football.

After the 49ers beat the Dolphins, a few of us kids stayed around to party. Lori started telling a story about herself. After all these years, I don't remember the story, but I remember how she told it—how animated and entertaining she was, nothing like the shy girl that I thought I knew in my world history class. In the middle of her story, Lori jumped up—only she couldn't jump. I don't think she got more than a couple of inches off the ground before dropping to the floor and bursting out laughing. She didn't seem to take herself seriously. I liked that. At that moment, seeing the glint in her eye, I was in love.

Lori was easy to be around. I was attracted to her carefree attitude. She was so unlike anyone else in my life; so unlike me. We sat for hours after our dates, talking in my car. She told me about her religious convictions, one of which was no sex before marriage, which was more than okay with me. I told Lori about my anxiety and the panic attacks, and the first time she witnessed them firsthand was during an outing to an amusement park. We climbed into the tiny cabin on the Ferris wheel, and when I heard the door snap shut, I felt that pang in my gut. That was always the start of it. Soon, an electric current was spreading through my body. The Ferris wheel seat swiveled and rocked, crushing Lori and me together. I felt the walls closing in, and my heart took off racing. My lungs felt like they were exploding. I crouched over, gasping for air. I don't know how long it lasted, probably only a few seconds, but I was certain I had doomed the relationship until I felt her hand on my back. Whatever was happening was okay, she said.

Lori was unlike any of the other girls I knew. She wasn't part of the popular crowd, and it wasn't something she aspired to. She didn't live for boys. She seemed more mature and naturally gravitated more toward older people. I'd call her an old soul. She preferred sitting in our kitchen and talking with my mom to attending high school socials. She had a special proclivity for people our parents' and grandparents' age, and they were immediately drawn to her warmth and compassion. I liked that about her. It made me feel safe.

We dated junior and senior year, but I wasn't completely surprised when she broke up with me after senior prom. Lori was pragmatic. We were headed to college. She wanted the freedom to be able to explore and experience everything her new independence had to offer. I was heartbroken, of course. We were both headed to the University of California, Davis, that fall, and I couldn't imagine seeing her but not being with her. We decided to remain friends and would occasionally jog together. Sometimes I helped her with her chemistry homework. My hope was that she'd change her mind and decide that she couldn't live without me, but I was gutted when she mentioned she had a crush on another guy. I stuck around anyway. Better to have a friendship than no relationship at all, I decided. But things with the other guy faded out, and Lori and I found ourselves being drawn back together. By sophomore year, we had picked back up the romantic relationship that we had started in high school.

In hindsight, it is clear now that we didn't have that spark that people talk about, but we were just comfortable with each other. Lori gave me a sense of stability I wasn't used to in my life. She cared about me the way family members care about one another. I couldn't imagine my life without her. And at the end of our junior year at UC Davis, I proposed. I'd saved up from my job flipping burgers at McDonald's and picked out a tiny marquise-style diamond ring. "Will you marry me?" I asked, nervous as all get-out.

She hesitated for a moment, then smiled.

"Yes," she said.

BY SENIOR YEAR, I WAS HAPPY. My plans for starting the rest of my life were in place. I was over school and in a hurry to get on with the next chapter. To me, that meant being married and working and living independently, finally free and on our own.

With graduation and a wedding fast approaching, I was in a scramble to find a job. My major was biochemistry, and in 1990, biotechnology was a big up-and-coming field. UC Davis held a career fair that May, and I attended to learn about sales rep jobs in the pharmaceutical industry.

Standing in line waiting to talk to a biotech company, I glanced around. Something flashed in the corner of my eye. A man lying on a kitchen floor, his head in a pool of blood, stared back at me from a TV screen in a nearby booth. Others turned their heads to avoid the gruesome scene, but I couldn't look away. I was spellbound. "What in hell is that?" I wondered, hastily leaving the line I was in and heading over to that booth. The person behind the table introduced himself as Victor Reeve, head of the renowned California Criminalistics Institute, a training and research center in the Department of Justice. Reeve was a middle-aged guy with a receding hairline, large aviator glasses, and a rumpled tan suit and mismatched tie. He'd been a criminalist for more than twenty years and, little did I know, was one of the best in the business. But at the time, I didn't even know what a criminalist was. Reeves explained that a criminalist was a forensic scientist who used their scientific expertise to help solve crimes.

"That's what I want to do," I told him.

It was the first time I had felt excited about a possible career. I hadn't thought about *Quincy* for a long time, but all of the passion I'd felt watching the TV show flooded back. I walked out wide-eyed and keen to start solving crimes. I spent the next morning at the campus job center going through binders with job postings from potential employers. One was for a forensic toxicologist with the Contra Costa County Sheriff's Office. It wasn't a criminalist position, but I would be working in the crime lab. It was a start. I decided to give it a shot and apply. If I got the job, at least I'd get my foot in the door of a crime lab. My application was followed by a visit to the government complex in Martinez to take an oral exam. I left feeling like I aced it. A week later a letter came informing me that I'd ranked fourth out of some fifty applicants. I finally found something I thought I could be really good at, and I was being given the chance to find out.

And yet weeks passed with no word from the Sheriff's Office. I'd been so sure that things would work out, but my hopes dimmed with each passing day. I turned my attention to our wedding. It took place as scheduled on a sultry Saturday at the end of August. By then, I'd converted to Lori's conservative approach to religion. We'd been attending church services together regularly since we'd gotten back together, and the ceremony took place at our Protestant church on base. Lori looked beautiful in a white wedding dress. I wore a tux. Watching her walk down the aisle on her father's arm, I felt so proud that she was about to become my wife. I couldn't recall ever feeling happier. We chose traditional vows. *I, Paul, do take you, Lori* . . . My hands shook trying to place the ring on her finger. The kiss was chaste and sweet. When I looked back at my mom, she was wiping away happy tears.

I felt the importance of the moment. I wanted to be married, and now I was. It was a significant milestone in my life. A reception followed under a huge white tent in Lori's parents' backyard. It was an elegant but simple afternoon affair. A champagne toast but no wild dancing or smashing cake in each other's faces. We were happy and in love, and a little bit jittery about the wedding night. We spent it at the Holiday Inn in town before driving to Mendocino on the northern coast for a honeymoon. I had just gotten a new camera to document the trip. We took pictures of sunsets and palm trees, and each other, holding hands on the beach, sunburned, beaming. Only after we got home did I discover there was no film in the camera.

We settled into an apartment in Vacaville that Lori's parents helped us to get. I was still working at McDonald's and certainly not making enough to support us. Still, it was such an exciting time in our young lives. We were on our own, in our own place. The rest of our lives were ahead of us. Lori got a job with an interior designer, and I found a better job at a local warehouse, stocking scarecrows in preparation for the annual pumpkin patch at a road stop restaurant called the Nut Tree. Six weeks into it, I was out on the warehouse floor when I got called to the phone. "Who is it?" I asked. "Dunno," my boss said. "She said something about Contra Costa County." I grabbed the phone out of his hand. "This is Paul," I said. The crime lab supervisor was on the other end of the line. "Are you still interested in the position?" she asked. "Absolutely!" I said yes before she finished the question. We set a date for a follow-up interview, and I thanked her for the opportunity. Hanging up the phone, I ripped off my apron and yelled "I quit!" almost dancing out the door.

4

Lab Rat

1990

"Do you want to see the lab?" Kathy Holmes looked almost sheepish when she asked. Kathy was the supervising criminalist in charge of the county's drug and alcohol unit, twenty or so years my senior, who'd been working as a criminalist since the mid-1970s. It was the day of my follow-up interview, and she was about to introduce me to her world—the one I'd imagined as a kid watching *Quincy*.

I followed her out of her office on Escobar Street and around the corner to a dilapidated block that looked as if it hadn't seen a can of paint in decades. Martinez had once been a thriving retail center but was now a down-on-its-luck industrial town. We approached a washed-out sign painted on a brick facade that read MARTELLACCI'S GOLDEN STATE BRAND DAIRY PRODUCTS, long since gone. Kathy stopped at the awning. There was no signage outside, only the street number, 726. "This is it," she said, almost apologetically.

"The lab?"

It wasn't much to look at on the inside either, she said, pulling open the door. In fact, it was kind of pitiful. I walked into a long, narrow office suite with mustard-yellow partitions separating gray metal desks. All of it looked as if it had been pulled out of storage. The actual crime lab was all the way at the back, in a cramped, windowless area next to the bathroom. It was the fall of 1990, and the radio sputtered news about the recently launched Gulf War. I would soon learn that, at the insistence of the senior guy on staff, news radio was on all the time. Nothing about the Castro Street lab resembled where Quincy's loyal lab rat, Sam Fujiyama, tested crime scene evidence on TV. But I couldn't have cared less. I was spellbound. I imagined myself coming to work there every day, testing blood and urine samples for drug and DUI cases. It was all so fascinating and exciting. The microscopes, the spectrophotometer, the contents of the test tubes that could determine someone's fate.

I tried to play it cool, but being in a real crime lab was perhaps the most exciting moment of my life up to that point. "We'll be in touch," Kathy said, shaking my hand.

It was a torturous twenty-four hours before I got the phone call from John Murdock, the county's chief of forensics. "We'd like to have you join us," he told me. I was going to be the county's new drug analyst. That same night, I ran out and bought a pair of khaki pants and a navy blazer.

My life was playing out just as I had planned. I was married and had a respectable job. From day one I loved going to work. It gave me such a sense of purpose and pride. Everyone around me was so bright, and there was so much to learn. I was an eager student. The people pleaser that I was, I always tried to anticipate what Kathy expected of me before she could ask. Some of my coworkers accused me of being her favorite, and I'd bristle at the notion, but secretly, I didn't mind. And if it were true, I wanted to make sure it stayed that way.

Lab testing, itself, was pretty cut and dried, but I absorbed myself in the study of drug analysis and addiction. I had never used drugs in high school or college, so learning about the effects of stimulants, depressants, and hallucinogens was fascinating to me.

Part of my job entailed testifying in drug cases. Six months in, I was called to give expert testimony in a juvenile case. It was my first time testifying, and I felt fully prepared. It was a simple marijuana possession case, nothing complicated, and I'd had some in-house training in court-room testimony. Walking into the courthouse, I was confident that things would go smoothly. But my anxiety had other ideas.

Sitting on a bench outside of the courtroom, waiting to be called, I felt that familiar pang in my gut. My heart started skipping and my hands trembled. *Oh no,* I thought. *Not now.* I knew that court testimony was going to be a big part of my job. It was one thing when this happened in a social situation, but if I were to suffer a panic attack on the stand, it would ruin my career before it had even begun. Desperate to calm myself down, I remembered the breathing exercise the psychologist from my high school days had taught me. "Concentrate on the moment," she'd said, "not what happened in the past or what may happen in the future. Stay present. And breathe."

"Paul Holes!" The bailiff waved me into the courtroom. I took a deep breath and slowly exhaled. *Stay in the moment. Breathe.* I walked into the courtroom and took the stand. I continued focusing on my breath rather than taking in the courtroom around me. "How did you receive the evidence?" the prosecutor asked, walking toward me. I signed the chain of custody. I checked the taped seal on the baggie containing a small amount of green leafy material to make sure it hadn't been tampered with. I weighed the evidence and performed the standard Duquenois-Levine test, the screening for the presence of cannabis. Yes, I could say quantifi-ably that the evidence was not oregano, I said. It was marijuana. Then it was the defense attorney's turn to question me. "How many times have you qualified as an expert before?" he asked. I was twenty-two and looked twelve, an observation that wasn't lost on him. "Never," I said honestly. I was young, but I knew my stuff, which gave me a kind of confidence that I hadn't known before. The judge, satisfied with my credentials, qualified me as an expert. I passed my first test.

AFTER A YEAR OF WORKING IN the lab, I started getting the itch to move up. That seems to be a common theme in all aspects of my life. My mind is restless, and I'm in constant pursuit of the next thing. "You're always after something else. Something more," Lori told me many times. It was true, but without that constant stimulation and upward motion, my anxiety kicked in. I was and still always am on high alert for a challenge, and each one dissolves into the next because the last is never enough. That's who I am. I'm not sure it makes for much peace of mind—in fact, I'm pretty sure it doesn't—but the intense need for more drives me in everything I do. I guess it was inevitable then that I'd quickly tire of the daily grind of a lab scientist and start looking for the next shiny object.

It didn't take long to find it. I would often slip away from my lab on Castro Street and walk the five blocks to the lab on Escobar, where the criminalists worked. These were the guys who got to go out to crime scenes to sweep for evidence and analyze it in the lab. I wondered what it would be like—the challenge of figuring out *how* a crime happened. Their stories were real-life thrillers. I'd meander into their unit whenever I could get away, and eavesdrop shamelessly while they compared notes about working homicides and recounted details of scenes they'd investigated.

Poking around one afternoon, I discovered a treasure hidden in plain sight—the crime library. It was about the size of a truck container, like something you'd see on the back of those cross-country rigs, and right in the center of the Escobar lab. The walls were covered in worn paneling, and black floor-to-ceiling metal shelves held decades' worth of books and journals that covered the gamut of forensic and investigative subjects. I saw titles about crime scene investigation, the newest genetic technology, and serial predators. Many of the books looked like no one had taken them off the shelf in years. For me, it was like discovering gold.

Under flickering fluorescent lights, I began pulling books off the shelves and leafing through them, dog-earing pages I wanted to come back to. It wasn't long before I came across a blue cloth edition of a book entitled *Medico-Legal Aspects of the Ruxton Case*. The illustrated book detailed the landmark case out of Britain in which a highly regarded medical doctor named Buck Ruxton killed his wife and nursemaid, dismembered their bodies in an effort to conceal their identities, and dumped the body parts a hundred miles from his home. It wasn't so much the gory crime story that pulled me in, but how a team of investigators, pathologists, and forensic scientists all worked together using novel techniques to solve the crime. The case was dubbed "the Jigsaw Murders" to reflect the exhaustive efforts to put the pieces of the puzzle (and the bodies) together and identify the victims. Dr. Ruxton was found guilty at trial and later hanged. These books opened a whole world for me. Now that I had a taste of what was possible, there was no way I was going to be stuck analyzing drugs and alcohol blood levels for very long.

Once I was past the new employee trial period, I wandered down to the library almost every day. I wanted to soak up everything I could. Whether it was a science journal or a book about crime scene processing, I dove right in. My interest didn't end when I closed the book or finished the article. I was still thinking about it through dinner and until I fell asleep. Whatever I read rolled around in my head until I'd absorbed every detail. I was happiest when I was in that place. I imagined it was what a good drug high must feel like. When my brain was immersed in something that challenged me, I was almost euphoric.

Over the next three years, I consumed everything I could about investigative techniques, the psychology of criminality, the minds of serial predators, and—along the way—cold cases. For my twenty-fifth birthday, my parents sent me two books, *Crime & Human Nature* and *Sexual Homicide: Patterns and Motives* by Robert Ressler, Ann Burgess, and John Douglas. By the time I finished *Sexual Homicide,* I had figured out what I wanted to do.

I wanted to become a criminal profiler.

And Lori wanted to start a family.

5

Moving Up

By the fall of 1993, Lori and I were both on our way to fulfilling our dreams. Our daughter, Renee, was born that September. She was a beautiful baby, with a perfectly round face and apple cheeks, just like her mom. Lori had been working at a car dealership but left her job to stay home with the baby. And a few months later, a position for a criminalist opened up. It was the first time one of these jobs had come up in ten years. I was twenty-six and short on qualifications, but I knew that with my energy and thirst for knowledge I could learn quickly. I couldn't wait another ten years for someone to retire, so I applied, as did fifty others. First, I had to pass an oral exam, which meant taking questions from a panel of experts. Think quick, or you're out.

You are assigned a homicide case as a rush case with the results being needed within three days. You expect the examination to take six to eight hours. After working two hours on the case, you are called to court to testify. You spend the rest of the day in court. At 9 P.M. you are called to investigate a homicide scene. You spend most of the night at the scene.

The next morning the detective requests you begin work on his case right away. Tell us how you would approach these assignments to ensure that the work is completed within the requested time frames.

I managed to keep my cool and nailed the oral test. All of the time I'd spent in the library and reading in my room late into the night had paid off because despite my lack of experience, I got the job. I was on my way to becoming a deputy sheriff criminalist. A CSI. I was so happy. And Lori was happy to be at home with our new baby. Everything felt right.

For the next five months, I trained at the police academy. The transition from civilian life to the strict militaristic environment of the academy was an absolute culture shock. It was boot camp with classroom time, and all consuming. Every morning, I had to show up for formation at zero dark thirty with my uniform pressed, my shoes shined, and my brass polished. All of this with a six-month-old baby girl at home. That meant getting up and out of the house before anyone else was awake. Days were jam-packed with grueling physical and academic challenges. We jumped walls, learned how to shoot, and studied the law while the drill instructors barked commands.

My primary drill instructor's name was Bagwell, and he had bug eyes and a thick dark mustache. He seemed to take pleasure in riding us hard. Early into the program, another instructor gave us a course on alcohol intoxication. As an exercise in class, she explained how people of different ethnicities react to alcohol. One of the students called her out for using a negative stereotype when she said that people of a certain race tended to react faster and more dramatically to alcohol without providing any scientific backing. It was a tense moment. I'd had plenty of experience in alcohol impairment training during my years in the lab, and I thought I could help. Walking to the blackboard, I drew a graphic of alcohol metabolism. I pointed out that alcohol dehydrogenase converts ethanol faster in certain people. The problem, I explained, was that the metabolite acetaldehyde built up to toxic levels, which caused side effects such as a flushed face and wicked hangovers. Both my instructor and my classmate thanked me for explaining. As I was sitting back down, somebody in the class yelled out "Spock!"—the geeky science officer on *Star Trek*. The nickname stuck with me for my entire time at the academy.

After those long and grueling days, I'd go home, broken down and bone-tired, and spend the evening preparing for the next day of torture and testing. Needless to say, my circumstances were less than ideal for life with our daughter, and Lori bore the brunt of the responsibilities at home. Renee was a difficult baby. She couldn't be put down without screaming, and sleeping through the night was rare. The only thing that seemed to placate Renee was riding in the car, so I'd drive her around the neighborhood after dinner until she fell asleep in her car seat. Inevitably she'd wake up when I carried her back into the house. That left Lori to take over, because I needed to spend evenings polishing shoes and ironing my uniform for early inspection. Lori was overwhelmed, and I tried to do what I could to help, but it wasn't enough.

For those five months, my entire life was the academy. It was mentally and physically rigorous. My long absences, both physical and emotional, created tension in a marriage that had already been showing cracks. I remember one day, Lori and I were out on the patio arguing about something—probably the stress she was under because I was gone so much. Renee was crawling by, and we were so immersed in our own frustration that we didn't see her crawl to the edge of the patio and off a step. Renee started crying, and Lori became distressed. "It's your fault," she said, as our daughter screamed. I didn't know how to respond, so I turned and walked back into the house.

All of my life, I handled stress that way. When the conversation got tough, I walked away. People took it for indifference, but it wasn't. It was fear. I could spend all day studying the most evil of killers, but it was emotional conflict I was terrified of. I was afraid of rejection, afraid that facing the conflict head-on would push my loved ones away. So instead, I pushed the feelings deep down inside myself, hoping that if I ignored them, the trouble would disappear. I didn't know it then, but I was only driving those I loved away from me, only isolating myself further behind the walls I was beginning to build around myself.

6

EAR

My life changed again in October 1994. I had graduated from the academy and was officially a CSI, going out to crime scenes and analyzing evidence. With tensions with Lori increasing, when everyone else went home, I'd stay behind in the library, reading books about serial killers and homicide, sometimes late into the night.

It stood to reason that at some point, I'd start running out of things to read. I was rummaging around the shelves one day, desperate to find something new—a book I'd overlooked or a study I had missed—when something caught my eye. Pushed off into the corner was a file cabinet, the typical office model, putty in color with four or five stacked drawers. How had I never noticed it before? Judging from the coat of dust on top, it hadn't been opened for a while.

Tugging open the top drawers, I saw what I expected to find: random, outdated administrative stuff, old handwritten lecture notes, and cassette tapes of people presenting at forensic conferences long ago. But the bottom drawer was heavier than the others. I felt the weight as I dragged it open. The sound of the manila folders flipping forward reminded me of the shuffling of a deck of cards. Each one was labeled in red marker with the letters "EAR."

I pulled out the first file. On top was a copy of a police report with the numbers "261/459" in the upper left corner, the California penal codes for rape and burglary. The crime had taken place sixteen years earlier in Concord, a residential suburb of San Francisco, Berkeley, and Oakland. Dated October 7, 1978, the typed report began: "Dispatched to the above location on a report of a hysterical female on the phone, saying that she had been raped, and she and her husband had been tied up. I arrived and found the wife standing at the front door completely unclothed. Her hands were tied behind her back. [She] told me her husband was still tied up in their bedroom." The attack had occurred sometime past midnight, after the young couple had put their one-year-old daughter to bed and gone to bed themselves. The husband was awakened first, by what felt like something at his feet. Opening his eyes, he saw a man wearing a ski mask standing at the foot of the bed, a flashlight in his left hand, a handgun in his right. "I just want money and food, that's all," he snarled. That's when the wife woke up. "I'll kill you if you don't do what I say. Get on your stomachs."

Reading on, I quickly realized that money wasn't the intruder's only ambition. His goal seemed to be to terrorize and control. He ordered the couple to put their hands behind their backs, then bound them at the wrists and ankles with shoelaces he pulled painfully tight. Putting a knife to the woman's neck, he said, "I'll kill you if you don't do everything I say." His voice was "a whisper through clenched teeth," the husband recalled. For the next thirty minutes, while the stranger wandered through their house, they lay there helpless. I could only imagine the dread they felt, wondering what was going to happen next. *The baby. What if he finds the baby? Will he hurt her? Is he going to kill us?* The fear the couple felt leapt off the pages of the police report. I couldn't look away.

The intruder eventually returned to the bedroom carrying dishes from the kitchen. Placing them on the couple's backs, he said, "If I hear these, I'll blow your fucking heads off." *This guy is a sadist,* I thought. *He gets off on causing psychological terror.* I was already starting to develop a psychological profile in my head.

The couple endured another few minutes of listening to drawers opening and closing and kitchen cupboard doors slamming, as the intruder continued to roam through the house. He was back again, suddenly and quietly. The only clue that he was at their bedside was his breathing, heavy and quick, almost as if he were hyperventilating. Cutting the woman's feet loose he ordered her: "Stand up! Don't you look at me, or I'll cut your fucking head off." If she didn't do everything he told her to do, he said, he would kill her, her husband, and their little girl. Having my own infant daughter, I could only imagine her panic. Self-preservation is innate in all of us, but the instinct to protect our kids is perhaps even stronger. The woman did as she was told, and he pushed her toward the family room. There, he blindfolded her and ordered her to lie on her stomach on the carpet in front of the fireplace. He turned on the TV, sound off, and draped a small blanket over the screen. I imagined her dry mouth, heart tearing at her chest. She recalled that he smelled "like cinnamon."

She heard the thud of his knife dropping on the coffee table, then the soft clomp of his feet as he padded back to the kitchen. Dishes clanked. *Thud. Thud. Thud.* She strained to hear every sound. He was headed to the bedroom, presumably to place more dishes on her husband's back. Just like that, he was beside her again. "If you don't give me a good fuck, I'll kill everyone in the house. I'll cut off your baby's ear and bring it to you." His voice was menacing, evil. As she lay there, frozen, she heard the slash of material. She felt him rip off her nightgown, piece by piece. He masturbated over her. She was stunned when, just before he sexually assaulted her, he called her by her name. "I've been seeing you for a long time," he said. *Where?* she wondered. Did she know this man? For the next hour, he raped her. Afterward, he crouched in the corner and cried.

In the attached case summary, one of the investigators had scribbled the words "East Area Rapist." EAR.

I was shocked. I closed the file and opened the next.

Six days after the October 7 attack, a five-minute drive away, another family was attacked in the middle of the night. The twenty-nine-year-old woman and her thirty-year-old boyfriend were sleeping when they were awakened by the sound of their bedroom door being thrown open. Standing in the doorway was a man shining a flashlight in their eyes. Imagine waking up from a dead sleep with a flashlight blinding you. Part of training at the police academy was learning to use the flashlight to disorient an attacker. *Dominate his face. Shine a light in his eyes, and he'll likely be blinded for three or four seconds, enough time to get control.* A fleeting thought crossed my mind: this guy was using a law enforcement tactic to control his victims.

This was a brazen, confident attacker. Having stunned the couple, he immediately began barking orders. "Don't move or I'll blow your heads off," he said, jaw clenched. He ordered the boyfriend to roll over and place his hands behind his back, then he threw a handful of shoelaces at the woman and directed her to tie his hands. An act of cowardice, having her restrain her boyfriend? Or another way of terrorizing her?

With the boyfriend bound, he ordered the woman on her stomach and bound her wrists and ankles. He placed a gun to the boyfriend's head at the same moment the woman's seven-year-old daughter came into the bedroom. When she saw the ski mask, the young girl screamed, and the gunman pushed her into the bathroom and told her to "stay there and be quiet." To prevent her from escaping, he piled furniture in front of the bathroom door and returned to the bedroom and ransacked it.

When it was finally quiet for a stretch, the couple thought the intruder had left. No such luck. He had quietly returned to the boyfriend's side of the bed, draped a blanket over his head, and placed dishes on his back. "If you move, I'll drive this knife into your back," he warned. He then proceeded to force the woman out of the bed and into the living room, just as he had in the previous attack. There, within earshot of the boyfriend, the attacker wrapped a towel around the woman's eyes and ordered her to "play with it" before repeatedly raping her. Then he was gone.

I had studied serial predators by day in the lab and by the light of my bedside lamp while Lori and the baby slept, and I knew enough to recognize that this was a different cat. It wasn't a sex act or inflicting physical injury that aroused him. Psychological terror and control fed his emotional and psychological needs.

The similarities between the two cases were stunning. He awakened his victims in the middle of the night by shining a flashlight in their eyes. He tied them up, threatened their lives, and raped women while their young children were nearby. He whispered obscenities as he was attacking them. He piled dishes on the men's backs. The dishes were his alarm system. "If I hear the dishes rattle, I'll cut off her ear and bring it to you." He was chillingly bold. It was a huge risk to attack two people, especially when one was a man. The kinds of cowards who raped women rarely took that kind of gamble, yet this offender seemed to seek it out.

I dug back into the drawer and pulled the third file. I couldn't stop reading.

EAR had attacked eight times in Contra Costa County between the fall of 1978 and summer of 1979. Then, just like that, the reports ended.

I filed the reports back in the cabinet and clicked off the light. Driving home, I thought about him obsessively. I couldn't get the case out of my head. I felt like I had started reading an unputdownable thriller and couldn't wait to see what the next chapter would bring. I'd read plenty about serial killers and cold cases, but this one felt like mine.

"You won't believe what I found today," I told Lori that night as she was preparing dinner. "There was this serial rapist back in the seventies . . ."

"Stop!" she cried. "I don't want to hear about that."

I'd been so excited to talk about my discovery, and she'd shut me down. I was disappointed and dispirited.

A FEW WEEKS LATER, I WAS on a flight from Oakland to Los Angeles, a brand-new CSI headed to a meeting of the training and resources committee for the California Association of Criminalists. I was reading the conference materials when someone took the seat beside me. "John Murdock!" I said. Murdock was the former chief of forensics for Contra Costa County. He was a big deal, with years in the field, and highly respected around the country. He was the big boss when I was hired and had made the call offering me the job. But I didn't know him well, even though I had taken a crime scene investigation course from him at Diablo Valley College in Pleasant Hill the year prior. I was intimidated, and a bit tongue-tied at first, but we eased into conversation. We'd been chatting for a while when, about halfway through the one-hour flight, I brought up the files I had found.

"Who is EAR?" I asked

He quickly turned toward me.

"The East Area Rapist! I was on the original task force," he said.

"Was the case ever solved?" I asked.

"We tried so hard, but the guy just disappeared," he said.

John proceeded to tell me about his role in coordinating and evaluating the evidence collection in the case. Then he dropped a bombshell. EAR's crime spree wasn't unique to our county, he said. "The cases started up in Sacramento."

It was at that moment that I realized I had stumbled upon something much bigger than I had been able to gather from the file cabinet in the library.

"The case isn't solved?" I asked.

As the plane descended into Los Angeles, John shook his head. "Unsolved. Never did catch the guy. That would be a good case to figure out."

EAR had disappeared in 1979. A sixteen-member multi-jurisdictional task force had tried and failed to identify him. The fact that no one had been able to solve the case was a challenge I couldn't resist. Some people might call it hubris, and maybe it was, but at that early point in my career, it never occurred to me that I might fail to figure out a case that had eluded the best criminal minds for decades. I knew I could solve it.

7

CSI

I was forced to tuck the EAR files back in the cabinet and focus on my job. It was the mid-1990s, and my promotion to the deputy sheriff criminalist position meant I started going out to crime scenes instead of just spending all day in the lab. Now, this wasn't a typical CSI position, which normally involves collecting evidence, taking photographs, and briefing lead investigators. My job was very much a hybrid position because of its scientific component. I viewed evidence with the eyes of a forensic scientist, assessing and collecting it in a manner that would be optimal for when I returned to the serology lab to examine it. DNA testing was just starting to emerge in criminal cases, so I was training in that as well. Soon, the crack epidemic would invade our territory, as it had in cities all over the country. Gang-related homicides skyrocketed. Drug labs were everywhere. Suddenly, I was out in the field all the time. The workload was so demanding that I was almost always on the road. New crime scenes popped up day and night—often when most people were sleeping. I was usually the one who caught the calls because I was junior staff. Honestly, that didn't leave much time for a wife and a kid. They were tough times.

The scourge of illicit drugs was spreading to every station of society. It swept from the poor urban areas of our county to the affluent suburbs. It robbed kids of bright futures, parents of their beloved children, and families of their happy homes. I saw the damage every day. What I neglected to see was the damage my time away was doing to my own home.

My first callout as the lead CSI was to a crime scene in Pleasant Hill, a town that bordered Martinez. Climbing into my work jumpsuit, a hand-me-down from an older colleague who had died a few years prior, I holstered my sidearm, grabbed my metal clipboard, and headed out with a partner from the lab. It was a sweltering August morning in 1995. The report was of a dead man behind the county library in Pleasant Hill. Driving to the back of the building, I saw the body, a bicycle resting on top of it. The library janitor said he thought it was a homeless man from the area. As we awaited the coroner, I eyeballed the body. The clothing was loose and masculine, but the socks were pink. "Pink socks?" I said to the detective standing beside me. When the coroner arrived, I turned the body over. The face was feminine, and the hair stuffed into the knit cap was long. "This isn't a guy," I said.

The victim was a young woman dressed in men's clothing, a trick to keep men away. She had once been a promising athlete and a budding musician before, somewhere along the line, probably in high school, she'd taken a wrong turn, met the wrong guy, and ended up addicted to methamphetamines. In her midtwenties, she landed on the streets. She'd come from a family that loved her and hoped that one day she would quit drugs and return to them. Instead, she ended up brutally bludgeoned to death with her own bike. It would take a year, but her killer, unable to live with his secret, ultimately turned himself in to the police. He'd come across the woman behind the library. He wanted sex. She didn't, so he beat her to death.

I made sure to get the girl's name, Julie. Driving away from the library, I had a hard time getting the vision of her crushed face, pine needles stuck to it, out of my head. Such promise erased in an instant. I took it personally.

I wasn't back at the lab long enough to even change out of my uniform when I was on the road again. "There's been a massive double in Orinda," my supervisor said. A restaurant owner and her daughter had been shot to death in their home. "You're going back."

The case was too big for an apprentice, which I was at the time, so I was assigned to assist. Orinda was only a ten-minute drive from Pleasant Hill, but it was a completely different world. A suburban oasis, with pricy real estate and top-rated schools, it's been called one of the best places to live in California. The houses sit on sprawling lots and are usually hidden from view. My partner and I arrived on scene in midafternoon. The ranch-style home was blocked from view by tall trees in the middle of the semicircular driveway. The perfect spot to commit a crime without being seen, I thought, walking past a green Volkswagen convertible that was parked outside the front door. The ideal place for the offender to blitz the victims as soon as they got out of the car.

Inside was messy and cluttered. Old newspapers and magazines were stacked in the hallway inside the front door next to where a woman's body lay facedown. She looked to be in her early fifties, fully clothed, her hands bound behind her back with an electrical cord that had been ripped from a lamp in the next room. A few feet away was an older woman's body, also facedown, her bloody cheek stuck to an Old Navy shopping bag. She, too, was bound at the wrists, and her fingers were wrapped around the bindings, as if at some point she had been trying to free herself. The scene was bizarre, partly because of the contrast between the neighborhood and the crime. Murder wasn't supposed to happen in places like Orinda, where the American dream was taken for granted, and when it did, the circumstances always seemed to be curiously weird. The community was still recovering from the fatal stabbing a decade earlier of a popular high school cheerleader by her teenage rival. Now a mother and daughter from a respectable, well-to-do family? It would send the town reeling.

Up to that point, most of the homicides I'd worked were gang members fighting turf wars in the west end of the county. They didn't get much media attention. This case involved a popular local restaurant owner and her daughter in a "this doesn't happen here" kind of town. That brought out the mics and cameras. It was a good story, and my first high-profile case, made so by the status of the community and the victims. In all of the crime scenes I'd worked in lower-income neighborhoods, I'd never seen a news truck. A poor Black kid is bleeding out in the middle of the street, a victim of gun violence, and his grief-stricken mom is wailing over him, but not a single reporter is there to tell their story. Here, every time I walked from the house to the crime scene van, cameras whirred, and reporters shouted questions. It was my first lesson in the harsh reality of what the media covers and why.

THE MOTHER AND DAUGHTER IN ORINDA were hardworking women who'd lived good lives. Sometime after they'd left their restaurant the previous night, they'd been attacked. Family members discovered their bodies after they hadn't shown up for work that morning. *Why would someone want to hurt them?* I wondered, looking at their lifeless bodies splayed out on hallway tile. They looked so small and harmless. The mom was dressed the way you'd think someone in her seventies would be: skirt, blouse, nylons, and flats. The daughter wore jeans, a striped sweater, and white Converse sneakers. A few hours earlier, they'd been preparing authentic Mexican food for their loyal customers. They'd left the restaurant around midnight, and sometime after that, someone tied them up in their own home and shot them multiple times in the back of the head. They could have been my family, or yours.

Examining the bodies, I put myself in each of their places at the time of the killings, something I did at every crime scene. I could see them, likely sitting in the hallway while the offender was going through every room, pulling out drawers, opening cabinets, looking for anything of value. They can see each other, but they can't help each other because they're tied up. I wonder how long they were sitting there, bound and terrified. When they are finally forced onto their stomachs, does the offender tell them what is about to happen? The fear they must have felt gives me a chill. There's no way to tell who was killed first. I hear the mom's final plea the way her daughter might have. *Please don't kill us; take what you want; just don't hurt my daughter.* I see the daughter's tears when she realizes that her mom is about to be killed. Or had the daughter already been shot? I feel the mother's desperation as she struggles with the bindings, trying to free herself, when—*pop-pop-pop.* Her last thought on this earth is "My daughter is dead." Both women had been shot multiple times, the bullets entering the backs of their heads and exiting out their faces. It had all of the elements of a gang-style shooting. Gently, I lifted each of their heads and dug the bullets out of the floor, then collected the spray of shell casings around the bodies. When the coroner arrived, we put the bodies into body bags and removed them from the house. I was nearly blinded by the camera lights as we pushed the bodies into the coroner's van.

Once the bodies were taken away, the hunt for more evidence resumed. The house was cluttered, whether from hoarding or ransacking, which made the search more of a challenge. I combed the scene well into the night, and we still had days of work ahead of us. We decided to leave and return in the morning. By then, I was going on seventy-two hours with pretty much no sleep. *I can't afford to nod off on the freeway*, I thought. Home was too far of a drive only to turn around and come back again in a couple of hours, so I decided I would stay the rest of the evening at the lab.

It was the dead of night when I parked the van behind the office.

The city lights bounced off the waves of fog rolling in from the bay, casting ghostlike halos. Walking from the van to the building, I heard what sounded like a maniacal cackle. I quickly looked up, just in time to see the outline of an owl, backlit by the refinery fires burning bright in the distance. Some Native American tribes see owls as a symbol of death. *This is surreal*, I thought, picking up my pace, *even for a guy who just rolled back from a gruesome murder scene.*

Martinez was right off the water, so even August nights could be chilly. Inside the building was even colder. I walked to the crime library, looking for a spot to sleep, and decided on a narrow sliver of floor between the conference table and the wall. The carpet was thin and stained from age, and the floor felt like ice. I lay down and covered myself with my puffy Sheriff's Office jacket. It was pitch-dark, and things, I don't know what, creaked. Lying there, I remembered a story that some of the maintenance guys told, about a worker who, as legend had it, went under the building one day to fix something and never came out. They claimed they heard there was a skeleton down there. I closed my eyes and tried to sleep, but my mind raced between Pleasant Hill and Orinda. Thoughts swirled in my head. Around and around they went. *What do we know? What do I need for tomorrow?* Eventually I fell asleep, awaking at daybreak with both arms numb from lying on the hard floor. I hadn't even called Lori to let her know I wasn't coming home. I would get tunnel vision when I was drawn into a case. I was so focused that I wasn't even thinking about my family. It was the first of many of those nights.

8

Abernathy

On the days I did make it home, after dinner with Lori and the kids, I usually locked myself in my office, which doubled as a storage room, and worked on my cases. I was beginning to realize that as skilled as I was at the science of homicide, it was the victims' stories that drew me in, that turned my cases into obsessions.

At around eight on a chilly February evening in 1997, I had just settled in behind my computer, ready to dig into a case file, when I was called back to the lab for a 187, the penal code for a murder. A father and his twelve-year-old son had been shot to death in their home in Hercules, a town on the coast of San Pablo Bay that most would consider idyllic. I was the criminalist on call, so I gathered my things and prepared to return to the lab. Little did I know that this routine crime scene call would turn into my first real homicide investigation.

Lori was sitting on the floor in the family room watching one of the TV shows she liked, maybe *Melrose Place*. Pictures of the kids were fanned out around her for a photo album she was putting together. By then we had two kids, Renee, who was four, and our son, Nathan, who was one.

We'd been married seven years at that point. We weren't unhappy, but something was missing. I think we both thought having another child would breathe life back into our relationship. It's not like we argued a lot, but we had drifted apart. Lori's world was the kids and her church. I was focused on my work, which left little time for anything else. She tried to get me involved in activities with our friends, but I had nothing in common with them, nor they with me. I gave it several tries. We'd go to a church gathering, and I'd quickly become bored with small talk about kids' activities and local sports. I couldn't connect with others because no one wanted to hear about things like the rancid stench of a decaying corpse or what blood and brain matter patterns revealed about a homicide. Who could blame them?

I'd long since stopped trying to talk to Lori about my work because I knew it upset her. "To you, once they are dead, they are science," she said, holding her hands over her ears. "To me, they are human beings, and I don't want to know what one person can do to another. It horrifies me." That was my cue to escape to my office. Lori had nicknamed it my "cave."

It frustrated me that Lori didn't understand how affected I was by the tragedies of others. With my work, I buried my emotions because it was required in my field. You have to show that you can handle the kinds of things we see every day. My way of doing that was to concentrate on the science and box up my emotions somewhere safe in my brain. Only a robot could look at a dead infant and not feel something. I wasn't very good at expressing my feelings, but I was no robot. My heart broke with every victim, but rather than break down and cry, I focused on what might bring them some kind of justice.

My parents saw trouble ahead in our marriage, even before Lori and I realized that we might be mismatched. My dad encouraged us to take the Myers-Briggs personality test, a questionnaire that identifies a person's psychological type. He'd taken it himself and thought it was a useful resource, both as a look inside us and a tool to help identify and understand our differences. Lori and I followed his suggestion. We answered the questions on the test and scored on total opposite ends of the spectrum. She fell into a classification of people who were tuned in to others' emotions, empaths who were led by their heart. I landed in a rare category of "introverted thinker," a "just the facts" kind of guy who felt plenty but had trouble expressing emotional warmth and could give the impression of being aloof. If you believe in personality tests, and I'm not sure that I do, Lori and I were polar opposites by virtue of our wiring and the way our minds perceived the world. She believed that people were good by nature. I thought she was naive. I argued that most people were well intentioned, but there was still a segment of the population that was just evil. Seeing what I had seen, how could I not? Our views of life were so fundamentally at odds, there seemed to be no middle ground.

That was never clearer to me than three months earlier when we had attended a Christmas play at Lori's church. The auditorium was full of people there to see *A Night in Bethlehem*, most of them strangers to me. The lights dimmed just before the curtain rose, and Renee took Nathan off to play. Lori seemed to think nothing of it, but I panicked.

"What's wrong with you?" she whispered, clearly irritated that I was scanning the crowd trying to find them.

"You just let our kids go running off somewhere, and I can't see them," I replied.

"These are all Christians, Paul," she whispered under her breath.

I was exasperated. "Even Christians do bad things," I said.

By then, I'd had my share of experiences with the dark side of humanity. At crime scenes and in the autopsy room, I'd seen what people can do to one another. I'd studied serial predators and knew that people with religion were as capable of atrocities as anyone. In fact, just a few years prior, a serial killer known only as BTK had terrorized people in Kansas while also playing the role of model citizen. When he was not torturing his victims, he was a pillar of his community, a Boy Scout leader and president of his church council. Congregants from his church described him as a good Christian. Days before his arrest, he delivered spaghetti sauce and salad to a church supper, so I knew that psychopaths hide in plain sight, that they disguise themselves with families and jobs and, yes, even religion. Those were the type of people I thought about when I couldn't find my kids. I knew too much not to be on high alert.

LORI BARELY LOOKED UP FROM HER collage of family photos as I said a quick goodbye and headed back to the lab. There, I picked up the crime scene van and headed west on Route 4 toward Hercules to my next obsession. The house was in a neighborhood that one local newspaper described as more accustomed to having streets roped off for a block party than a criminal investigation. Hercules hadn't had a homicide in two years and never a double. It was ten o'clock when I arrived at the address on Dunham Court, but the house blazed from the inside with bright crime scene spotlights. Two patrol units, lights pulsing, sat outside. I parked the van on the street and crossed the yellow crime scene tape. Hercules sergeant Bill Goswick gave me a quick rundown of what he knew. The victims' names were Neal Abernathy and his son, Brendan. Their bodies had been discovered by Neal's wife, Brendan's mother, Susan, when she got home from work a few minutes before six. They were still inside.

Processing a crime scene is a painstaking procedure that involves a meticulous search for anything that might be of an evidentiary nature. A single hair or drop of blood can make the difference between a solved case and a cold one. The work is often grim, and I prided myself on my ability to stay vigilant. The goriness didn't affect me, and I'd seen plenty— mutilated bodies, blown-out brains, maggots, just about any horrific visual of what can happen to a person after they die—and I've always been able to handle it. The intentional killing of a child was different, and this was my first.

Like so many homicide scenes, this one painted a picture of life as happy and normal, until it wasn't. A drinking glass on the coffee table. A black jacket draped over a kitchen chair. A set of keys tossed haphazardly on the kitchen table, next to a bowl of half-eaten salad and a couple of ketchup packets from McDonald's. I was met inside by Detective Sue Todd. A chain-smoking blond woman with piercing blue eyes, Todd was a good cop but a novice when it came to homicide investigations. In fact, this case was her first. She looked angry, as if to say, "Who does something like this?" She took a deep draw on her cigarette and nodded toward the family room. The victims were sprawled out on the floor.

My brain switched to crime scene mode. Unattached. Analytical. You don't show weakness, even if it means putting on an act. The father was facedown in a pool of congealed blood, a gaping hole in the back of his head. His wrists were tightly bound behind him with yellow audio cable that stretched down and wrapped around his ankles. Deep abrasions on his skin suggested that he had fought against the bindings before he was killed. The boy was slumped over the back of his father's legs with his arms stretched up over his head, almost as if he were sleeping. His hands were bound with the same kind of cable, but loosely. He could easily have pulled out of them if he'd had an opportunity. I wondered why the shooter had tied him so gently. Did that imply an emotional connection? An existing relationship? Or was it that the offender had shown him some mercy because he had a pang of conscience about killing a kid?

I went to work, dusting for fingerprints and footprints, cutting blood-stains and brain matter from the carpet, collecting trace evidence with tape lifts, scraping spatter from the walls, photographing every room. As the night stretched on, I was hit with a wave of melancholy. It sounds

strange, but after spending so many hours in the house, I felt like I'd gotten to know Neal and Brendan. The picture of them at a sporting event,
with Brendan resting his head on Neal's shoulder. Their shared computer
games. Brendan's typically messy boy's bedroom. Neal's shaving kit. The
smell of the clean clothes that had just been laundered and folded in neat
piles. The half-empty McDonald's soda sitting next to Brendan's computer that he'd never had the chance to finish. I went in cold, but with
each new discovery, I was developing more of an emotional attachment
and finding it harder to maintain my distance. Instead of seeing scientific
bodies, as I usually did, I saw a boy and his dad. I couldn't get out of my
head the image of my own son Nathan lying on the floor.

When the coroner arrived at sunrise, we turned the bodies over. Only
then did I see that Brendan was leashed to his dad. The offender had used
the father to anchor his son in place and prevent Brendan from being able
to get away. I gasped. It was a ghastly detail that felt right out of a horror
movie. The boy had died instantly when a single bullet passed from the
back of his skull through the front, burrowing in his right arm. Remarkably, his facial features were intact. His mouth was slightly open, revealing the braces on his teeth. There was something so contradictory about
braces and such a malevolent act. Kids weren't supposed to die, especially
not that way. I shook my head, trying to shake off my sadness.

The critical moment was when I discovered that stains from Brendan's
brains and blood were found on the carpet beneath his father's body, which
told me the boy was killed first. Neal hadn't died right away. Expiratory
blood from his nose and mouth was evidence that he was still breathing
after he was shot. Not only had he witnessed the murder of his son; he
had lingered after that fatal bullet lodged in his brain for who knows how
long. What kind of God allows such cruelty? The sequence suggested that
the killer was exceptionally callous and intended to cause Neal great emotional suffering before he killed him. Clearly, he had succeeded.

So often, the random shootings carried the signature of gang violence. Gang members frequently "dome" their victims. Doming is when the shooter stands over his victim and empties the gun into his or her head. It's intentional overkill. He wants to be sure that when he walks away the victim is dead. The Orinda restaurant owner and her daughter had been domed by a gang during a robbery. I believed the Abernathy attack was not Orinda. The offender or offenders went to this house with a single intention, to kill the father and his son. This appeared to be an execution, with both victims shot once through the head. But why?

AT FIRST GLANCE, THE ABERNATHYS LOOKED like everyone's next-door neighbors. They lived in a standard California subdivision home and drove sensible cars. Susan was a chemist at Chevron, and Neal owned a car repair shop, which he ran mostly from home so he could help with the kids. Brendan was a brainy kid, a precocious twelve-year-old who spent hours playing computer games and was more comfortable with his parents' friends than his own classmates. Susan Abernathy described a life in which she and Neal still spent romantic moments together doing things like picking daffodils from their garden and soaking in a hot tub with lavender blossoms "until we were all wrinkled." They had their problems like everyone. Sometimes she thought he was a bit lazy, and he'd suffered from bouts of depression. Friends described her as the dominant partner and Neal as passive to a fault; he would do pretty much anything to avoid confrontation.

By Susan Abernathy's account, the morning of the murders started out routinely. The alarm sounded at 6 A.M., and Neal and Brendan stayed in bed while she got ready for work. She kissed her husband goodbye and left home at 7:10 to carpool to her office with a colleague.

At 2:30 P.M., Neal drove Brendan to the dentist for X-rays. By three o'clock, they were on their way home again. Two hours later, Susan packed up her briefcase and collected her colleague for the commute home. She dropped him off at home at 5:30, then stopped for gas. It was 5:47 when she pulled into her driveway on Dunham Court. The family dog, a corgi named Annie, greeted Susan. She had taken only a few steps inside when she saw Neal and Brendan lying facedown on the living room floor.

At first, she thought the red stain under Neal's face was juice. Maybe he'd gotten sick, and her son was kneeling over him trying to help? She took a few steps closer before she realized the juice was blood. Her family was dead. She tried dialing 911 from the kitchen phone, but the phone was dead, so she ran to the next-door neighbors for help. Al Flanagan was cooking pasta in his kitchen when Susan came in. "I think my husband and son are dead on the living room floor," she said. "Call 911!"

By the account provided by Al's wife, Tina, to the investigating detectives, she was upstairs changing out of her work clothes during all the commotion and only became aware there was a problem next door when she came downstairs. By then, Al and Susan were back. Susan was sitting calmly at her kitchen table, but Tina's husband was frantic. "There's been a double murder next door!" he cried. It took a minute for Tina to grasp what he'd just said. When she did, she reached out for Susan. Susan was unresponsive, cold even. She said she was expecting a friend for dinner and needed to make a call. Tina overheard her calmly leaving a message on the answering machine. "Hi, Craig, this is Susan. I have to cancel dinner tonight. Neal and Brendan are dead. I'm going to go to the hospital. I'll see you later, and sorry about dinner." Sue Todd later listened to a recording of the call and described Abernathy's tone as "chipper."

Sirens screamed, and red flashing lights flooded Dunham Court, alerting neighbors that something dire had happened on the cul-de-sac. After the bodies were removed to the morgue, my team and I continued to comb the house for evidence overnight and into the next day. Each of the items was placed in its own paper bag, labeled, sealed, and inventoried—the bag and tag—for the trip to the lab where it would be itemized and analyzed. Whoever killed Neal and Brendan was meticulous in covering their tracks. The only useful evidence I found was a glove fingerprint, which was next to nothing.

The Abernathy house was in disarray, drawers were left open, and papers were shuffled around, but I didn't believe this was a burglary gone sideways. In the Orinda case, where burglary was the motive, the offenders had torn up the house looking for valuables. In the Abernathy house, despite the mess, nothing of value had been taken. Expensive jewelry and electronics in plain sight had been left behind. The scene looked staged to me. In my opinion, the motive here was to kill Brendan and Neal.

Susan Abernathy arrived back at the house just past noon, accompanied by two cops from Hercules PD. Before she arrived, I made sure to place cardboard over the bloodstained area where the bodies had been, so as not to further traumatize her.

In my crime scene work, I'd seen mothers who'd lost their kids, and it was always heartrending. A few months earlier, I'd witnessed a mother come up to the crime scene tape where her teenage son had lain in the street dead, the victim of gang violence. The woman could barely stand as she wailed with grief.

Susan Abernathy's behavior was unlike any I had ever witnessed under the circumstances. I watched, like a fly on the wall, as she walked in the front door, flanked by the local detectives. To me, she seemed more like a potential home buyer than a victim who had just lost her world. Maybe she was just in shock, I thought, but I took note of how detached she seemed, even a little giddy. She bopped from room to room, pointing out minor discrepancies. Papers on Neal's desk looked disturbed, the telephone answering machine was missing, and Brendan's backpack was nowhere to be found. Nothing of real value had been taken, she said. Standing at the juncture of the murder scene, she paused, looked over at the cardboard covering the stains where the bodies had been, raised her hand to her mouth, and, in a squeaky voice, said, "Oops."

It seemed like the kind of response you might expect if she'd walked in on her son kissing a girl or stepped into an occupied stall in a public restroom. This was the very spot where her husband and only child had suffered the last terrifying moments of their lives, the place where they'd taken their final breaths, where she'd seen their ravaged bodies only a few hours earlier. *Oops?*

When a family member is not sufficiently emotional after a homicide, it can be a red flag to investigators. But I never like to judge the conduct of someone suffering from the trauma of losing a loved one to violent crime. I'd been on the job long enough to know that people respond in unpredictable ways to trauma. I had to remind myself that bizarre behavior did not a murderer make—and Susan Abernathy's just kept getting stranger. In the interrogation room at police headquarters, she asked detectives if she could "act out" what she remembered from the night she found the bodies. Rising from her chair, she demonstrated how she got out of her car and walked to the front door. At that point, Sue Todd walked into the room. Susan Abernathy turned to look at her. "We're just at the good part, and you almost missed it!" she said, before returning to her story.

"You can't make this stuff up," Sue Todd said to me afterward, taking a deep drag on her cigarette.

"Maybe this is just her way of handling tragedy," I said.

"Could be," Todd agreed. "But you can't deny that she's peculiar."

"No, there is no denying that," I said.

. . .

MY ROLE IN THE ABERNATHY CASE should have ended when I wrapped up the crime scene, but I'd gotten a taste of detective work and liked it, so I edged my way in. Hercules was a small department with limited resources. I offered to help Sue Todd in any way I could. While she did the daytime detective work, piecing together the story of the family's life and interviewing people connected to them, I dug for information on friends and associates on a home computer I'd built with PC parts collected from garage sales. (That's the nerd in me.)

At night, by the light of my computer screen, I looked up names given to me by Sue Todd. I focused on statements made by the family's circle of friends. There was plenty to be suspicious of. The inner circle was made up of colorful characters who believed in things like shamans and spells and spirits. Most were from Susan and Neal's college days, and others they'd met socially through the Society for Creative Anachronism (SCA), a group that reenacted medieval times, wearing period costumes and acting out battles with sticks and swords. (The Abernathys had two swords, one under their bed.) I keyed in on two of their closest friends. One, a computer whiz who boarded with the family for a time, had a criminal record. He had a job installing the same stereo audio cables that were used to bind Neal and Brendan. During questioning, he admitted to Sue Todd to having a sexual attraction to Susan Abernathy. Nine years before the homicides, in January 1988, California Highway Patrol found him sleeping in his car on a remote road in Ventura County. A search of his car revealed an arsenal of weapons—multiple firearms, bomb components, and a stolen part from a stinger missile system. He told the officers he worked for an aerospace and defense corporation. He was also carrying a bulletproof vest and a copy of the book *Cop Killer*. He was arrested and charged with weapons possession. Two months later, in a nearly identical scenario, he was arrested and charged again, this time by San Bernardino Sheriff's officers. He looked suspicious to me.

Another person of interest was a former college roommate of Neal's who had recently come back into the Abernathys' lives and was among the last people to see Neal and Brendan alive. On the day after the murders, he'd written that he was mourning the death of his best friends. "This was a planned execution," he wrote. *How could he have known that?* I wondered. Was he speculating? He didn't have an alibi for the day of the homicides. Another name to add to the list of possible suspects.

As tips came in, the list of possibilities continued to grow. New theories were advanced. What were we dealing with? Based on Neal's victimology— which included business contacts with convicted felons and a somewhat unconventional lifestyle—the list of possibilities was broad. We narrowed in on two early tips. Both involved alleged business associates of Neal's.

One I'll call Garrett Barr was a customer at Precision Tune, Neal's car repair shop. An anonymous caller claimed that shortly after the homicide, Barr had been at a local Moose lodge bar spouting off about Neal "deserving what he got." The two men had previously tangled over a six-hundred-dollar car repair bill. Barr threatened to kill Neal because he was unhappy with the work the shop had done on his car. I dug into Barr's past and learned he'd once been suspected in another homicide case, although no charges had been brought. Friends described him as a braggart, a bigmouth, and a liar. The tip was certainly worth pursuing.

The second lead centered on Michael Riconosciuto, a computer genius who was serving a prison sentence for running a methamphetamine manufacturing facility in Washington state. Through his attorney, Riconosciuto, who had family connections to Hercules, claimed he held the key to the Abernathy case. Sue Todd spoke to Riconosciuto. His story was that he had been a CIA operative, commissioned by the U.S. Justice Department to create a back door into a private case-management computer program used by government prosecutors called INSLAW PROMIS (Prosecutors Management Information System) so it could be used for covert intelligent operations against foreign governments. Before he went to prison, Riconosciuto said, he tasked Neal Abernathy with hiding a stash of secret documents and millions of dollars' worth of valuables. Neal, he said, hid the goods in a container in a storage facility in Emeryville under a false name. Reconosciuto identified a man with mob ties and said it was he who had either killed or ordered the hit on Neal because of Neal's knowledge of the container. Brendan was collateral damage.

With every new lead, Sue Todd and I volleyed theories back and forth, but for me, the case always went back to our original hunch: the answer to the crime was closer to home.

On the night after the killings, Susan and her parents had dinner at the Flanagans'. Tina Flanagan would tell police that over coffee, Susan's mother said that she was proud of how strong Susan was; Susan had told her she was ready to get on with her life and intended to get married again. That weekend, Susan echoed these comments in an announcement she made at an open house at the Flanagans'. She stood and thanked everyone for their support, saying she intended to get on with her life. She was returning to her maiden name and planned to renovate the house and move back in as soon as it was done. At this point, her husband and son had been dead only a few days. What she really wanted, she said, was for the crime to be solved so she could move back into her house.

Three weeks after the murders, in early March, an anonymous letter was sent to the Antioch Police Department. It read: "Regarding the Abernathy shooting in February: There are no tears from Susan over her dead son and husband and a large insurance policy with a new man waiting in the wings—wait and see." The letter was signed, "Someone who knows."

At the end of March, Hercules PD returned the Abernathys' house key, and renovations began. Three months later, the work was done, and Susan moved back into her remodeled home. Over the Fourth of July weekend, she showed up at a block party and introduced a man she called her "new boyfriend" to the Dunham Court neighborhood. By then, some of the neighbors had seen the new man coming and going during the previous couple of months. Kent Truscott was an old friend of both Neal and Susan from their days at UC Davis. He had never married and didn't have children. They'd kept in touch over the years. Susan told the neighbors she lucked out because he was available and interested in having a relationship.

I have a saying that a homicide investigator is wrong until they're right. In every case, numerous suspects are developed. With each suspect, you believe there is enough evidence until there isn't. This happens often. It's not uncommon to believe in your gut that you know what happened yet not be able to meet the burden of proof, but I was still new to the job, and this was the first time it had happened to me. I wish I could say the job is the way it is portrayed on TV, where we swarm in, and by the end of the hour the bad guy or woman is in custody. It isn't. Sue Todd and I worked the Abernathy investigation relentlessly. We had plenty of compelling information that led in many different directions, but we still didn't have the answer we needed to close the case. Who killed Neal and Brendan Abernathy? We couldn't say. The evidence just wasn't there.

Garrett Barr agreed to submit to a Computer Voice Stress Analyzer. The test results were mixed. His alibi was that he was at home taking care of his children when the murders took place. His wife could neither confirm nor deny his story.

Michael Riconosciuto had a reputation for telling half-truths. His story was partially validated when INSLAW, the computer company, sued the U.S. government for stealing and tampering with its software and Riconosciuto was called to testify about his role in "customizing" the INSLAW

PROMIS system. But we were never able to establish any connection between him and Neal Abernathy, nor were we able to confirm telephone calls and correspondence he claimed to have had with Neal. Sue Todd wrote in the case file: "Until such time that Riconosciuto chooses to come forward with full disclosure, it is my opinion that to continue to investigate this venue would be an exercise in futility." My belief is that Riconosciuto was using the Abernathy case to try to have his prison sentence reduced.

Susan Abernathy took a polygraph and denied any involvement in the murders. The administrator of the test determined she had been truthful, but a polygrapher from the California Department of Justice challenged the finding. He was of the opinion that Abernathy had been deceptive. The test result was changed to "inconclusive."

If suspicious behavior was a crime, the whole Abernathy circle would have been taken into custody. Neal's former roommate's polygraph results were inconclusive. He said he was home alone when the murders took place, that he'd left work feeling ill. During a break in the polygraph process, Sue Todd saw him point his fingers at the door, as if he were aiming a gun, and heard him say, "The nightmare is just beginning." When he was later asked what he meant, he said he'd been thinking about the grief he'd suffered over the death of his wife and knew that the same process was just beginning over the loss of Brendan and Neal.

Kent Truscott retained a lawyer and has always refused to be interviewed by investigators. Without his cooperation, we were left to depend on information from other sources. He married Susan Abernathy and moved into the Dunham Court house, where the murders had taken place.

Eventually, the Abernathy file was moved to the cold case room. After Sue Todd retired from Hercules PD, I continued to revisit the case, usually on the anniversary of the murders, February 19. It haunted me that I hadn't been able to crack my first real homicide investigation. Three years earlier, when I had first discovered the East Area Rapist files, I found myself wondering, *How can someone just let these cases sit? How can it be that no one has ever solved it?* It was naivete on my part. A staggering number of homicides went unsolved, more than a third nationwide. If they were easy, they would have been solved. Now I had my own "old and cold" to add to the pile, and it bugged the hell out of me.

I never stopped thinking about Neal and Brendan Abernathy. I'd awaken in the middle of the night asking, "What did I get wrong? What am I missing?" On those nights when I was turning the case over in my head, unable to sleep, I'd pacify myself by remembering that the case was not black and white. We had no scientific evidence. No usable DNA. No shoeprints or fingerprints. No bodily fluids besides those of the victims. No witnesses. Only a glove print that proved useless. If the case were possible to solve, I believe I would have solved it. We had theories, just not enough evidence to prove or disprove any of them. But that doesn't mean we won't.

A criminal analysis of the case done by the California Bureau of Investigation in 2004 concluded: "It is unlikely the victims were killed by a total stranger. We believe the killer can either be found in the victims' social network or had some relationship with the surviving family member." I still believe that's where the answer lies, and I continue to reexamine and reassess. I don't look at the case as a defeat. It's ongoing. As long as I'm breathing, I'll continue to circle back. *Maybe this time I'll get a break.* That's how I think about it. And if it isn't me, it will be someone else. Sometimes an offender gets lucky. But there is always new science, advancing technology, jogged memories, guilty consciences come home to roost.

I remind myself there is always tomorrow.

9

Connecting the Dots

It was exciting taking on more investigations, but I was still itching to return to that filing cabinet in the basement. And the only way I could get back to those EAR files was to go rogue. Working on a cold case, even one that had paralyzed the state for years after the attacks stopped, wasn't in my job description. I was building my career as an investigator, and we had more active homicides than criminalists to handle them. If I wanted to work EAR, that meant stolen moments on nights and weekends, pulling out the files when I thought no one would notice. It was taking a risk, but I told myself that the end would justify the means. What was a little bit of deception, if it meant unmasking the monster?

During those stolen moments, I'd learned a lot about the predator. He'd cut a wide swath of fear across Northern California, terrorizing communities along an eighty-mile stretch of the north-south corridor between Sacramento and Contra Costa Counties. It galled me that someone could commit the atrocities he had and possibly still be out there, able to live a normal life.

I spent months poring over those case files and doing what research I could, but there came a point when I realized I had to visit the crime scenes to see what I'd read in the case files. I had to physically be where he had been to try to figure out why he chose certain places, certain victims. It was the only way I would be able to get inside his head. And so I began the next phase of my investigation, spending weekends driving to the addresses in Sacramento County where he had gotten his start.

SITTING IN MY CAR OUTSIDE THE HOUSE on Ladera Way in Fair Oaks, I was transported back to the week before Christmas 1976. On that day, the house shimmered with festive lights. The fifteen-year-old girl inside was home sick with a cold. She'd decided to stay behind when her parents went to a holiday party. Her sister was working, so she was alone in the house. Dinner was pizza. She set the oven timer for ten minutes and retired to the living room to practice the piano while she waited. It was only a moment or so later when she heard what sounded like a crack or a thump. She froze. *What was that?* She always heard noises when she was home alone. *Ignore it; you're overreacting.* What about those silent phone calls the family had been getting lately, sometimes three or four a night? That had frightened her. *Don't jump to conclusions.* She resumed playing piano. "Make a move and I'll kill you," the man said, pressing a knife to her throat.

He pushed the girl from the living room and down the hallway, past her parents' bedroom, and outside to a picnic table in the backyard. He wore gloves. She could barely catch her breath.

"Sit down," he commanded in that terrifying, guttural whisper. "You'll be okay. I won't hurt you. I'm going to tie you up to a post. If you try to look at me, I'll kill you."

She couldn't move. He shoved her down on the picnic table and tied her legs and pulled off her slippers and threw them across the yard.

He walked back into the house, leaving her there, bound and shaking in the cold night. She could hear him in the kitchen, opening and shutting drawers and cabinet doors. "Oh shit," he said. "Oh damn." *What was he looking for?* The oven timer buzzed, and he turned it off, just as if it were his kitchen and his pizza heating in the oven. He was in control.

A few minutes passed, and he was there beside her again. He grabbed her, pulled her to her feet, and pushed her inside the house. He raped her on her parents' bed.

"This is wonderful, just great. Isn't this good?" he taunted her. A knife at her throat, she nodded.

He continued his sadistic game, moving her back and forth between the house and outside, tying and untying her between assaults. The depth of his cruelty was stunning.

After an hour and forty minutes, tires screeched, and he was gone.

The attack was listed as Attack No. 10 on what would become the official EAR list.

From the car, I wondered why here? Why her? Most of EAR's attacks were in clusters, but some, like this one, were geographically isolated. This attack was also different in that it happened at 7:30 P.M. rather than the middle of the night. Was it random, or did EAR have knowledge of the family and their movements? As predictable as he could be, striking repeatedly in the same neighborhoods, sometimes he was totally unpredictable.

NEWSPAPERS DOCUMENTED EAR'S TRAIL OF TERROR with grim headlines. EAST AREA RAPIST ATTACKS AGAIN. SECURE ANTIRAPIST LOCKS URGED. Neighborhood watches were formed. Gun sales soared. Guard dogs were employed. "The boogeyman" was out there somewhere. He upped the ante a month after the *Sacramento Bee* ran a story, in March 1977, and mentioned that he'd never attacked while a man was present. Less than a month later, he broke into a home where a couple was sleeping. He was a vindictive bastard. *I'll show you who I am.*

A woman and her boyfriend were asleep in her bedroom in Orangevale. Her kids were sleeping in another room. She woke up to see a man shining a flashlight in her eyes.

"Don't make a sound," said the voice behind the light. "Wake him up." She had to know who he was. Everyone in Northern California had EAR on their minds.

The woman obeyed and shook her boyfriend. She hoped her kids didn't hear what was happening. The boyfriend started to get up from the bed.

"Stop. Don't move. Lay on your stomachs," EAR said.

He threw a rope to the woman and ordered her to tie her boyfriend's hands while he held the muzzle of the gun to his head.

"Don't look up. If you see me, I'll have to kill both of you," he said.

With the boyfriend bound at the wrists, EAR took the same type of rope and tied his feet together, then bound the woman's hands behind her back.

"I'm going to tie you up in the hallway so you can't untie each other," he told her. Holding a knife to her back, he took her to the family room and made her lie down on the floor. He wrapped a towel around her head, then went to the kitchen, retrieved a cup and saucer from the cabinet, and went back to the bedroom and placed the dishes on the boyfriend's back. If he heard the dishes rattle, he warned, he would kill everyone in the house.

EAR returned to the family room with a pair of high heels he'd gotten from the woman's closet. He put them on her feet and proceeded to repeatedly rape her while her boyfriend lay incapacitated in the next room.

"I'm going to go have some cheese," he said afterward. As she lay naked and bound, she heard him open the refrigerator and then the sound of him chewing. He was inflicting psychological torture.

Before he left, he went back to the bedroom. Bending down close to the boyfriend's ear, he whispered: "Next place, next town."

EAR had flawlessly achieved his first attack with a man present, a practice he didn't divert from throughout the rest of the series. *Fuck you,* Sacramento Bee. He had to have thought about how he would accomplish getting the two adult victims under control while minimizing the risk to himself. In his mind, he delineated a process that he put into action and it worked, minimizing the threat of—and in many ways emasculating—the man. The forethought spoke to his intelligence and his arrogance.

From that point forward, more than two-thirds of the remaining attacks happened when men were present. EAR was purposefully choosing to enter and sexually assault a woman while the man was inside the house, an unusual characteristic of a serial predator, I thought.

EAR STRUCK THIRTY TIMES OVER TWO years in Sacramento County before moving our way in early October 1978, striking twice in the same week. For a month before he first appeared on October 7 in Concord, neighbors reported prowler sightings, barking dogs, and open gates. He was targeting his next victims.

For a spell, he seemed to be prowling young girls. One of his youngest victims was a case of ours, a thirteen-year-old named Mary from Walnut Creek who was awakened at 4 A.M. on June 25, 1979, by the masked intruder. As her father and sister slept nearby, he attacked her amid the rainbows, unicorns, and heart posters decorating the walls of her girlish bedroom, promising "instant death" if she didn't sexually satisfy him. When he was finished with her, he tied her up. "If I hear one word out of you, I'll kill you while I looky-looky for money, money, money," he sneered. By the time she was able to cry for help, he was gone.

She was Victim No. 47. That fall she started eighth grade.

WHILE THE EAR CASES HAD HAPPENED in the late '70s, it was now 1997, and DNA testing had changed the game. To get used to this new technology, we'd started practicing on non-probative sexual assault evidence kits—that is, sexual assault evidence kits from crimes that had passed the statute of limitations and were about to be destroyed. I asked Karen Sheldon, my supervisor, whether kits were done in this East Area Rapist cold case I was interested in. And if they were—it was a huge "if"—could we use those for practice in the lab with this new DNA technique? She knew of my interest in the case and agreed.

"Okay," she said. "Go ahead."

I felt like I'd been set free. I could come out of hiding with my EAR work.

I returned to the files to scrutinize the police reports for each of our EAR attacks. In my search, I discovered that sexual assault kits had been kept in three of the suspected EAR cases. If they still existed and hadn't been destroyed over the decades, they would be stored just down the street in the Sheriff's Office Property Room. Back in the late 1990s, the Contra Costa County Sheriff's Property Room was located in an old two-story warehouse on Escobar Street in Martinez, California. At the time, it was overflowing with evidence, and at one point, it was even the subject of a grand jury investigation that resulted in a critical report detailing major flaws in managerial oversight and resources that could potentially compromise cases. Sheriff Warren Rupf assigned a dedicated manager to supervise and overhaul that resulted in a move to a modern facility and the hiring of Property Room management. But those improvements occurred *after* I went to the old facility looking for EAR evidence for the first time. Property wasn't the kind of place you'd want to go unless you had a good reason, but I always looked forward to my trips there. The anticipation of discovery made me giddy.

The Property Room process can be broken down into three main phases: intake, storage, and disposal. As evidence is collected and submitted, it is labeled and placed in the appropriate storage location. Hundreds of new items come into the Property Room every day, which means that if everything were retained, the facility would have run out of space long ago. Therefore, evidence that was no longer needed was routinely destroyed. The statute of limitations for sexual assault cases committed in California in the 1970s was six to eight years, which meant that evidence collection from our EAR cases would likely have been purged years ago. It was a long shot—that a usable sample was still on file and capable of producing enough DNA for a profile—and, under the best of circumstances, all it would accomplish would be to prove scientifically what investigators had already concluded anecdotally years before: that the same person was responsible for all three attacks. Still, it was an exciting prospect, to prove beyond any doubt that at least three of the attacks believed to be EAR's were linked.

I left the lab and walked the few blocks on Escobar Street to the Property Room, a two-story windowless cinder block cube behind a chain-link fence with barbed wire. Angel, one of the Sheriff's specialists working at Property, buzzed me in.

"What can I do for you, Paul?" she asked.

Angel had been there forever. She knew the Property Room inside out. I gave her the case file number, and she went off to pull the relevant property cards—three-by-five-inch index cards that listed a case number, an offense, and a description of correlating evidence. Angel returned with several small stacks and placed them on the counter in front of me. The cards were labeled with the same red "EAR" scratched across the top. Sifting through them, I saw that each was labeled "Do Not Destroy." I couldn't believe it. The evidence had been kept.

The Property Room had been a hollow rectangle when the Sheriff's Office leased it years earlier, and a metal serrated deck had been installed for more floor space. Older rape cases were stored upstairs. I followed Angel up, the *clank, clank, clank* of our shoes on the metal steps echoing from floor to ceiling. The air smelled stale, and the grayish-white fluorescent lights cast a sterile glow over the space. Wall shelves were piled high with tattered envelopes and crumbling paper bags containing old evidence. Crushed in the middle of the room were yellowed boxes stacked taller than me. The bottom boxes sagged from the weight. Most had been chewed through by rats and other rodents.

Angel pulled the first box and went back to fetch the second and third while I started on the first. Inside the box, I was hoping to find a manila envelope with a semen-swabbed Q-tip sealed inside a tube. I opened the box, and there it was, a little bit worse for wear, but it was there. I continued my search, carefully looking through everything Angel brought me. The second box produced another sample. I felt like I'd hit the jackpot when I found all three—two vaginal swabs and a neck swab. I could barely contain my excitement, but I knew my challenge was just beginning. I still didn't know whether these samples contained enough usable DNA to render results.

During my DNA training, I'd learned about the things that cause samples to degrade. Age and heat topped the list. The twenty-year-old kits had been kept in an area that could easily exceed 120 degrees on the hottest summer afternoons. But I didn't let that dim my hope. With all three swabs in my possession, I thanked Angel and headed back to the lab to get the process rolling. It was June 16, 1997.

By early July, I had my answer. By some miracle, the DNA hadn't degraded fully, and the results were conclusive. The original investigators had been right in their assessment that the three cases had been the work of a serial rapist. The swab with semen from one of the victim's necks cinched it. It was the cleanest sample of the three and gave me the most DNA.

Having absolute proof that it was the same person who had committed the three attacks was a significant step forward in a case that had been stagnant for so long, and I was proud to have been the one to make this discovery. But the real prize was that, using sperm extract from all three rape kits, I was able to create a DNA profile for the elusive EAR in the lab, which could help us identify a suspect. The next step was compiling an official list of former suspects so that we could begin the process of looking for a match.

"LIEUTENANT LARRY CROMPTON" WAS A NAME I'd seen repeatedly in my EAR research. Crompton had been a member of the original Contra Costa County EAR task force, and judging from the record, I figured he knew as much and probably more about the case than anyone. I hoped he would be able to tell me which names on my list had been the top suspects. Then I would go and get their DNA and solve the case; simple as that. I called Crompton in July 1997. I still have the notes. I was a young, low-level guy, and he was ranked up in the stratosphere of law enforcement. His stature gave me pause, but I didn't let the intimidation stop me from trying to get the information I needed. Lucky for me, I could tell right away that Crompton would be an ally. EAR had stopped attacking in Contra Costa County twenty years earlier, and Crompton's involvement had ended a short time later, but the case was still fresh in his mind. He recited case numbers and dates as if he'd been on it yesterday. When I asked if he'd be willing to rank the list of suspects I'd pulled together, he hesitated. "We never had a real good suspect," Crompton said. "We had a lot of suspects for sure, but the best ones we were able to eliminate." There went my plan.

But then he said something that stunned me.

All of the EAR attacks I was aware of were in Northern California. "We always thought he went down south and started killing," Crompton said.

"South? . . . Killing?"

When he was actively investigating EAR, Crompton had consulted with a psychiatrist to try to better understand the predator he was pursuing. "You had better catch him," she'd said, after reviewing the case. "He is going to kill, and he wants to kill." EAR had shown a predisposition for killing in at least one of the rape cases. In Attack No. 7 he'd run a knife up and down the victim's naked body. Another psychological assessment found he was likely fantasizing about cutting into her and that he was capable of evolving into a killer. Crompton told me he believed EAR did go on to kill. He'd been pursuing that avenue in late 1979 after a law enforcement buddy whispered in his ear that Santa Barbara in Southern California had a couple of cases that matched EAR's MO. One was a homicide. But when Crompton tried to connect the dots, Santa Barbara shut him down.

Back then, even more than now, the culture of sharing information between jurisdictions was very territorial. Why let someone else take a shot at solving something you couldn't? It was ego driven and political, and I'm certain there were many crimes that went unsolved because of a lack of cooperation between agencies.

"I never understood why they shut the door so fast," Crompton told me. "We heard there was an issue related to Governor Reagan running for president, and they didn't want the negative attention of a serial rapist moving into their area."

When I got off the phone with Crompton, I called Santa Barbara.

I wish I remembered the name of the detective I spoke with, but I can't seem to shake it out of my brain. What I do remember, clearly, is thinking that nothing had changed in the time since Crompton made the call. The detective was disinterested and dismissive when I explained why I was calling.

"I think there could be a connection," I said.

"Nope," he replied. "We don't have anything resembling that."

He knew the history of EAR and about the inquiries from up north way back when, but any hope I'd had of him revisiting the case was dashed when he told me, point-blank, "Our cases are not related to yours."

I don't easily take no for an answer when it comes to my cases, but I also knew when I'd hit a dead end. I was about to end the call when, either because his memory had been jogged or I had worn him down, he said. "Orange County might have something. Irvine is doing something with DNA."

I didn't know what he was talking about, and he wasn't interested in elaborating, but I decided to follow through, to eliminate the thread I'd begun to pull, if nothing else.

I called Irvine. After getting tossed from one person to the next, I landed at the desk of Detective Larry Montgomery. The gods must have been with me that day, because Montgomery was full of information and willing to share. He said Irvine PD had two homicides that had been tied together by DNA. One was from 1981, in which a female was bludgeoned to death in a sleeping bag inside her home. The other was in 1986—an eighteen-year-old girl killed the same way. Those two cases had been tied to a third Orange County case in which a newlywed couple had also been bludgeoned in their bed. By linking the homicides, they had developed a DNA profile of the killer, but they didn't have a name—the same situation I was in with EAR.

Mary Hong, at the Orange County Sheriff's Crime Lab, had done the DNA work, Montgomery said.

My next call was to Mary Hong.

I told her I was just doing due diligence on a rape series from up in Northern California and wanted to see if her DNA profile matched mine. I fully expected to eliminate any connection, and then I could move on from this brief Southern California distraction.

The use of DNA technology by law enforcement was less than a decade old in 1997, but it had already started to undergo changes. The British geneticist Alec Jeffreys had employed DNA technology (RFLP—restriction fragment length polymorphism) over in Britain in 1988 to solve the sexual homicides of two teenage girls. The technology he used had risen out of academia—genetic tools that had been employed to study various aspects of the human genome. These tools acted like genetic scissors, cutting the DNA strand into pieces of different sizes depending on each individual's genetic sequence. Jeffreys and his associates recognized that if enough of these pieces were made and sized, they would form a DNA profile that could be used to identify whose DNA had been left at a crime scene. It's akin to forming a DNA "barcode" unique to each person. Jeffreys's test had led to the arrest of the true perpetrator in England and showed that the wrong suspect was in jail. The promise of DNA typing reverberated throughout law enforcement and forensic science.

Jeffreys's technology was employed in casework around the globe, and though it was successful in many cases, it had an inherent weakness: it needed a lot of DNA from a crime scene to be able to work, and that DNA had to be relatively pristine. Think of DNA like a long strand of beads. As it is subjected to environmental insults, such as sitting out in the sun or exposure to bacteria, the strand breaks down into smaller and smaller lengths until each one is too short for the technology that Jeffreys invented to work. Forensic DNA samples, especially those that are decades old like the ones from the EAR cases, often have too little DNA or are too degraded to bear results.

Fortunately, another tool—this time from the biotech sphere—became available to forensic scientists: polymerase chain reaction. Instead of cutting the DNA the way RFLP did, PCR replicated it—a molecular copier—and could produce millions of copies identical to the DNA found in a forensic sample. Not only could it work with much smaller amounts of DNA; it also worked with degraded DNA. Incorporating the PCR process was a huge leap forward for law enforcement.

The PCR process, though, does not produce a DNA "type" the way RFLP does. It just makes a bunch of DNA. In 1997, the technology was still in its infancy and had not yet been standardized, which meant that crime labs across the country were all employing different ways to produce a DNA type based on the PCR process. The technology I used on the EAR samples looked at a very specific area of the DNA called DQα. The DQα profile was developed using an old "dot blot" method, where specific areas of a white nylon strip turned into blue dots to indicate what DQα type was present in a sample. EAR had a DQα of 2, 3, but so did many other people. Though this technology was exciting, it was still very limited in terms of its power of discrimination.

At the time my lab was doing DQα testing, another typing technology was taking root—STRs (short tandem repeats). This technology exploited areas of the DNA where there was a stutter in the sequence, short areas that repeated over and over again. Different people have different numbers of repeats. The STR technology also looked at many more regions across the human genome. Its power of discrimination was far greater than that of DQα and is now the technology that has become the standard used by law enforcement labs everywhere. However, in 1997, when I called the Orange County Sheriff's lab, that wasn't yet the case.

Mary Hong told me her cases had been linked by STR tech, so I knew it was a solid link—no doubt the same offender for all three. My lab was still using the older PCR technology. Fortunately, Mary had also done some of the older PCR-based DNA testing, which showed that her offender had the same DQα type as EAR. The problem for me was the PCR marker by itself was not very discerning, and based on just that one DQα marker, I couldn't conclude that her cases and mine were committed by the same offender.

I promised Mary that once Contra Costa's DNA technology caught up with Orange County's, I would be giving her a call back.

I never thought it would take four years to make good on that promise.

10

The End of a Marriage

My panic attacks had begun to sneak up on me in the middle of the night. I'm an erratic sleeper anyway, but now even those times when I was able to doze off were disrupted by terrifying jolts of alarm. The disruptions had gotten progressively worse as I had begun to acknowledge how alone I felt, even within my marriage with Lori. I'd awaken plagued by feelings of foreboding, and soon I was curled in a ball on the bedroom floor, sweating and panting, certain I was about to die. Lori was a deep sleeper and usually slept through it. Once the symptoms subsided, I'd be up all night pacing the floor, fearful that if I lay my head back down on the pillow, another attack would follow.

Lori and I had started seeing a counselor, but we hadn't seen much progress. Each session seemed to be a repeat of the last, with my wife shaking her leg nervously while the counselor attempted to prod my feelings loose.

"I love my family, but I don't know what I'm doing wrong," I'd say. "I don't know how to be who Lori wants me to be," I'd say.

"Who do you want to be?" the therapist asked.

What kind of question was that? "A good person. A productive person. Someone who has a purpose."

"And who are you?"

I'm Paul, dammit. What do you want from me?

TRYING TO FIGURE OUT HOW TO answer felt like turning the pages of a book when you don't know how to read. I truly couldn't comprehend what was being asked. *How can we get you to connect? You must know how you feel about that. Dig deeper. Close your eyes and think about what you're afraid of.* I was pretty good at interpreting evidence, but decoding my own feelings was like playing chess with missing pieces.

Sometimes it felt like we were just picking off scabs during those sessions. Old wounds were opened. Hurt feelings spilled out.

Lori cried. "You slept at the office and never even called to let me know you weren't coming home."

I complained. "I need more affection."

She recoiled. "I can't do that until you change."

I withdrew. "This is who I am. I became who I had to be to win you, and then I couldn't keep up the facade anymore."

"You're a good person," Lori said one day. "You have a genuine desire to put people's minds at rest by helping them to know what happened to their loved ones. You have a good heart. But somehow that compassionate, loving person doesn't make it home to me."

Lori blamed my work for what she described as my transformation.

"He's dealing with a very dark profession, and he has started seeing things differently," she told the counselor. "He has lost his way."

My work wasn't my job, I explained. It was my purpose. My worth. My reason for choosing to exist on this earth. How many times had I heard the story of someone who'd checked out because they'd lost their intention?

Their significance. I was useful in my work. I felt like I was making a contribution when I could bring a victim some peace of mind. And I was good at it. How could I stop being that person? It was who I was. I wasn't lost. I was right where I was supposed to be. The only place I felt lost was at home.

"I want my wife to be my soul mate," I said.

"And what is a soul mate?" the therapist asked.

"Someone to do things with," I said. "Someone to talk to."

She looked at me kindly. "But you're not around enough to do things. And most people don't want to listen to stories about things like babies being put in boiling water." The sessions always ended the same. I left feeling empty. Lori was frustrated and upset at what she called my selfishness. I felt like I was married to someone who couldn't engage about something that was core to me—my work.

After years on and off, I decided I wasn't going back to that room. If we still couldn't figure things out after all that time, what was the magic pill? For all of my aptitude for analyzing crime, I couldn't figure out how to be successfully married. How was it that two good people with two great kids couldn't make it work? It didn't compute in my logical mind. But it felt like there was no "us" anymore, so why continue to pretend?

But I couldn't say that to Lori.

"I'm going to take a break from counseling," I said, after our final session.

"Then I guess I'll go alone," she said.

The car ride home was tense.

Lori stared out the passenger window.

"The therapist says you're the most complex person she's ever had in counseling," she said.

"Do you want to stop to eat before we go home?" I asked.

I saw tears on her cheeks. I didn't know how to respond.

We spent the next few weeks in virtual silence. Lori accused me of being cold and aloof. I came home one night, and she followed me upstairs.

"If you can't tell me things will change, I want out," she said.

She was brave enough to say what we were both thinking, but it still hurt.

I felt numb. I left that night and took a room in a seedy motel in Martinez, around the corner from work. Going from a five-bedroom, three-bath home, noisy with the chatter of kids, to a single room with thin walls in a place that charged by the half day was humbling. The room was clean enough, but worn, with threadbare carpeting and a queen mattress warped from years of use. My neighbors were a mix: people who were down on their luck; hookups; travelers who'd exited off Highway 4 too late at night to find someplace decent. I'd once worked a homicide in a room down the hall from mine—a guy killed during a drug deal gone bad.

After a few nights at the motel, I ended up going to my parents' house to stay. Here I was, thirty years old, two children of my own, and sleeping on my parents' exercise room floor, thinking, *Oh my God. What am I doing?* At the same time, I knew it was on me to figure things out if I wanted to change the direction of my life, whether that meant in my marriage or outside of it.

I had probably been out of the house for a week or so when I went to see Lori's parents to explain. "Lori and I have been struggling," I said. Luckily, they were understanding. "We just want everyone to be happy," her mother responded. Over time, the frosty relationship with Lori thawed, and I moved back home to be closer to the kids. But in reality, we were only pretending to be a family, with Lori living downstairs and me taking the upstairs loft. Divorce was not something either of us took lightly. I was raised Catholic, and Lori's faith and upbringing prohibited it.

A few months later, my parents were over for dinner. I tried to act as though everything was happy. I didn't want them to know that we were continuing to struggle. I went into my home office for something, and my mom followed me. "We know you are having issues in your marriage," she said. "I want you to know that whatever decision you make, we're okay with it." Tears welled up in my eyes. Hearing those words was a huge relief. My parents would still love me, still accept me as their son if Lori and I didn't work out.

Lori and I continued to go through the motions for several months, but the tension between us grew once more. One day, I pulled into the driveway after being out on a case for days and saw her trying to push my new electric lawn mower through the thick grass I'd neglected for weeks. Her cheeks were bright red, and her lips were pursed. I could see that she was seething. I had just stepped out of the car when she turned toward me, her voice barely containing her rage. "Why would you buy a stupid lawn mower that can't even handle our front lawn?" she cried. I knew something had finally snapped. I went inside to my cave, and she took the kids to her mother's.

It was a tumultuous time for both of us. Lori said that whatever happened between us would have to be my decision. She would not take the initiative to leave the marriage since it was against her religion. I went back and forth in my head. One day I would long for a chance to look for real romance, the next day I'd convince myself that I loved Lori and needed to try harder to keep our family together. It went that way for months. I didn't know what it would take to push me in one direction.

ON AN AFTERNOON IN MAY 1997, as Lori and I were still living in this limbo state, I responded to a report of a body buried on a hillside off North Rancho Road in El Sobrante, a small, weathered community about twenty miles from San Francisco. A man had alerted a local detective to a wild story told to him by a buddy at a local bar. The story began something like

"Guess what my dumb brother has done?" After a couple of beers, it spun into a nasty tale of murder. The informant said the storyteller was a guy named Ray Holmes. Ray told him that, six months earlier, his brother, Dale, had come home in a panic and said he had "a problem." Dale and Ray were two years apart, thirty-one and twenty-nine respectively, and lived at home with their mother in El Sobrante. Dale had a fondness for "dating" sex workers out of San Francisco. Unfortunately for him, the women he chose weren't looking for love, and after one rebuffed his suggestion that she be his girlfriend, he pulled a knife and stabbed her to death.

The "problem," Dale told Ray, was the body. It was in the front seat of his pickup parked outside in the driveway. *What was he going to do?* Ray reluctantly agreed to help Dale dispose of the corpse. The brothers drove to the end of their street and buried it on the side of a hill. *Then what happened?* the informant asked, incredulous. Life went back to normal, Ray said, but six months later, Dale came to him a second time with the same dilemma. Another sex worker, stabbed to death because she had rejected Dale's desire to be her boyfriend, was stuffed inside the pickup. "This time, you're on your own, pal," Ray told Dale.

Going it alone, Dale drove the body a few miles away, where he dumped it on the side of the road and covered it with piles of debris. That had been two weeks earlier. Ray hadn't notified the authorities about the murders. Instead, he went to the bar and opened his mouth, not knowing his drinking buddy would alert law enforcement.

The Holmes brothers were taken into custody and interrogated, eventually giving up the locations of the bodies. A San Pablo PD detective, decked out in a suit and tie, was digging into the hillside at the end of North Rancho Road when Sheriff's Office decomp dogs arrived. He wasn't having any luck finding the grave of Dale's first victim, a young woman who had been a month shy of her twentieth birthday when she disappeared just before Christmas. It was summertime by then. A decomp dog sniffed out the spot, stopped, and pulled on a toe sticking out from the dirt. We grabbed our shovels and started digging there. It didn't take long to unearth the body. The brothers had wrapped it in plastic and buried it in a shallow pit, in the midst of dense green vegetation.

Waiting for the coroner to arrive, I looked out over the slope of the underbrush and thought, *This guy killed two women. Maybe there are others buried here on the side of the hill.* I aimed to find out. I pushed through the bushes looking for evidence but found nothing.

The hard work began with the coroner's arrival. A body starts to degrade after death. This one had been decomposing underground for six months, most of that time during the rainy season. With the coroner and the deputy standing at the head of the grave and me at the foot, we lifted the woman's body to get it into a body bag. Dead weight is real, and she was heavy. The deputy slipped on the damp soil, jostling the body. We were on a steep slope, and decomposition fluid ran out of the plastic wrapping onto the ground, forming a puddle. One of the dead woman's legs dropped down into the pool of foul liquid, splashing it up on my face and my leather crime scene boots. The stench was unimaginable. As we were loading the body in the van, a couple of miles away the second body was recovered. The brothers were taken into custody and charged with the killings. I donned my yellow body suit and searched the areas for evidence that might be connected, then combed the house where they lived with their mother, looking for anything that might be relevant. The mother bred Saint Bernards, and there were seventeen dogs running loose in the house. The place reeked of dog feces and was infested with fleas. I could see them jumping out of the carpet. Oh, the glamorous job of the homicide investigator. You never see things like that on TV.

That weekend, I began to itch. We were visiting my in-laws when I noticed a red spot on my right wrist. *A flea bite,* I thought. On Monday,

I woke up with oozing pustules on my neck, arms, and lower legs. That's when I realized: the vegetation I'd pushed through, looking for more bodies. "It must have been poison oak," I told Lori. I was scratching and oozing. Torture, but I had to go to work. The only thing that helped was the steaming hot water in the shower. The burning felt better than the itching. After I'd dried off, I wrapped gauze around both arms to prevent the pus from dripping onto my clothes, then finished dressing and headed out to the lab, fidgeting and trying not to scratch the whole drive. I was miserable.

It went that way for a couple of days. Even when I was able to drift off to sleep, the itching woke me. Lori was a deep sleeper, so my incessant scratching rarely disturbed her, but I was operating on short spurts of spastic sleep. Midweek, I came home, still in the depths of despair, wanting to rip my skin off. Lori was in the master bathroom, applying mascara. The tub was filling. "Mom and I are going out," she said, never looking away from the mirror. When she finished putting on her makeup, she turned and hurried past me. "The kids need a bath," she said over her shoulder as she left the house.

I was hurt and mad. Besides being completely sapped, I worried about exposing my kids to my poison oak. I got it. Lori needed a break after being home day after day with a toddler and an infant, and I was their dad. But her lack of compassion for my condition made me feel resentful and, truth be told, unloved.

For a long time, I'd gone about life not allowing myself to think about how empty I felt, assuming, I guess, that the marriage would somehow magically fix itself. Even if it didn't, there was always tomorrow, I told myself. In retrospect, I understand it took both of us to get to the point where neither of us had empathy for the other's challenges and frustrations, but that night was the moment that I realized the love was gone. As I bathed the kids and tucked them into their beds, it finally became clear to me that I could no longer live in denial. I didn't want to pretend anymore.

That fall I left home for good. Lori was sitting outside by our front gate, tears running down her cheeks. I hesitated. "I'm leaving," I said. She shook her head. "I don't understand what you want from me," she said. I didn't know whether that meant she didn't want me to go or that she'd given up, too. "It's too late," I said. Driving away, I felt a combined sense of guilt and relief.

11

Antioch

1998

I arrived on the scene after midnight, a little more than an hour after a father had killed his two little girls and then himself. I had spent the evening, like most, at Lori's house. I'd been living on my own for a few weeks in a small apartment in the picturesque town of Benicia, about thirty miles from Vacaville, but we agreed we'd do whatever it took to ease the disruption our separation had on our kids' lives. Ironically, I'd been more engaged with them since I'd moved out. Earlier in the evening, the kids and I had been playing a game of floor gymnastics, which had become a favorite after-dinner routine. I lay on the floor with my legs in the air as the kids circled around me, giggling. They took turns diving toward me, and I'd grab their little hands and push them up into the air on my feet and then over onto the sofa. It was what my dad did with my brother and me when we were small. At about the same time we were romping around, the little girls' father had barricaded the three of them in their home. He'd promised hostage negotiators he wouldn't harm them. He'd been reading to them and letting them watch cartoons, he said.

Hours later, standing over the body of one of the young girls, I wondered what she had seen before he took her life and then his own. Bugs Bunny? Scooby-Doo? I stared at her shoes, a tiny pair of sneakers with cartoon characters and Velcro straps. Maybe I'd focused on them a moment too long. "What is it?" asked the newcomer to the lab, a rookie scientist named Sherrie who was still learning the ropes of crime scene investigations. I didn't realize she was watching. "My son has the same pair," I whispered. I had to stop myself from picturing one of my kids lying there, shot in the head. *Shut it down*, I told myself as the image flashed in front of my eyes.

THIS WAS A REVENGE KILLING. A father, distraught over his wife saying she wanted him out of their lives, deciding to have the last word. The two little girls had lived with their mother in a modest home in a tired neighborhood in Antioch, a Bay Area suburb. Antioch had a seedy reputation, fueled mostly by crime-infested neighborhoods and street gangs.

The father was a fugitive in a gang-related murder.

The 911 call came in just before 6:10 A.M. on Friday, July 11, from the girls' mother.

"1300 Putnam! My two little girls!"

By then, the fate of the kids had already been fixed. The mother had been able to crawl to the front door and escape when the shooting started, leaving the little girls in the house with their raging father and his arsenal of weapons. I did my best to leave any judgment out of my work, but I couldn't help but wonder, who leaves their kids in such peril?

Lori and I worked so hard to not let our differences get in the way of our love for our kids. She was a devoted mom, and I was trying to be a better father. Why hadn't these little girls been cherished beyond the problems between their parents? I wondered. On the last day of their lives, they had been nothing more than objects, pawns in a deadly game of power and control with no one to keep them safe. It really is the luck of the draw, isn't it? The way children come into the world, who they are born to, whether they will be nurtured and protected.

SWAT had arrived within minutes of the call for help. The girls' father took a few shots at the officers to let them know he meant business. He was dressed for the mission, wearing camouflage and toting three guns. Negotiators did a valiant job of keeping him talking through all of Friday and late into Saturday night. He'd assured them he was taking care of his girls. He was feeding them hot dogs and Pedialyte. The littlest one had a diaper rash, and he was putting ointment on her, he said. They were okay. Just when the negotiators thought they were making progress, he switched from relatively calm to hysterical and announced that the standoff was over.

"Ten, nine, eight, seven, six . . ."

"Listen Carlos, why don't you talk to your mom?" the police negotiator pleaded.

"Five, four, three, two . . ."

"Carlos!"

"Tell her I love her," he said.

"Carlos, we can get your mom to talk to you, all right? Carlos?"

He was crying. "I'm so sorry, girls. I love you. NaNa, I love you."

All three were in the master bedroom. The TV was blasting, but nothing was loud enough to mute what was happening inside. The little girls were crying. At some point, they were looking into the eyes of the person who was supposed to defend them, to protect them with his life if he had to—a man who, by all accounts, adored them—and now he was aiming a gun at their heads with his finger on the trigger.

The cops heard what sounded like muffled gunshots. They shouted to him again.

He was shrieking. More shots followed. "What is wrong with me? . . . What the fuck is wrong with me?"

"We can get through this," the negotiator said, trying to reassure him.

"No. Oh my God. What am I doing?"

"Carlos, talk to me. Carlos."

A final shot rang out. Silence followed.

SWAT waited before lobbing concussion bombs into the house and storming inside. It was right around midnight. Forty-two hours had elapsed since they'd begun bargaining for the kids' lives. The father and the toddler were pronounced dead in the bedroom. The four-year-old was clinging to life. The paramedics tried to keep her heart beating, but she died on the way to the hospital. Homicide involving young ones is wretched, but having a child die while you're trying to save her was something I didn't want to fathom.

By daylight, the SWAT team was long gone, but the street was swarming with curious neighbors and reporters with tape recorders and mics. My team and I had worked through the night processing the crime scene. The house was in shambles, maybe because that's the way the family lived, or maybe because it had been a shitshow in there during the previous two days. The kitchen sink was piled with dishes, and a year's worth of mail was stacked everywhere. Phone messages were written in Sharpie on the walls. We worked around the mess, sifting through everything, collecting dozens of spent cartridges and bullets, the vestiges of circumstances gone terribly wrong.

Two days later, I was loading the last of the evidence bags into my car when I noticed a woman standing on the sidewalk on the other side of the police tape. Her face was swollen from crying, but I recognized her as the mother of the murdered little girls, from photographs scattered around the house. Happy family photos that belied the terrible truth, as they so often do.

She waved me over.

Tears spilled down her cheeks, and she said, "I have to bury my girls. My youngest had a doll she called Baby Doll. She dragged that doll everywhere, and it's somewhere inside. Please, I have to bury my baby with Baby Doll."

She was a young woman, but with deep lines etched in her face. I suspected she'd aged a lifetime overnight. Who wouldn't have? Any thoughts I'd had before about her leaving her babies behind in the house with their father while she escaped were quickly erased. My heart ached for her. I couldn't even think about losing one of my kids without being overcome by feelings of despair.

My thoughts turned to the little one on the bed. Now she had a name. Kavi, her mother told me.

"I'll find Baby Doll," I promised.

I went back inside and began searching. Kavi was going to be buried with Baby Doll if it was the last thing I did. I ransacked every room in the house, and when that didn't produce the doll, I went outside and rummaged through the dumpster. Dejected and fatigued, I was starting to lose hope when, almost absentmindedly, I picked up a sports coat that one of the other investigators had tossed on a kitchen chair, and there it was: Baby Doll. I felt like I could breathe again.

Bone tired, I went home to my apartment and fell into bed. Soon, I was drifting off to another place. The blast of a gunshot breaks the calm. I see myself walking in circles, searching for my shadow. When I finally find it, I'm aghast to see that it is headless. I've blown my own head off.

My eyes fly open. I'm panting and my chest is heaving, as if I've just finished running a race. I get up from my bed, soaked in sweat. I walk to the kitchen, splash my face with cold water, and decide to pour myself a glass of red wine. I won't sleep for the rest of the night. I've seen things that are unimaginable to most people, things that I've buried deep within my subconscious. It has to be that way in order to carry on with my work. But I can't stop the horror from invading my dreams.

Tomorrow night, it could be that same nightmare. Or it might be the recurring dream I dread the most: one of my kids has gone missing. The last time, it was Nathan. I'm searching frantically when I see him standing at the crest of a steep hill. I know he's in danger. I run toward him, arms outstretched, screaming his name. *Nathan! Nathan!* I'm so close I can almost touch him when he disappears over the other side.

He is gone.

12

Conaty and Giacomelli

NOVEMBER 1998

The first thing I saw were his shoes. Wing tips, as shiny as black ice. I was crouched down on my hands and knees in a garage, scrutinizing a ski boat for possible evidence in the homicide of a teenage girl. I cranked my head slowly upward. Brooks Brothers suit. Starched white shirt and silk tie. California tan. Dark glasses. Buzzed silver hair.

"Inspector John Conaty, Pittsburg PD," he said.

I knew the name. Everyone did. Conaty and his partner, Ray Giacomelli, were a two-man homicide squad out of the Pittsburg Police Department. Their reputation as top-notch detectives preceded them. If anyone deserved a pass for pomposity, they did. They were the team that solved the trickiest cases and coaxed confessions from the most hardboiled killers. Badasses and best dressed. They'd earned their badges as inspectors, the highest-ranking detectives in their jurisdiction, and they were best friends. Remarkably, I'd never run across either at a homicide before then.

Conaty lifted his chin, a gesture that seemed to ask, "What's up?"

"I'd like to know what you've got," he said.

His voice was imposing, but I detected a note of amusement in there. I was about to learn that Conaty always had a quip or joke, even during the darkest moments. Especially during the darkest moments. Working homicide is survival of the fittest. In order to stay sane on the job, you need to crack jokes, or you'll crack up. And this was a tough one. Earlier that night, the body of a missing fifteen-year-old girl had been discovered in an industrial area along a lonely stretch of the Pittsburg-Antioch Highway. Every day for the previous week, helicopters had circled overhead as search teams, some with dogs, combed the area on foot. On the eighth day, the search ended. A volunteer had stumbled upon the body just outside the door to a landscaping company that employees and customers used every day. It was in a prone position against an exterior wall in the front parking area and was covered with scrap cardboard and plastic sheeting. Two wooden freight pallets had obscured it from view. The face and upper body were caked with mud and debris and crawling with insects.

It was one of those stories that stokes every parent's fears. A kid who made a foolish decision—in this case to walk home alone in the dark—and paid with her life. Lisa Norrell had attended a rehearsal for her best friend's quinceañera. She left the rehearsal early, shortly before it ended at eleven o'clock. Friends said she was upset with the boy she'd been paired up with. Her mother, Minnie, thought it was more likely that she was embarrassed because she hadn't mastered the dance steps. Nevertheless, Lisa didn't wait for her ride. One parent thought another was responsible for driving her. No one realized she had taken off from the practice hall to walk the four miles home. Not until Minnie awakened in front of the TV at 3 A.M. and Lisa wasn't in her room.

The two-lane Pittsburg-Antioch Highway was the most direct route from the dance hall to Lisa's house. It was scarcely traveled at night.

Witnesses reported seeing a girl matching her description walking along the stretch of road frequented by sex workers and their johns after dark, something she wouldn't have known. She didn't make it far from the hall, less than a mile or so. She'd likely been abducted near where her body was found.

I'd been called out as part of the backup team and assigned to process the garage behind the landscaping company. It wasn't expected to produce anything of an evidentiary nature, but it had to be thoroughly searched. In my experience, investigators, especially senior investigators, rarely checked what was happening at a crime scene. The evidence came to them, and they rolled from there. It was immediately apparent to me that Conaty didn't exploit his rank the way others with the title did. For starters, he was there in the middle of the night, which in itself was a rarity for someone in his position. I was just a reinforcement on the case, working on the periphery of the crime scene, yet he'd taken the time to check out what I was doing. It wasn't just in and out and back to the desk either.

I'd already spent several hours in the garage and was about halfway through my routine by then. My general visual search was complete, and I'd taken hundreds of photographs of the area and the boat that was stored in the garage, but I still needed to dust for prints and test surfaces for traces of biological matter. If any part of the crime had taken place in or near the boat, it wasn't immediately evident, and I doubted that it had played any role. I felt almost guilty telling Conaty that my search thus far had turned up nothing of consequence. He asked a lot of questions, which told me he was thorough in his work. I assured him that if there was something there, I would find it.

"Thanks for being here," he said, turning to leave. "Appreciate what you're doing."

He hesitated, then turned back to face me. It was kind of a Columbo moment. Pushing his hands into his pockets, he shook his head.

"This just isn't right," he said. "We are going to freakin' figure this out."

The tough guy had a heart.

I SAW CONATY A FEW HOURS LATER at the morgue. I was the criminalist assigned to the autopsy, and I had gone straight there from the crime scene. Conaty came in with his partner, Giacomelli, a few minutes later. They really did look like characters from a Hollywood script. Giacomelli was a little bit shorter than Conaty, with a bushy mustache and dark hair, but like his partner, fit and dressed to the nines in a suit that probably cost more than my mortgage payment. Conaty introduced us. "Good to meet you," Giacomelli said, extending his hand. His fingers were thick, and his smile seemed to hide behind his mustache.

The three of us made small talk while I prepared to document evidence that I had retrieved from the body before the pathologist came in. A criminal postmortem is a collaboration between the investigating agencies, the pathologist, and the coroner's office. It has a lot of moving parts and is much more complex than a clinical autopsy. Earlier that morning, Lisa's body had been transported in the coroner's van from the crime scene to the morgue refrigerator, where she'd been placed among a lineup of rolling tables parked side by side. On any given day the refrigerator room was a tableau of death. An elderly man who'd succumbed to cancer; a little girl who'd drowned; a suicide victim who'd taken a gun to his head; and now young Lisa.

The familiar *whoosh* of the automatic doors leading from the refrigerator into the autopsy room signaled the arrival of the body. The room went quiet as the gurney was rolled in. All eyes were on the victim. Her gray hoodie was still pushed up above her breasts, and her pants were down around her thighs, just as she'd been found. Her thick, brown hair was tied up in a scrunchie. Conaty and Giacomelli walked off to a corner and took seats under a dry erase board with tallies of homicides for each agency written in black marker. Pittsburg was about to update their count by one. In short order, the pathologist appeared, and we began our dance. My job was collecting evidence, his was to determine the way Lisa had died.

I eyeballed the clothing for transient evidence—things like hair and fibers that might be linked to her killer—and photographed anything I thought could be significant to the homicide investigation. I documented whatever I could without touching or moving the victim. It's a long, tedious process that can take up to four hours, and pathologists often become impatient with the wait. Once I was finished, the clothing was carefully removed from the body, and the pathologist began his visual observation. In a forensic autopsy, that's when it got real for most people, just before the cutting began. First, the pathologist noted and recorded all visible bruises and abrasions. The demarcation between the ligature marks and compound bruising and abrasions around the neck suggested she had also been manually strangled, he said out loud to the room. There had likely been a struggle. She was probably sexually assaulted. I cut the ligature from the neck, careful not to disturb the knot, and bagged it for evidence. I determined that a "blind swabbing" was in order, that is, not just swabbing obvious areas for DNA but places where salivary evidence might have been secreted during a sexual assault or transferred in a tussle. When the swabbing was complete, I scrutinized the skin for additional transfer hairs and fibers and plucked hairs from the victim's body for comparison in the lab. I then shaved and collected her entire head of hair to be able to collect whatever biological material might be lurking in there. It was a lesson I'd learned from FBI colleagues who'd worked the 1993 Polly Klaas kidnapping. Twelve-year-old Polly was snatched in the middle of the night from a slumber party in her California home by a knife-wielding intruder. Her skeletal remains, with her hair intact, were discovered two months later. Agents collected the hair and, using a light with ultraviolet rays, were able to find transfer fibers belonging to her killer, Richard Allen Davis. Had it not been for that crucial evidence, there might not have been a conviction in the case. After that, I'd made sure to include this technique in my repertoire.

During my examination, I noticed Lisa was missing one or two artificial nails. Hands and nails can hold important clues. If she'd been fighting her offender, they could offer trace evidence or DNA. Using clippers, I attempted to cut off the remaining fake nails. The nails were too thick, and I had to resort to using wire cutters. I got the jaws of the cutters around the thick thumb nail and started to squeeze when I heard the grisly sound of her real nail being ripped off. I was shaken. I felt like I was torturing the girl. I knew all eyes were on me. I couldn't show weakness. I just had to put away my emotions and finish the job.

The autopsy began. The pathologist's tray is a macabre assortment of cutting and chopping instruments, the worst of all being pruning shears that are used to crack the rib cage and access organs. I've watched hardened investigators run out of the room when they see the shears ready to be used. Our head pathologist, Dr. Brian Peterson, was a brilliant guy with a wicked sense of humor, and he liked to joke to ease the tension. ("He didn't need that spleen anyway," I'd once heard him say as he pulled the fist-sized organ out of a body.) During autopsies, there is normally a lot of gallows humor and chatter. Depersonalizing death is a coping mechanism for all of us. If you dwell on the process and what is taking place on the table, you aren't able to do the job. I knew story after story of rookies so traumatized by their first autopsies that they fainted. Some sought psychiatric help to be able to manage. The truth is, there's no bonding experience quite like it.

Giacomelli seemed content to sit back while we worked, but Conaty popped up to the table from time to time to ask questions. I was surprised that he was so knowledgeable about the medical aspects of the process. I later learned that he was a medical junkie. He listened compulsively to Dr. Dean Edell, a medical radio show host. He was book smart with a street attitude. The four of us had great chemistry. Brian told his jokes, and Conaty and Giacomelli cracked back. The banter was more like friends catching up over a beer. The two inspectors reminded me of Mel Gibson and Danny Glover in the movie *Lethal Weapon*. Conaty, boisterous and happy to be the center of attention. Giacomelli, a little bit reticent and content to play second fiddle. Conaty called Giacomelli Super Mario after the Italian American video game character. Quietly amused, Giacomelli chipped back. I couldn't help but chuckle, listening to their jousting.

They entertained us with war stories. There was the time they were interrogating a man whose boyfriend had been hacked to death with a meat cleaver. "He didn't care that the boyfriend was cut into pieces," Conaty said. "All he could talk about was his cat. Where was his cat? Could someone make sure his cat didn't get out during all the commotion? Finally, I said, 'You know, we're concerned about your cat, too, so I have arranged for your cat to be taken into protective custody.' He bought it! A cat in protective custody! After that, he loosened up and told us how he did it."

I inhaled their stories. Their uncanny ability to read people was their gift, I think. They could walk into an interview room, converse briefly with a suspect, and figure out exactly his or her weak point. From there, they developed a strategy. What does each do to maximize their chances of getting the person to talk? In some cases, the good cop / bad cop tactic worked. Other times, indulgence got results, as it had for them in the meat cleaver killing.

LISA NORRELL'S OFFICIAL CAUSE OF DEATH was manual and ligature strangulation. All joking ended as we left the morbid environment of the morgue. The mood was somber as the detectives pushed off to return to their investigation, and I headed for the lab. An innocent young girl had been brutally murdered. Her youthful virtue couldn't keep her from falling into the hands of danger.

After that day, Conaty and Giacomelli started coming around the lab to pick my brain about science and evidence and bounce around theories in the Norrell case. I always knew when they had arrived before I even saw them. I'd hear Conaty's booming voice at the front counter. Giacomelli's routine was to sit down and put his feet up on my desk. Same wing tips as Conaty, same mirror shine. Conaty always took the lead. "Okay, handsome," he'd say. "We're two knucklehead homicide guys, and you're the tutor. . . ." It wasn't long before I felt like an honorary member of their team. As much as they depended on me for an education in forensics, I devoured their investigative knowledge. I wasn't good at making friends— especially guy friends—but I wanted to know them better. Our common bond was our thirst for tough homicide cases. We shared a passion for our work. Conaty's mantra was "Homicide is like heroin. If you like heroin, vodka ain't going to cut it." I related to that. The challenge of solving a case was intoxicating. Once you were hooked, you were always searching for the next fix. Like me, Conaty and Giacamelli lived the job. They never hesitated to call me at home in the middle of the night from a crime scene. *How do we handle this evidence?* they'd ask. Or, *How important do you think this is to the case?* Conaty later said I'd taught him more about mitochondrial versus cellular DNA and mesenchymal tissue than he'd ever wanted to know.

One of the more memorable middle of the night calls came later in the friendship. The phone at my bedside rang at 2 A.M. Conaty was at a home in an upscale Bay Area suburb. What had started out as a missing person case may have just turned more sinister, he told me. I sat up in bed, my eyes blurry from sleep. He proceeded with the details. "It's a weird case," he said. A mother and daughter had gone missing from the home months earlier. "There's a little detached garage here, and there's this bar-rel bungee-corded to a dolly in there," he said. "I think we might have a body in the barrel." Now I was up and pacing. "Text me a photo," I said. The picture popped up on my screen of a barrel with a bungee cord. A missing woman? A barrel with the bungee cord on a dolly hidden in her garage? "Yep, looks like you've got a body in a barrel," I said. Sure enough, it was. At the morgue, lifting the top off the barrel, I saw the gooey blob of what had been a body immersed in some kind of sweet-smelling cleaning agent. The smell was nauseating. My job was to figure out how to get the body out of the barrel in one piece while preserving the evidence. As I se-cured chicken wire over the top of the barrel, Conaty pulled on his white bunny suit coveralls. I'd never seen him do that, and by then, we'd at-tended some pretty gruesome scenes together. Once he was suited up, we tipped the barrel to drain the fluid, then collected what remained of the body in a body bag. The mother had been shot by the daughter, her body left in the barrel for months. Her daughter remains a fugitive to this day.

Conaty and Giacomelli were deep in the weeds of the Norrell case when three women were brutalized and killed near the area where Lisa's body had been found. The women were sadistically sexually assaulted, murdered, and tossed out like trash along the same stretch of road where Lisa's body had been discovered. All three were sex workers. Law enforcement is of-ten guilty of placing less of a priority on cases in which the victim's death resulted from an illicit activity. But it was simple for me: everyone is some-one's child. They mattered. I don't know the circumstances that brought them to sex work—it could be abuse or addiction—and I wasn't there to judge. They lived in a dangerous world of cruelty and violence.

A different set of investigators were assigned to the three homicides. Concerned about their lack of experience—Conaty called them the B-Team—I'd kept abreast of the investigation and shared my thoughts with Conaty and Giacomelli about what I thought the investigators were getting wrong or missing. They had instantly focused on the boyfriend of twenty-four-year-old Jessica Frederick, the first of the sex workers to be killed. Her body had been dumped near an auto wrecking yard and salvage business in Pittsburg. What happened to Jessica should never happen to anyone. She'd been so savagely attacked that the coroner originally thought she'd been run over by a car. Her killer had used a serrated knife to torture her. The hair on the right side of her head and her right ear had been crudely chopped off. He gouged the knife into her stomach with such ferocity that her intestines spilled out. Jessica bled out. With his handiwork complete, he took a spark plug cord and tied it in a bow around her neck.

Investigators found specks of Jessica's blood on her boyfriend's comforter and on a paper towel in the trash in his apartment, as well as a presumptive positive test for blood in his kitchen sink, and this was enough to convince the B-Team that they had their guy. The boyfriend was charged with murder. Looking at the evidence, I wasn't convinced. That paper towel had not cleaned up five liters of blood, I said. I decided to do some digging on my own.

I learned that Jessica was one of those girls whose transition into the life that would ultimately kill her had been documented in mug shots. The first, taken when she was eighteen or nineteen, shows a pretty girl with a chubby face and a little-kid look about her. In the next, she looks the same, except she has a strung-out look in her eyes. Over the next three or four years, the heroin leads her to sex work, and you see that little girl harden. In her last mug shot, she is steely eyed and looking down the barrel of the camera, her expression a blur. She looks like she isn't even there. Two weeks later, she was torn up by a killer.

Jessica's boyfriend traded drugs for sex, and I knew that the blood in his apartment was not evidence of murder at all. It was blood patterns associated with shooting up heroin with a hypodermic needle. Jessica had obvious ulcerated sores on her arms where she had been injecting herself.

The sores could explain the blood stains on the comforter. In examining the paper towel, a serologist had found a fairly big stain, red with some green and a large amount of cellular material, which was more consistent with blood and pus from treating the infected ulcers in Jessica's arm than the extreme violence and total loss of blood found at Jessica's autopsy. Jessica had been beaten ferociously. Yet there was no blood spatter in the apartment. Even if there was, addicts mix their blood with heroin before they inject it. When the air is squeezed out of the syringe, blood sprays out. This often gets confused with blood spatter on walls from blows.

The criminalist who processed the scene had sprayed leucomalachite green—shortened to LMG—which turns green in the presence of blood. It had reacted positively around the kitchen sink, giving a green color around the faucet and in the basin. This meant that there had been blood there previously. However, LMG doesn't discriminate between human and animal. Cow's blood, simple beef, can give a positive reaction. I almost always get a positive LMG reaction around the kitchen sink area. It didn't mean the boyfriend had cleaned up the copious amount of blood that must have come from Jessica during her murder. Likely, it was from the last meal he had prepped.

The knife collected from the boyfriend had a tiny fleck of what the pathologist deemed to be mesenchymal connective tissue on it, and therefore they concluded that the fleck must have come from Jessica and the incision in her abdomen. Yet further DNA testing that I decided to process could not detect any human DNA. I processed the taxi that the boyfriend drove for a living. It was clean. So nothing in his car, and the evidence in his apartment was lacking. *Oh God*, I thought, *there's no evidence to charge this guy.*

I called the DA. "I can't tell you if he's good for Jessica's murder or not, but the evidence does not correlate with the violence she suffered."

The case was dismissed, and the boyfriend sued the police department—

not the act of a guilty man. Still, it haunted me. What if it had been him, and because of me, he was free to kill again?

If I'd learned anything over the years, it was that too many cases went unsolved, especially before DNA technology. The truth was, no matter how skilled the investigator or how devoted the team, sometimes there simply wasn't closure. Those were the cases that kept good cops up at night. Both the Norrell case and the sex workers homicides fell into that category. I know how frustrated Conaty and Giacomelli were when they hit a wall with every lead and were never able to give Minnie Norrell the answer to who killed her daughter. But in this kind of work, where there are often no easy answers, sometimes killers get away with murder.

While the Pittsburg cases were active, I'd tossed around the theory that perhaps we had a serial killer on our hands and that, based on geography and victimology, all four homicides were the work of the same predator. Four women had been murdered within six weeks. All were picked up and dumped off. I'd spent months digging into old homicide files and scrutinizing sex registrants looking for suspects. What emerged from my research was that Contra Costa County had been a hotbed for serial predators in the '70s and '80s. At least six suspected serial killers had been working in our communities, and fifteen homicides of women had gone unsolved. Two decades later, some of those same killers were still at large.

And I was going to find them.

13

Bodfish

It was the last day of June 1999, and just before noon, when my team and I left suburban San Francisco for the hills of Orinda. It was terribly hot—the kind of oppressive heat that melts tar—and we drove to what felt like a peaceful nature preserve, though one with some of the priciest real estate in the Bay Area. Riding shotgun in the crime scene van that day was our former intern, Sherrie Post, who had recently completed the police academy and returned as the newest criminalist on staff. Sherrie and I had recently begun dating. Sherrie was three years younger than me and had never married. I was attracted to her spirit. She was sassy and made herself laugh, and that made me laugh. Like me, she was passionate about the work we did. I admired her inquisitiveness and her thirst for knowledge. We clicked early on over our common interest in the science of homicide. I was her mentor and she was a bright and eager student. There was never a lull in the conversation when we were together. We'd bonded over our many talks in the crime scene van. She understood what I did, and she shared the highs and lows. I remember the moment I thought that she could be "the one." We were together at a drug lab. We'd pulled all of the chemicals from inside the house and laid them out on the back patio. Sherrie was taking the hazardous chemical inventory. She was suited up with bright-yellow crime scene booties and rubber gloves. I was across the patio, photographing the evidence, when I glanced over at her. She was completely immersed in her work, unafraid to get her hands dirty, so absorbed in the task at hand that she didn't even realize I had snapped a picture of her. *You know what, we click,* I thought. *She may just be that soul mate I've always wanted.* Luckily for me, the attraction was mutual. It was an exciting time for me when our work relationship turned to romance. Before then, Lori had been the only woman in my life that I'd ever felt really comfortable with. Now I realized that I could date someone else without fearing my next panic attack. Sherrie accepted me, warts and all. It was a confidence builder for me. *I can do this,* I thought.

Sherrie had already figured out from watching me work the Pittsburg cases in the evenings and weekends that everything, new relationships included, trailed behind work on my priority list. Today it was a homicide at 616 Miner Road. The initial information we received was vague. The name of the homeowner was Emmon Bodfish, a fifty-six-year-old recluse from a prominent Chicago banking family. Emmon had failed to show up for an appointment with his psychiatrist. The therapist contacted a relative, who went to the house at nine that morning and found a body inside. The first responding officer reported that identification in the victim's wallet confirmed it was Bodfish.

Miner Road was a rich person's enclave, a meandering thoroughfare with luxury estates obscured by oak woodlands. A writer once called it "the winding spin of old-money Orinda." While I drove, Sherrie made small talk. As usual when I was focused on a case, I checked out of the conversation and got lost in my head, silently ticking off tasks that needed to be done once we got there and matching names to assignments. Sherrie called it my scene-tude when I was processing a scene. I'd pull on my dispassionate mask, turn off everything else, and turn on my tunnel vision.

No. 616 was three miles in on Miner Road and up on a hill, completely obscured from view by the forest. We almost missed it. The property was several wooded acres accessed by a steep drive ending at a ramshackle ranch-style house. A shiny black Bentley in the garage was a heads-up that this was not going to be a typical case. I parked the van and assigned tasks to Sherrie and the two other criminalists on scene. "Okay, this is what we need to do," I told them. While my team went about their work—sketching the outside of the house, checking doors and windows for signs of forced entry, and preparing to dust for shoe prints and fingerprints—I walked toward what would be the strangest case of my career. It is the case that still follows me in my nightmares, more than twenty years later.

AFTER BEING BRIEFED BY THE LEAD detective, I approached the open garage. I didn't know much about expensive cars, but I knew Bentleys were an extravagance within reach of only the most affluent. The door leading from the garage into the kitchen was slightly ajar, and a strange buzzing noise came from inside. Likely an electrical issue, I thought, pushing open the door. I walked into the kitchen, which was neat and uncluttered. A Scapa scotch whiskey bottle on the shelf had a handwritten note attached that read, "Druid Property Hands Off. Stealing from the Gods brings bad luck!" *Strange*, I thought.

The buzzing sound got louder as I crossed from the kitchen into a large medieval-looking living room. It had dark wood paneling, chalices on the fireplace, and heavy red velvet drapes covering the windows. A ceiling fixture provided only a dim, eerie light. The stench was overpowering. I recognized it right away as decomposing flesh. Pungent and sickly sweet.

The smell of death. It saturates your clothes, your hair, even the interior of your car for days after you've been immersed in it. I'm sometimes self-conscious when I'm dealing with people in public after having spent time with a body because I'm sure they're sickened by the smell.

To my right, faceup on a sprawling Persian rug, was the body. A cloud of flies hovered around it. *Ah, that buzzing sound.* I swatted them away as they bounced off my forehead. Dried blood was spattered on the floor and on a bookcase beside the body. I noted what the victim was wearing, a white button-down dress shirt tucked into brown corduroy pants with a brown braided leather belt and a pair of old leather hiking boots. From the bluish-black hue of his face and hands, I knew the body had been there in the one-hundred-plus-degree heat for several days. The man I assumed to be Mr. Bodfish had been bludgeoned to the point of overkill, the blunt force trauma to his head so fierce that some of his teeth had flown out of his mouth and onto his shirt.

I went about writing my observations when—*Wait a minute!* Stepping over the body, I swore I saw his face twitch. He was lying there, absolutely still, but his cheeks were moving. Instinctively, I jerked backward. *Oh my God! He couldn't still be alive!* After a pause, I knelt for a closer look. The movement I'd seen was maggots feasting on his face. Large blue flies were laying eggs in the crevices where his head had been smashed in. That's about the time you tell yourself, "Just roll up your sleeves and do what you have to do." The developing larval stages of insects can help tell us the time of death, so I needed samples to submit to the entomologist for examination. Straddling the body, I dropped precariously to one knee until the victim and I were face-to-face. Using tape lifts, I collected trace evidence from the parts of the body that were exposed, then plucked up samples of larva and live flies, placing different species in separate small glass jars.

Those are the kinds of nasty details that never make it to the general public. The things that tend to dull the shine on the job. On TV you won't see LL Cool J or Chris O'Donnell scooping insect larvae from a decomposing body. I looked at it more like a lab experiment than ghoulishness while I was on the job. My subconscious, that was a different story.

To this day I have a recurring dream. I'm in the Bodfish house, looking around, when I lift up a rug and discover a trapdoor in the floor. I pull up the door and lean in, trying to see what's in the basement. Before I can focus, I see the shattered, insect-infested face of Bodfish rushing up the steps toward me. The sound of my gasp awakens me.

THE BODFISH HOMICIDE WAS A MIND twister from start to finish. I asked permission from the coroner's office to cut the clothes off before the body was transported to the morgue. That was an unusual request—normally a body is removed "as is." But in this case, the body was decomposing, which could lead to what we call the "body bag effect." I wanted to prevent a soupy mess from going into the body bag and contaminating blood evidence on the clothes. In the O. J. Simpson case, drops of blood on the back of Nicole Simpson's dress, which might have belonged to her attacker, were lost as evidence when she bled out in the body bag, obfuscating the random drops that might have proven definitively who her killer was. I didn't want that to happen here.

As I began cutting, my team stood at the ready with their cameras to document the evidence. The cutting process, in many ways, mirrored the procedure used by pathologists to open a body in an autopsy. I cut up the front of each pant leg and through the leather belt, then moved to the shirt and undershirt until I was able to splay the clothes open, the way a pathologist splays open a body to access the organs. Taking a step back, I looked at the entirety of the exposed victim. "Oh, hold on here," I said.

The victim had a vagina and scars from what looked like a breast reduction or double mastectomy.

If our victim wasn't Emmon Bodfish, who was it?

WE LEARNED THAT EMMON WAS A transgender man who lived a double life. Sometimes he lived as Emmon, and other times he lived under his given name, Margaret. I couldn't imagine how difficult it was for him, having to play both roles depending on where he was and who he was with. It was 1999, years before many people in the transgender community felt comfortable coming out. The Orinda property was Emmon's getaway. His primary residence was an hour west in Mill Valley, one of the richest counties in the country. In addition to family money, he had made his own fortune with a pool and plumbing business. Except for owning three homes, he lived frugally, with an occasional extravagance, such as the 1993 Bentley, which he'd bought new for $283,000 in cash, and the $100,000 Persian rug where he'd bled out. (His lawyer had a fit when he discovered sections had been cut out of it for evidence and crime scene cleanup. I heard he had it pieced back together in order to get something for it at auction.)

The Orinda house had become a more frequent retreat during the last years of Emmon's life, but the friends who once visited had slowly slipped away, most of them because he'd told them not to come around anymore. His only child, Max Wills, remained in his life. From what we could gather from distant relatives and former friends, their relationship had been fraught. Max was described as "odd," an introspective, gentle man who had never really grown up. Emmon often chastised him for his trust fund baby mentality. He was spoiled, lazy, and unmotivated, Emmon would say. He was thirty-three years old, and Emmon still gave him chores to do. Every week, Max drove the hour from his main residence, a condo in Sausalito owned by Emmon, to the house in Orinda to pull weeds and do laundry, gnashing his teeth while he worked. *Where had he gone wrong?* Emmon would ask. When he was Max's age, he had been a real go-getter. Max just sat around doing nothing.

Emmon had taken a vicious beating to his head. With his face and skull crushed in, he was unrecognizable. Cast-off blood patterns from the repeated blows made it certain the murder weapon had significant blood on it. Whatever had been used to inflict the blows to his head to kill him was nowhere to be found. It had been taken away from the scene. Judging from the height of perpendicular blood spatter on the bookcase, a blow had been inflicted while he was in a seated position. I saw no signs of defensive wounds, which I thought was unusual. Usually, someone who is aware of being clubbed instinctively tries to ward off the blows.

It was late afternoon by the time we wrapped the body in a sheet and zipped it into a body bag for transport to the morgue. At that point, I turned my attention to the Bentley. It, too, had stories to tell. From what we were able to piece together, Emmon had arrived at the Orinda house either on the twenty-third or twenty-fourth of June. Sometime before the homicide, which had likely occurred on June 25, he had apparently stopped at the dry cleaner and the grocery store. Clothes on hangers, still inside plastic sleeves, hung from the back seat grab handle, and a brown Whole Foods bag filled with fresh vegetables sat on the front passenger seat. My practice was to document everything at a crime scene, and that meant tagging all of the items in the grocery bag. One by one I pulled out the different items—lettuce, cabbage, turnips—and laid them out to photograph. Also tucked in the bag was a book entitled *The Fabric of Reality: The Science of Parallel Universes—and Its Implications*. It looked as if it was in the process of being read. Leafing through it, I discovered a folded piece of lined paper from a spiral notebook. I opened it and began reading.

Do first. Exercise. Sweep down cobwebs. Body exhausted, mal-coordinated, whining lots of skin and joint pain, wants to die. Violence. Body up, out of seat. Get broom. Whines and begs constantly and hurts all over. Begin sweeping down wall and ceiling eaves of porch and side. Some sense of accomplishment. Remember how I always wanted a home to care for and fix. Childhood hopes and dreams rush back. I feel love for my cabin and its beautiful surroundings. I could be happy. (Now body cuts in with double the pain and exhaustion and whining. Stumbles and goes weak in the knees.) Ignore it. I pick up a mug for a sip of soymilk. Right hand fails and lets go of mug. Spills milk. Now I have no more milk without driving to store and have a mess to clean up. I curse right hand and make it hold on to the mug as tightly as it can, despite muscle pain and exhaustion for 5 clock minutes. Then I curse at it more and make it work three or four times as hard, hauling scrub buckets of water and scrubbing for twenty minutes. I ask if it's enjoying its sick-act joke.

Tell body it's a stupid piece of shit that should be beaten to death. . . . How do I feel about my aliveness at this moment, the book asks? I hate it. I just want out.

Placing the letter next to the rest of the contents of the grocery bag, I thought, *Things here are definitely not as they seem.*

I'M NOT SURE WE WOULD HAVE gotten to know Emmon the way we did had we not had a unique opportunity to read his thoughts. Reticent in life, he was prolific with the pen and had kept diaries dating back seventeen years. I was living in an apartment in Benicia at the time, and I liked the freedom of being alone. At night, I'd spend hours on the bed or the floor, the diaries spread out in front of me, reading and making notes. They painted a picture of a conflicted, lonely man who longed for love and felt he never had it.

Emmon wrote copiously about his involvement in a neo-pagan group called the Reformed Druids of North America. Druidism is a religious practice rooted in nature and the worship of gods and goddesses from Celtic times. Reading up on it, I learned the faith was built on mysticism, magic powers, and rituals. Druids believed the soul was immortal and transferred from one human body to another for infinity. Until a few years before his death, Emmon had been socially active in the Druid world. He hosted gatherings for rituals at a stone and mortar altar in the woods behind the Orinda cottage. He had pictures of himself dressed in Druid garb and spoke of praying to Danu the goddess. As he became increasingly paranoid and reclusive, he banished even fellow believers from his life. He wrote about former friends as "sleazy, scuzzy, dishonest" and "hard low-class females" and "liar males."

For a few years, Emmon produced a newsletter, "The Druid Missal," and wrote under his name. I learned a lot reading his stories. He had a keen intellect and a vast knowledge of the history of Druidism. "The Druids of folktales were imputed with the power to create a magical mist to hide themselves. . . . In practice, there are different levels of making oneself invisible. At the first level is the crass psychological technique of diverting attention to something else while you quietly walk away. On the second level is the method actor's strategy of changing his emotional state, manner, and gait so that he seems to turn into (or turn out to be) someone or something other than who he was, and so to 'disappear' into the role."

Had Emmon wanted to "disappear into the magical mist"?

MAX WILLS HAD BEEN MISSING SINCE his father's body was discovered, which made him a prime suspect in the case. He turned up in the LA County morgue a few days later. At around five o'clock on the day Emmon's body was found, Emmon's former mother-in-law, Max's grandmother, had told Max about Emmon's death. He'd been staying with a friend in Santa Monica at the time and rode his bicycle to a local Travelodge, where he'd insisted on a room with a bathtub. A maid found him the following morning submerged in a tub full of water. A razor had been used to slice up his neck and slash his forearms.

The coroner's office in LA was in an industrial section of the county, away from the residential area. I arrived there with Sheriff detective Mike Hubbard, the lead detective in the Bodfish investigation. We were met by LAPD Lieutenant Debbie Peterson. "We've got this bizarre homicide in Orinda," I said. "The son of our victim killed himself, and he's here."

"I have the death investigator pulling the body," the lieutenant said. "It could take a while." There was a gift shop in the building, she said. Perhaps we could pass the time there? "A gift shop?" I asked. I'd never seen an operation like the one in LA. The coroner's office was enormous, with a gift shop chock-full of death souvenirs on the first floor. The shelves were lined with things like tiny coffins and miniature skeletons and T-shirts with kitschy sayings. My favorite souvenir had a chalk outline of a body with the catchphrase "When your day ends, our day begins." As George Bernard Shaw famously wrote, "Life does not cease to be funny when people die any more than it ceases to be serious when people laugh." Apparently so.

As the lieutenant predicted, it took time to locate Max. I could see why when we walked into the morgue. The freezer was down a long tunnel with tile floors, just like you'd see in the movies. It was the size of a ware-house. In Contra Costa County, we were able to store up to ten bodies at a time, and that was crowded. Here, hundreds of corpses wrapped in plastic and tied with rope on each end were stacked on shelves on top of each other. The scene reminded me of a carpet warehouse. Looking around, my boyhood memories of watching *Quincy* flooded back. It was because of the show that the first book I'd ever checked out of the Travis Air Force Base library was by Thomas Noguchi, the famous Los Angeles County medical examiner known as "the coroner to the stars." Noguchi was the inspiration for Jack Klugman's character in *Quincy*. In the book, Noguchi dished about the celebrities he had met on the autopsy table. Names like Marilyn Monroe, Natalie Wood, John Belushi, Janis Joplin, and Robert Kennedy. Now I was standing in the same spot I'd read about as a kid, thinking about those celebrities wrapped in plastic and stacked in piles along with everyone else. Death does not discriminate.

As I looked around, recalling scenes from Noguchi's book, Max was rolled out on a gurney and into an examination bay for us to observe. In my role as the lead forensics guy on the case, I pulled out my camera and began my examination of the body. I was stunned to see that Max hadn't been autopsied, which would have been routine in our morgue. He'd left a three-page suicide note, and that had apparently been enough for the busy LA authorities to rule the death a suicide. The only thing they'd done in the way of an investigation was to get a toxicology sample from a liver biopsy to determine if he had drugs in his system. If I ever want to kill someone, I'll do it in LA and make it look like an OD with a suicide note nearby. So easy.

Before heading home, we were given a bag of Max's belongings, as well as the suicide note he'd left behind. Partially written drafts were found in his motel room, suggesting he'd wanted to make sure he got the letter right. His parting words, addressed to "Friends and Family," revealed that Max, like his father, suffered from long-term depression and suicidal thoughts, but he'd been reluctant to act on them while his father was alive.

I had a friendly disagreement with the other investigators on the case about whether or not Max was responsible for his father's death. They continued to focus on him as the most promising lead. I didn't believe he was involved. There were reasons for doubt, of course. A piece of paper discovered in his home had a list of a dozen people "who should be dead," he wrote. Topping the list was his father. He didn't have an alibi for June 25, the day Emmon was killed. The last time he'd been known to be at the Orinda house was on June 22, three days before. Max had told his grandmother he'd gone straight from there on a camping vacation to Southern California. A friend could account for his whereabouts between June 26 and June 30, when Emmon's body was discovered, but his only alibi for the day of the beating was that he'd been camping alone some six hours south of Orinda. Aside from that, there was nothing linking him to the homicide.

From what I could determine, Max was a sensitive, vulnerable man, and even though he and his father butted heads from time to time, they loved each other. I read his "death list" as entirely different from wishing Emmon dead for sinister reasons. In my interpretation of his writings, he thought death was preferable to the pain and suffering of this life, and no one suffered more than his father. The list was made up of all the people he loved. When he wrote that they "should be dead," I read that as him wishing them peace. Max wrote in his suicide note that for years he'd contemplated killing himself but couldn't bear to hurt his father that way. I believed that. Once Emmon was gone, he was able to fulfill his desire to be free of that burden. Even if he had it in him to accommodate his father's wish to die, it didn't make sense that he would beat Emmon to death and then drive six hours to Southern California to kill himself. Why wouldn't he have just killed both himself and his father at the same time?

I was more inclined to listen to Emmon's voice from the grave than jump to the simpler conclusion based on a subjective list. Emmon had spelled out in great detail his misery with life and his wish to die. In his diaries, he described waging war on an alter ego he called BlDC, or Blue Demon Conscience. BlDC lived within his troubled psyche and was introduced very early in written thoughts and threads throughout Emmon's diaries, right up to the time of his death. From the age of six, he'd had an ongoing battle with the demon, he wrote, and wanted desperately to escape from it.

As I read, I realized that Emmon, in the course of these entries, was having physical interactions with BlDC. He was hitting himself in the head with different objects, including his wooden staff, a truncheon, and a rock. I came upon a photograph of him with linear marks on the top of his forehead, consistent with hitting himself in the head. He believed that the beatings were the only thing that could quiet the voice. But the demon kept coming back.

In May 1991, his obsession with quieting the demon took a different course. He'd concluded that his approach had been all wrong. The demon, he realized, relied on him to stay alive. "This is a new perspective," he wrote. "I leave the body, instead of getting BlDC to leave, or be quiet, or learn, 'I' leave, perhaps leave the body to BlDC for both of them to 'rot.' This insight/communication made me very happy."

The only means of escape, he wrote in June 1995, was to die a violent, unexpected death and leave the demon behind with his body.

Four years later, he did.

A coincidence? I didn't think so. I had a theory that Emmon had all but handed us the answer to his brutal end. I believe he orchestrated his death with a willing accomplice, perhaps another Druid follower or followers. It was curious to me that two pictures, both Japanese themed and in matching black frames, had been taken off the walls of the Orinda house. The picture in the homicide room had been removed from the frame, and it appeared as though someone had begun to peel the picture from the wood backing, as if they'd been looking for something but then stopped. The other painting, which hung in one of the bedrooms, was missing. I found a book on Emmon's bookshelf called *Poof! How to Disappear and Create a*

New Identity. In the margins of one of the pages, he wrote about setting up a Japanese bank account, then transferring the funds to a Swiss bank account. He was setting up a mechanism to hide money. Had he hidden banking information on the back of the painting so his hired killers could cash in? That is my theory.

The Bodfish case has never been officially closed. The county's homicide investigations unit put it on a shelf for another time. The general feeling was that Emmon was dead, which is what he'd wanted, and Max, the prime suspect, was also dead, so why put any more resources into the case? I looked at it differently. My feeling was that even if this was something Emmon wanted, and there was enough in his diary to conclude he was behind his own death, no stone should have been left unturned in our effort to identify who killed him. Emmon needed help. He didn't need to die. It was a heinous crime, and whoever had struck the fatal blows should be held accountable. And even if I'm wrong, and Max was involved, the evidence shows that someone else was also there and inflicted blows on Emmon. That person needs to be identified and caught.

I still think about the Bodfish case. It makes me sad that Emmon and his son were so desperately unhappy that death was the only way they saw out of their living hell.

Before his death, Emmon wrote: "New far more effective way to silence a demon. When BIDC mouths off, go silent. Don't speak. . . . Walk over to the nearest good solid object. Pick it up. Come back. . . . Then hit the demon in the head."

14

Serial Killers

In January 2001, I was promoted to supervising criminalist, a management position overseeing the entirety of the Sheriff's Criminalistics Unit. Many aspects of the job came naturally to me, and I liked thinking about budgets and process improvements. But little did I know that my days would be spent handling things like dress code violations and workplace romances—not the career I aspired to or got much satisfaction out of. One day, I was dealing with an accusation that a fingerprint tech in the stolen car unit was having dalliances with tow truck drivers in the tow yard. The next, I was having to inform an employee that the way she dressed was in violation of the county's dress code. Getting into someone's personal business was foreign to me, and I felt like I had landed in an alternative universe. I didn't care if someone's skirt was more than three inches above the knee as long as the work was getting done. By March, my anxiety was kicking in again. I was doing things I didn't want to do, or dreaded doing, and I was feeling the pressure. I couldn't stand it. It was do or die. Do something different or die behind my fancy new desk.

On the bright side, I quickly realized that being promoted gave me the autonomy to pursue what I'd had to sneak around to do before. Namely, delve into cold cases. I discovered I could pick and choose the administrative chores that needed to get done and still take on unsolved homicides without worrying about who was looking over my shoulder. Employing someone dedicated to cold cases was a budgetary luxury most agencies couldn't afford. Cold case units were the exception rather than the rule, despite the fact that the number of unresolved homicides were growing exponentially across the country every decade. The last number I heard was that four in every ten cases went unsolved.

It frustrated me that so many homicides were solvable but for the time it would take to solve them, and unresolved cases continued to pile up. Before the Pittsburg cases cooled off, I'd tossed around the theory that we had a serial killer on our hands and that all four homicides—Lisa Norrell and the sex workers—had been the work of the same predator. Circumstances that had once favored predatory attacks had changed since then. DNA technology, behavioral science, and interagency communication were all novel back then. Behaviors had changed—women rarely hitchhiked anymore, and people routinely locked their doors—but the compulsion to rape and kill had not.

I've seen statistics indicating that some two thousand serial killers are operating in the United States today. Most are not loners and outcasts. They can and do function as your friendly next-door neighbor. They know that what they're doing is twisted, and they can stop for periods of time, but the urge to kill is stronger than the fear of being caught. I counted at least six active serial killers in our county in the 1970s and '80s.

One name stood out among the rest, not just because he was still a suspect in at least ten unsolved homicides, but also because he was still relatively young and coming up for parole after serving twenty-one years for murdering three women. Phillip Joseph Hughes Jr. was a monster even among monsters. His file contained hundreds of pages of psychological reports that documented his madness. In kindergarten, he mutilated his classmates' dolls, and by eight years old, he was having fantasies about dead bodies, which he described as "more like mannequins." Therapy followed, but both he and his parents decided it was a waste of time. In middle school, he started killing small animals, and in high school, he was slipping out of his house naked in the middle of the night, breaking into neighbors' houses, and stealing bras that he'd take home and put on, then watch himself in the mirror as he stabbed the cups with a knife.

His warped sexual proclivities had escalated by the time he turned twenty. He practiced sadomasochistic sex and would choke his first wife, Suzanne, into unconsciousness. Nothing serious, he would later say, "just broken blood vessels." There were times he attempted to hang or drown her—with her permission, of course. He often didn't remember the actual sex, but the near-death scenes, those were crystal clear.

Phil graduated to murder in his early twenties, maybe even earlier. His first known killing was in 1972. He'd offered a ride home from a local Kmart to nineteen-year-old Maureen Field, a former neighbor of his. At some point, he stabbed and strangled her and, with the help of his wife, dumped her body at the foot of Mount Diablo—in the same area where the body of missing fifteen-year-old Cosette Ellison had been discovered two years earlier. A composite of a man Cosette was seen talking to when she got off the school bus, just before she disappeared, matched a Polaroid of Phil wearing his favorite fishing hat, but there was no hard evidence linking him to Cosette's murder.

IN 1974, PHIL AND SUZANNE KIDNAPPED another fifteen-year-old, Lisa Ann Beery, at knifepoint and took her to a house they were house-sitting. Hughes stabbed and raped the girl, and Suzanne once again helped him bury his victim. The body was found five years later in a shallow grave on a hillside in Phil's hometown.

His third murder conviction was for the 1975 homicide of Letitia Fagot, Suzanne's coworker at a local bank. Letitia and her husband had recently moved to the suburbs to escape rising crime in San Francisco. She'd mentioned that her husband was away on business, and she was alone in their new home for the first time—information Suzanne offered up to Phil. The following morning, he drove to her house, attacked her with a hammer, then raped and strangled her.

I thought Suzanne was also a victim. Phil had complete control over her, and she was terrified of him. As noted forensic psychiatrist Dr. Park Dietz has written, I also viewed her as a "compliant victim of a sexual sadist." The guy was a lunatic, a fantasy-motivated killer of the worst kind. I discovered a cache of photographs of women in various death scenes that were confiscated from his house. All were nude or partially clothed. In some, they appeared to be stabbed. In others, they were strangled with ligatures, or hanging. Studying the photos, I realized it was Suzanne in every shot. She'd been posing.

Suzanne eventually left Phil and got a conscience. In exchange for immunity, she provided details of the three murders she knew of and confessed to helping dispose of the two bodies. She told detectives she posed in death scenes because Phil told her he needed to look at the photos to keep himself from carrying out his urge to kill. She fed Letitia Fagot to Phil after he confessed his urge to kill a former girlfriend. "He was becoming more upset, and he didn't want to kill her for fear he would get caught," Suzanne said. "So he wanted to use other people to relieve his anxiety and tension." That time, Letitia was the sacrificial lamb.

Based on Suzanne's testimony, Phil was convicted in 1980 of all three murders and sentenced to concurrent terms of twenty-one years to life in prison. Under the law, he was eligible for parole beginning in 1986. He'd come up five times since then and been denied each time, but at fifty-three years old, he was only a stroke of luck away from being free. His next hearing was scheduled for July 25, 2001, a month away. Experts had diagnosed Hughes with "necrophilia, antisocial personality disorder, and possible paranoid schizophrenia," but all agreed he was legally sane. "It is clear that he appreciated the criminality of his behavior in that following all of the killings he went to great lengths to dispose of the bodies and conceal the behavior from the authorities, and also he 'arranged' for victims, knowing full well the criminal nature of his intent. . . . He is required to render the other individual helpless or even dead in order for him to feel adequate."

Hughes, another expert concluded, "is a menace to society of the highest order."

Guys like Hughes don't rehabilitate. He was deranged and, I had no doubt, still as dangerous as he was way back. I petitioned the prison to allow me to attend the pending parole hearing and was granted permission. I wanted to see Phil, to feel the evil of his presence. The night before the hearing date, I drove the 250 miles to San Luis Obispo, along the Central Coast, and took a motel room near the California Men's Colony, where Hughes was serving time. A commotion in the motel parking lot kept me from falling asleep, and I tossed and turned all night in anticipation of coming face-to-face with the madman I'd learned so much about. Early the next morning, I badged up and set out for the prison. I was struck by the contradiction of the location of the Men's Colony. It was as if the giant cinder block building behind razor wire had been dropped into the middle of nature. I envisioned the psychotic serial killer gazing out of his cell window at the green hills against a blue sky with birds fluttering past. Studying the landscape, I was reminded of San Quentin. I'd always wondered whose idea it had been to build the walled behemoth on the scenic shores of the San Francisco Bay.

I was checked in and escorted to a waiting room with family members and the Contra Costa prosecutor who prosecuted two of the three cases against Hughes. Members of all three families were there. Maureen Field's brother and sister; Lisa Beery's sister and father; Letitia Fagot's husband. I tried to imagine what it was like for the families, all this time later, to have to be there and relive that terrible time in their lives. *They should not be going through this*, I thought.

The families welcomed me. Joe Field was a teenager when his sister Maureen went missing twenty-nine years earlier. His memory of that time was crystal clear, he told me. When Maureen was gone for three days, the home phone rang. His father answered. "Hello, Mr. Field," a man said over a staticky connection. "Your daughter is dead, and I'm the one who killed her." Joe remembered his mother falling into his father's arms crying, "My baby! My baby!" What kind of sick person does that? Taunts the family of a girl he had just murdered. Phil later admitted to making the call.

His account of the murder was not quite like Suzanne's memory. He hadn't offered Maureen a ride, or at least that's not the way he remembered it. His recollection was that he saw Maureen being chased down by someone else with a knife. He watched from his car as the man stabbed her, then push her to the ground and strangled her. That's when he took chase, he told investigators. "The guy ran off, and I ran after him for a very short distance and then ran back to the girl, who was lying on the ground. And there was blood all over her, and she asked me in the name of God to kill her." Of course, he obliged. He didn't want her to suffer, he said. Before Maureen took her final breath, "She said she forgave me," he said. Her family believed that was the only part of his story that was true.

People who knew Phil talked about what a good liar he was. Like any good liar, he always weaved enough truth into his fabrications that they seemed feasible. In Maureen's case, he tried to make himself out as the hero who had attempted to save her rather than the beast who had terrorized and killed her. I think the reality is that Maureen got off of work at Kmart, and while she was waiting for her father, who was late picking her up, Phil came around. He offered her a ride. He was a familiar face from the neighborhood, so she accepted the ride. At some point during the ride, she realized she was in trouble. She got scared and ran. Phil was the man chasing her down.

TWO YEARS LATER, PHIL AND SUZANNE abducted Lisa Beery near her home in Oakland. I'd bet my firstborn that there were others in between. Lisa was a tiny girl, five feet and a hundred pounds, a high school sophomore who sang in her church choir. Her mom had sent her to the local convenience store to cash a check. Lisa decided to thumb a ride. Wrong place, wrong time. The couple came along and kidnapped her at knifepoint. Before the parole hearing began, Lisa's sister, Linda, talked to me about how torturous it had been for the family, waiting five years for the body to be found. Five years of looking at every face in a crowd. Of expecting to see Lisa each time the front door opened. Once, she said, she was at an outdoor event and caught a glimpse of a girl who looked just like her sister. She ran up behind her and grabbed her shoulder. The startled stranger turned around. "I'm so sorry," Linda said. "I thought you were someone else."

When the parole board convened, we were all ushered into the hearing room. The board was made up of three members. *So much power*, I thought, looking from one face to the next. *Let's hope they use their authority properly*. I knew too many cases of killers being freed by bleeding-heart parole boards, only to go out and kill again. The panel could just wave their wands, and Hughes would be free to resume his treachery. What a terrible injustice that would be to an unknowing society.

At that point, I felt as if I knew Phil very well. His file was thick with police reports, trial transcripts, and psychiatric reviews. I'd read his affect was flat and that even when he was describing slicing and beating women to death, he was unemotional and detached. Matter of fact, really, from what I could tell. During interrogations, he often answered questions with questions. When he did answer, he was maddeningly vague.

"How was the girl killed, Phillip?"

"I'm not sure, but there was a knife involved."

"Is the knife still at your house?

"I think so."

"How was the girl cut?"

"I don't know, but there was blood all over."

"There was blood all over?"

"Yeah."

Phil's defense in all three homicides was that he didn't remember the killing part. He recalled bits and pieces of the encounters, but he claimed no memory of how or why he'd taken the women's lives. He claimed Suzanne had given him the details, and he believed her. Machiavellian. That was Phil Hughes.

I wondered what he looked like now. Did he still have the smirk like the one in his mug shots? Would he be somber? Smiling? Insipid? Compulsion is like addiction. How, I wondered, was he handling withdrawal from the murder cravings? Did his skin crawl? Did he suffer from wild mood swings? Irritability? Anxiety? How did he exhibit control now? How did he release his latent rage? What would his demeanor be when he was in front of the parole board? I wondered. He'd been incarcerated for nearly twenty-one years, which made the parole hearing all the more pivotal. Phil obviously thought he was getting out soon.

The hearing room door creaked open, and all heads turned. Adrenaline shot through me like an arrow, and the hair on the back of my neck bristled. Phil's attorney strode in, a thick file under his arm. I felt the weight of the tension in the room. The door slammed shut behind him. I looked from one family member to the next. I knew we were asking ourselves the same thing. *Where is he?*

"Mr. Hughes has waived his right to be here," the attorney said. Looking from face to face, I saw shattered expectations. The frustration and anger from family members was palpable. How long had these poor people been preparing for this painful day? What courage it took for them to be there again, for the sixth time, and willing to face down the predator who had tortured and killed someone they loved. Many of them lived in fear of Hughes, but they hadn't let that keep them away. They had come because they didn't want other families to have to live through the darkness they had.

Even though they had managed to get on with their lives, the anguish from the past was never far. And the persistent possibility of Phil getting paroled was a constant reminder that no one and no place was really safe.

I listened intently as family members spoke.

"She was just a little girl who sang in the choir."

"Everyone loved her."

"Maureen would have gotten married and had kids."

"Because of Phil, we don't have grandkids."

"Letitia was a beautiful wife."

Hearing their stories was when all of this became real to me. This was no longer about pursuing my cold case hobby in stolen moments. These were real people who had been sentenced to a lifetime of grief. I cared about them. This truly was my life calling. Sorrow had been woven into the fabric of their lives by a psychopath with an insatiable urge to kill. Like him, they were at the mercy of an unpredictable system, but unlike him, they'd done nothing wrong. And he didn't even have the courage to face them. *What a coward*, I thought. Being with the victims prompted a significant shift in the way I thought about cases. I'd interacted with devastated family members at crime scenes, but this was my first experience with grieving families who were still raw with sadness twenty years later. Cases never went cold for them.

Parole was denied.

On the four-hour drive home, I'd developed a master plan. I vowed to do whatever I could to help those families leave Phil in the past. His next chance at parole was five years away. That gave me time to dig into other homicides. Phil needed to have another case hung on him to ensure he stayed where he belonged, and I aimed to find it. It would be leverage. Capital punishment was again back in play in California, and if I could find a death penalty eligible case, we could use it as leverage. The state could offer Phil a deal. In exchange for a confession, the death penalty would be taken off the table, and he would be offered a plea bargain of life without parole. Phil could continue to watch the birds from his prison cell without checking off the days to the gas chamber—and the families of his victims would be one step further in their healing by knowing they would never have to attend another parole hearing. It was the same strategy used that year to get the notorious Green River Killer to come clean about all of the women he'd killed and where they were buried.

WITH THE CLOCK TICKING, I BEGAN to investigate Hughes in earnest. It was logical to review the unsolved cases that law enforcement had always attributed to him but could never prove. I started with the 1978 Armida Wiltsey homicide. Armida was a forty-year-old wife and mother who went for a jog around the Lafayette Reservoir in the East Bay on the morning of November 14, 1978. Her husband was away on a business trip, and she'd dropped off her ten-year-old son at school. When she didn't pick him up that afternoon, neighbors reported her missing. A search was launched, and a cadaver dog located her body sixty feet off a popular jogging trail.

She'd been raped and strangled, her body left in the bushes, her son left without his mother. Phil had always been Suspect No. 1.

In studying the case file, I found reason for encouragement. The original criminalist at the homicide scene noted a speck of blood underneath Armida's fingernail. Armida must have been fighting back and scratched her attacker, and a tiny amount of his blood lodged under her nail. The criminalist back then determined the blood spot was too small to test. Now, twenty-three years later, we had the sophisticated equipment that could produce a DNA profile from that speck of blood. My adrenaline was pumping. I was confident the blood evidence would match Phil's DNA. It was the slam dunk I needed.

I collected the fingernail with the blood sample from the Property Room, then planned my next step. First, I'd get Homicide up to speed on the particulars of the case so that when the lab analyses came back, we'd get Phil arrested. Once he was charged with the murder, we'd talk to the prosecutor about offering him a deal in exchange for information about other homicides he'd committed. We'd close the Wiltsey case once and for all and put Phil behind bars forever.

I got the ball rolling by submitting a request to have the blood under the nail and the hair analysed for DNA, then waited on pins and needles for the lab results. I assigned Sherrie to do the work. I couldn't concentrate on anything else but getting the results. Finally, she came into my office with a paper in her hand. "And?" I asked, certain I already knew the answer.

"It's not him," she said.

I'm blank after that moment. I was so traumatized that I've erased it from memory. What I do remember is the crushing feeling of knowing there was still no justice for Armida Wiltsey and her family, and the families of all of Phil's other victims would be forced to endure the hell of more parole hearings. It was one of those days when the only remedy for my misery was cracking open a bottle of cabernet.

I was at a loss. The male DNA under Armida Wiltsey's fingernails was in all likelihood her killer's, and it didn't belong to Phil Hughes. *Now what?* I wondered. Feeling gloomy, I turned to my friend and colleague Roxane Gruenheid to commiserate. Roxane was a detective with the Sheriff's Homicide Unit, a robust woman with a thick Bronx accent who shared my passion for cold cases. "I'm frustrated," I said. "I just eliminated Phil Hughes in the Armida Wiltsey case." Roxane let out a sigh. "Let me take a look at the case file to see if anything jumps out at me," she said.

I returned to the list I'd compiled of all the unsolved homicides Hughes was suspected of, looking to see if there was another case with biological evidence. There was one. The name on the file was "Waxman, Cynthia."

THE SUN SHONE BRIGHT ON APRIL 22, 1978, the perfect day for a game of ball at the local high school. Eleven-year-old Cynthia Waxman and her cousin Stephanie had gone with Stephanie's father, Steve, to a baseball game at the Campolindo High School athletic field that Saturday. Times were different then. The world looked safer. Kids had more freedom. No one thought twice about letting their girl or boy walk to school, or the store, or play on the playground alone. So there was nothing unusual about Stephanie's father allowing the girls to search for a stray kitten they'd heard about. Moraga was the safest town in Contra Costa County. The idea that something sinister would happen to your child just wasn't something parents worried about. Of course, at that time, the community had no idea there was a serial killer in their midst. Phil Hughes hung out in Moraga. Rheem Valley Bowl, his favorite haunt, was a block south of the ballfield. Moraga was his hunting ground, but it would be another year before his wife turned on him.

The girls walked a quarter mile down the well-traveled Moraga Road toward a dirt driveway leading to a local farm, the area where the friend had spotted the stray. Cindy waited on the sidewalk while Stephanie walked down the dirt drive looking for the kitten. There it was, a little black cat. It was almost as if it had been waiting for the girls to come. "I found it!" Stephanie cried, scooping up the kitten in her arms. Cindy was waiting excitedly for her cousin to climb back up the driveway. Stephanie later recalled. "Oh Steph!" Cindy cried. "Please let me hold the kitten." Stephanie later recalled, "And then is when I petted it about three times, and then I brought it up to Cindy."

The girls sat on the sidewalk, playing with the kitten, when Cindy decided it must be hungry. "Steph," she said, "go ask your dad for money so we can buy cat food." It was about a four-minute walk back to the ballfield. "Dad! We found the kitten," Stephanie said, running up to her father. "It's hungry and needs food." Steve handed his daughter a five-dollar bill, and she took off running back onto Moraga Road. But when she got to the spot on the sidewalk where she'd left Cindy, Cindy was gone.

The ball game lasted a couple of hours, and afterward, Steve and Stephanie drove to Cindy's house to make sure she was there. Cindy's parents had been at an ice-skating recital for their younger daughter, Pamela. No, Cindy hadn't been home since they'd gotten back, they said. At that point, Cindy had been missing for nearly three hours, which set off alarm bells. Everyone took off in different directions. They searched the high school and the market where the girls would have gone for cat food. They checked Steve's apartment complex and scoured Cindy's neighborhood. They checked the farm with the dirt drive. At 3:18, the Waxmans called police to report their daughter missing. While they waited for help to arrive, Cindy's mom, Bonnie, asked Stephanie to lead her again to the last place she'd seen Cindy. This time, Bonnie noticed the grassy area beside the sidewalk was matted down. She made her way through the underbrush for about thirty feet when she came upon a small clearing bound by bushes and small trees. A foot and a leg poked out from vegetation, leading Bonnie to her child. Cindy lay on her back, a rope tied in a tight knot around her neck. Her hands were crossed in front of her and bound at the wrists. Her green knee socks had been pushed down around her ankles, but her red, white, and blue–striped dress seemed to be intact. Bonnie ran back out to the road, screaming, "Call the police! Someone murdered my child!"

No one in Moraga felt safe after that.

Stephanie did her best to help with the investigation into Cindy's murder, but her interrogators had an agenda, and their suggestions became her story. Detectives at the time were convinced that a local teenage boy who'd been in the area was likely the killer. The same kid who'd come forward to say he'd see a man come out of the bushes near where Cindy's body was found. Investigators called it a diversion tactic. He was blaming someone else to take the focus off him. After they had prodded the ten-year-old for hours with loaded questions, she came to the same conclusion. The teenage boy had killed her cousin. It takes a highly trained interviewer to get answers from a traumatized child. Kids look at the world in a different way. Their primary concern is "What are the ramifications for me if I say something? Will I get in trouble with my parents?" There's a way to get them to give you the facts. Reading the transcripts of the interviews with the traumatized youngster was like reading a textbook on spin control.

DESPITE THE BEST EFFORTS OF INVESTIGATORS to pin the murder on the local teenager, the case went nowhere. It was shoddy police work, and Cynthia Waxman was ultimately relegated to the cold case files. But families never forget.

There were multiple tragedies in the Waxman case. First, little Cynthia lost her life. And for her mom to find her body? What could be worse for a parent? Cynthia's father, Lorin, said that in the years following his daughter's murder, he would often drive by the crime scene, squeezing a stress ball, blasting classical music, and screaming, "Why?" The stress of losing Cynthia, and the way she died, tore her family apart. And Stephanie?

With cold cases, everything is frozen in time. Decades pass. Faces age. Memories fade. It's a strange phenomenon, getting to know a cast of characters from the cold case files, then meeting them in real time. Stephanie obliged us by coming downtown to share her memories of that day, twenty-three years earlier. The ten-year-old I heard on the interview tapes, a frightened little girl who muttered her answers to interrogators, was now a poised woman in her midthirties. The meeting took place in a small conference room at the Sheriff's Field Operations Building. I accompanied Detective Sergeant Steve Warne, who'd suggested I be there. Warne and I had a good working relationship, and I'd shared my knowledge of the Waxman case with him. He read the file and suggested we bring Stephanie in. It was a highly unusual move, inviting me, the science guy, to take part in a witness interview. Homicide cop and criminalist required vastly different skills and personality types that were often in conflict. Nerdy science types and hard-nosed investigators rarely clicked. What I also had in my favor was that I'd quietly elbowed myself into so many investigations by then that the detectives had come to value my judgment as one of their own.

Warne took the lead with Stephanie. He began by asking her to recall undisputed facts in the case. The baseball game. The kitten. Asking her dad for money for cat food. After Stephanie had recounted everything she remembered about Cindy's disappearance, Warne pulled out a cassette tape and popped it into a player. "This is your interview from back then," he said as he pushed Play.

The voice of ten-year-old Stephanie—soft, sweet, scared—hummed on tape, and the grown woman stared blankly at the player, listening to her own voice. When it got to the part where she changed her story to implicate the local teenager, she shook her head furiously. "No!" she cried, putting her hands up to her mouth. "That's not right! He was never there." Stephanie's tears turned to sobs, and Detective Warne pushed Stop while she regained her composure. She had never meant to get the boy in trouble, she said. Decades later, we were watching that ten-year-old girl recognizing the impact of implicating an innocent boy in her cousin's murder. It was gut-wrenching.

The teenage boy had long ago been replaced as the lead suspect when Phil Hughes was charged with the three similar murders two years after Cynthia was killed. Once his role as a serial killer came to light, his name shot to the top of the list of suspects for all of the homicides with similar MOs. Still, the local kid had never been formally exonerated in Cynthia's murder. I wondered what it was like for him, living in the shadow of a murder for so many years. Now, for the first time, the only person linking him to the crime was recanting her claim. More fodder for the case against Phil Hughes.

Studying the Waxman file, I determined there was a good chance the killer's DNA was somewhere in evidence. Modern DNA technology could possibly give us clues that were missed two decades earlier when the sophisticated science was just developing. Perhaps the killer's imprint was on the rope he'd used to restrain and strangle Cynthia. The nylon rope told me that the homicide had been a crime of opportunity. The killer hadn't brought it with him. It was tied to an old barbed wire fence in the underbrush. He'd stumbled upon it when he was lurking in the bushes and burned off two pieces. One for each little girl. I was certain that he'd meant to kill both. My theory was that he was driving along Moraga Road and saw Cynthia and Stephanie playing with the kitten. He parked his car nearby and snuck back to the spot through the bushes, but only Cynthia was there by the time he made it through the brush. He lured her into the brush, used the rope to bind her hands, raped her, and then strangled her with the second piece, the one he'd meant for Stephanie. Crime scene photos and the autopsy report revealed that Cynthia had suffered massive vaginal trauma. Perhaps, I thought, he had left semen or saliva evidence behind.

Once again, I trekked the eight blocks from the lab to Angel in the Property Room on Escobar Street. The Waxman evidence was in a large cardboard box with all of the items inside tucked into brown paper bags. The original masking tape on the box had yellowed and curled and had obviously been taped over many times over the years, but the evidence was in decent shape. I retrieved Cynthia's clothing, the red, white, and blue dress, the green socks, white underwear, the blue-and-white-striped tennis shoes and headed back to my office, hopeful I was on the right track. I sent off the evidence to the lab and waited, confident Phil Hughes was about to be dealt his fourth murder conviction, and this time his sentence would be life without parole. As planned, he'd never get out of prison.

During her examination of Cynthia's clothing, the DNA analyst discovered a semen stain on Cynthia's underwear, a large stain, several inches across, that had been missed back in 1978. I would later learn that the original criminalist got a positive acid phosphatase reaction on the stain but decided it wasn't strong enough to be useful (attributed it to the potential elevated acid phosphatase activity often seen in prepubescent girls' vaginal fluids) and didn't pursue it. Once again, I was reminded not to rely on what was done in the past. Always revisit the evidence. The new analyst was easily able to generate a DNA profile from the semen stain. I was ecstatic. I was certain the case would be solved. The profile was uploaded into CODIS, the FBI's database of local, state, and national DNA profiles of convicted offenders. CODIS searches take time. I went about my job, the Waxman case secure in a separate compartment in my brain.

Several weeks passed. I walked into the lab one day, and Dave Stockwell, our top DNA analyst, called me over.

"Hey, Paul," he said. "I got a hit on Waxman."

You know how people talk about their heart dropping to their stomach? It's an awful feeling, as a torrent of hormones and neurotransmitters wreak havoc on your body. My heart took off, and my face flushed to a deep red. "Who is it?" I asked. Stockwell must have enjoyed seeing me squirm. He stood up from his chair and sauntered over to the printer, grabbed a piece of paper, and handed it over. The name at the top was "Charles Jackson." Not Phil Hughes? How could it be? How could the Cynthia Waxman murderer not be Phil Hughes? It had his name all over it. The ruthlessness. The wantonness. His territory. How could every investigator who had ever looked at the case have come to the same bungled conclusion? How could the obvious be a mistake? How could I have been so wrong?

Pour me another drink, please.

Charles "Junior" Jackson. Why did that name sound so familiar? Jackson was known as the East Bay Slayer. A handyman known to cruise for odd jobs in an old, beat-up truck, he had a lifelong rap sheet of burglary, rape, assault, and child molestation. He had been paroled a month before he killed Cynthia Waxman. In 1982, four years after he killed her, he was convicted of raping and murdering a Contra Costa woman and sentenced to life in prison. He had since been linked to the murders of seven women and one man in our county between 1975 and 1982. It was uncanny, really. A known serial killer hung out within a block of where Cynthia was raped and murdered, but a different serial killer literally just passing by had committed the crime. Cynthia was the only known child Jackson had killed, at least that we knew of. I was disappointed to learn he had recently died of a heart attack in Folsom Prison. The only justice Cindy's family would get was the resolution that came with finally knowing who had killed her.

I moved on.

I was already following leads in other cold cases when I got a call from Roxane Gruenheid, my detective friend who'd promised to look at the

Armida Wiltsey file a few months earlier. "Hey, Paul," she said in her raspy Bronx dialect. "I looked at that case. And I think this Darryl Kemp looks interesting."

I remembered Kemp's name from the Wiltsey case file. He'd been questioned two weeks after the murder following an arrest for peeping into people's windows nearby. His parole officer tipped investigators that the paroled sex killer might be worth looking into, but Kemp's girlfriend, who'd been his prison pen pal, said he'd been with her on the day Armida Wiltsey was killed. It appeared from the file that the investigators bought that alibi and moved on, but not before criminalist John Patty, out of an abundance of caution, collected a sample of his hair. It was amazing foresight on his part.

I headed straight to the Property Room again and dug through all of the boxes until I came across one with Kemp's name. The strands of hair were tucked in a paper bag inside. I turned over the hair standard to a DNA analyst to see if she could generate a genetic profile. The profile from the hair matched the DNA from the speck of blood under Armida's fingernail. Cold case closed.

I couldn't wait to tell Roxane. She was sitting in the hallway outside of the courtroom where she was waiting to testify in a different case when I called. "Darryl Kemp's DNA profile matched the blood under Armida's fingernail," I said, as court sounds rang in the background. Court is a place where a level of decorum is expected. I heard Roxane hoot and holler. "Fucking YAY!" she cried.

Roxane tracked Kemp to a prison in Texas, where he was serving time for his most recent aggravated rape conviction. He had previously been on death row in California for the rape and murder of a nurse in Los Angeles but was spared execution when the California Supreme Court overturned capital punishment. He was paroled in 1978 after serving eighteen years. Four months later, he ambushed and killed Armida Wiltsey on the jogging trail. Sometime after that, he moved to Texas, where, in 1983, he raped and choked six college students after breaking into the home they shared. Kemp was now sixty-seven. Since the age of eighteen, he had only been out of custody for eight years, and those were gifts from lenient judges and parole boards. He was about to come up for parole again when he was slapped with a murder charge in the Armida Wiltsey case.

Kemp was extradited back to Contra Costa in 2003. He slept through his trial and was sentenced once again to die. Armida had been murdered a week after Californians voted to reinstate the death penalty. Kemp is now eighty-five and still on death row at San Quentin State Prison. He will likely never be executed.

Hughes is seventy-four and remains incarcerated at the California Men's Colony prison. He continues to be denied each time he comes up for parole. He married a pen pal and helped her raise her two children from his prison cell.

The Phil Hughes odyssey was a significant teaching moment for me. In an attempt to keep him in prison for the rest of his life, I had inadvertently exonerated him in two of the murders for which he was presumed guilty. Lesson learned: As long as someone is looking, there's a chance for the case to be solved. Even if it's not the case you originally set out to prove.

I was disappointed that I wasn't able to pin another murder on Hughes. At first, I did what I always did when I didn't get results I'd expected. I doubted myself. But then I thought, *Wait a minute, is that what this is all about? Getting the bad guy?* Yes, as long as it's the right bad guy. The outcome of little Cindy's case wasn't what I'd been expecting. But Darryl Kemp will never be up for parole again. Those families will never have to see his face. And that is the truth. It was always about getting the truth. I could live with that.

15

EAR Breakthrough

It was 2001, and four years had passed since I had developed a DNA profile for the East Area Rapist. It had been that long since I had compared notes with Orange County criminalist Mary Hong about a serial predator she had in Southern California. We'd found similarities between EAR and their guy, who they called the Original Nightstalker, or ONS. Both were active at around the same time, and both were sexually motivated predators who attacked couples in their beds. I put more weight on the differences, though. EAR was a serial rapist whose signature was placing dishes on his victim's back, which ONS didn't do. ONS committed serial rapes, but he'd also bludgeoned couples to death.

There had been nothing at that time that caused me to say, "Oh! This is the same guy!" I would have dug further into a possible connection, but some of the agencies that had investigated ONS put up roadblocks when I made inquiries about their cold cases, and the DNA profile Mary had developed with Orange County's sophisticated equipment was incompatible with the more rudimentary testing capabilities I was working with back then. Without the next place to turn, I'd determined I couldn't justify spending my time chasing a rapist who had apparently stopped attacking years ago, especially not when I'd concluded we had an active serial killer in the Norrell/Pittsburg sex workers murders. If my theory about those cases was on target—that at least some had been committed by the same person—the perpetrator was a public safety threat and the case had to take precedence over everything else.

I'd promised Mary I'd get back to her when our lab caught up with hers. It had taken years, but we were finally able to do the standardized STR DNA testing in our lab. We received an incentive grant from the federal Office of Criminal Justice Program to develop DNA profiles for the FBI's fledgling CODIS program—a national database of DNA profiles for known offenders and unsolved crimes. The grant amount was relatively small but enough of a boost to our budget for us to work on unsolved cases and upgrade our DNA procedures.

Standing in the hallway of our Escobar lab, a group of us brainstormed cold cases we could apply to the grant. I hadn't thought much about the East Area Rapist since I'd hit that dead end in 1997, but the case popped into my head that day. "Oh!" I said. "Can we use it to do EAR?" A discussion began. The EAR cases were not homicides, and all of his rapes were past the statute of limitations, which meant he couldn't be prosecuted even if we were able to identify him. My next question was, "Can we realistically spend grant money on a case that is going nowhere?"

Dave Stockwell, a droll DNA analyst, wasn't keen on the idea. Stockwell was a by-the-books kind of guy. "I don't know if that case meets the spirit of the grant," he said. I understood his reservation, but my boss, Karen Sheldon, overruled him. "Yes, we should do it," she said. "If anyone says anything, it's on me." I was back on the case.

I assigned Stockwell to redo the DNA analysis I'd done on the three EAR cases in 1997, using the new technology to generate a modern profile. Stockwell was a brilliant forensic scientist who had transferred up from the San Bernardino Sheriff's crime lab in Southern California two years earlier. He was the brains behind our transition into the new DNA technology. If you had a question, you went to him, and he'd ask you questions until you came up with the answer.

Stockwell went to work on my EAR cases using the new STR testing. He came back and informed me that the three cases shared the same STR profile, an expected but still reassuring result, as STRs were much more discriminating than the old profiles I had been creating. Out of due diligence, I asked Stockwell to contact Mary Hong so we could finally compare EAR's DNA fingerprint to her Original Nightstalker profile and close that book. For every investigation, there are steps that need to be taken and items that need to be checked off before you can move on. The comparison with Orange County's profile was one more thing to cross off my list of things that needed to be checked out. One more detail to eliminate in the long search for EAR's identity.

Stockwell disappeared to the back of the lab, orders in hand, and I went about my daily routine of reading and signing off on lab reports. That same afternoon, I looked up from my desk, and he was standing just inside my office door. "I spoke with Mary," he said, with about as much enthusiasm as if he was about to tell me the specials at the local deli. "The profiles matched."

I was gobsmacked. "What?" I asked in disbelief.

"The profiles matched," he repeated. "She has four homicide cases with the same profile as our East Area Rapist. It's a perfect match."

Stockwell was never one to get amped up. For him, this was just another case he would write up before moving on to his next project. For me, it was the culmination of a lifetime fascination with serial offenders and a textbook example of a predator evolving from a rapist to a killer.

I sat there for another moment, too stunned to move. When I recovered, I grabbed the phone and called Mary. "Mary. It's a match?" I asked.

I'm in my Class A uniform walking away with Ben after a Sheriff's Office inspection on May 18, 2007. This photo sat on my desk for years before I retired. (Sherrie Holes)

Doing drug analysis at the Castro Street lab in early 1991. Still new to the job, I was ecstatic after having floundered in college. I would quickly become bored analyzing drugs, but at this point I couldn't have been more excited to have finally started a career in forensic toxicology. (Paul Holes)

On a break with a few of my police academy mates out at the Sheriff's Department's firearms range circa June 1994. When not at the academy, my days were spent polishing my brass and shoes, ironing my uniform, and studying for our constant tests. But this was also a tough time, as my days away led to me being absent as a husband and father. (Paul Holes)

I'm holding my oldest child, Renee, while Lori (far left) is giving Nathan a bottle at the baby shower the office held for us circa 1996. This was a hard era for our marriage, as I was being called out numerous times almost every week to handle homicides, officer-involved shootings, and drug lab scenes. Shortly after this photo was taken, we would reach the breaking point in our relationship. (Paul Holes)

My partner and I had just finished excavating Dale Holmes's first victim from a shallow grave on the side of a hill in El Sobrante, California. She had been killed and buried six months prior. (crime scene photo)

I'm sifting through ashes containing the remnants of Dale Holmes's two victims' clothing, which he burned in his fireplace at the impound located inside of the old Sheriff's Property facility. The vehicle that both women were killed in can be seen in the background. Though you can't see it, I was suffering from a severe case of poison oak. (crime scene photo)

With my oldest child, Renee, standing in front of her science fair project, "Crime Scenes, DNA, & Different Tissues," in April 2005. (Sherrie Holes)

Sherrie helping to process a drug lab circa 1999. I took this photo, as I was so smitten with her. Lori and I were separated at the time of this photo, but because I couldn't figure out what was going to happen with my marriage, Sherrie had moved on. (Paul Holes)

Pittsburg PD Homicide Inspectors John Conaty (left) and his longtime partner Ray Giacomelli circa 1998. These two became my mentors and great friends. To my knowledge, this is the only photograph of the two of them together. This photo was taken right around the time I first met them, during the Lisa Norell investigation. Always dressed in expensive suits, Conaty later confided in me that this habit was quickly driving him to the poor house, as he constantly was having to replace suits and shoes that would get beat up during investigations. (Paul Holes)

With Sherrie at an after-hours lab function early in our courtship. (Paul Holes)

John Conaty and myself on April 17, 2019, after I gave a presentation on the Golden State Killer at the Contra Costa County District Attorney's Office. (Paul Holes)

Sherrie and me after she accepted my marriage proposal at Mirror Lake just below Half Dome in Yosemite on February 14, 2004. (Paul Holes)

A family photo taken in my Vacaville backyard on November 4, 2007, after Juliette was born. My mom and dad are on the right. (Paul Holes)

Me with all four of my kids during a hike in the Vacaville hills in March 2010. When I had previously taken Renee and Nathan on this hike, we had run across the skeletal remains of a dead cow. This time, I took the time to point out what could be discerned from the remains. Ben and Juliette got to see those remains but they had been scattered. It was quite the lesson on the cycle of life for the kids. (Sherrie Holes)

Crime scene photo showing the general location where Regina Stamps's body was found in Pittsburg, California, on March 26, 2001. In the lower left, Ray Giacomelli can be seen furthest to the right talking to the Pittsburg officer who is pointing in the direction where the victim was located. (crime scene photo)

Serial killer Phil Hughes wearing his hat after bowling at the Rheem Valley bowling alley in Moraga in 1971. His friend Jill took the photo. She remembers that at one point, Phil gave her a necklace, and when he went to put it around her neck, his hands were shaking. She thought at the time it was nerves, but in hindsight, she thinks he was probably resisting the temptation to strangle her. After I met with Jill, she sent me a very nice letter with a picture of her family, thankful she was alive to have such a beautiful family and life, knowing she very well could have become one of Phil's victims. (Jill Voeghtly/Phil Hughes trial record)

A school portrait of eleven-year-old Cynthia Waxman, who was killed on April 22, 1978, near Campolindo High School in Moraga by serial killer Charles Jackson.

The ski mask (in a plastic bag) that I was convinced would solve the East Area Rapist case. It had been collected by original investigators back in 1979 after having been left by my railroad suspect Robert Lewis Potts. (Paul Holes)

The view from the front door of the shed in which Jaycee Dugard was held captive for several years after Phillip Garrido abducted her. I took this photograph while investigating the crime scene on August 31, 2009, five days after she was found. (Paul Holes)

Three pages of torn-out notebook paper containing two essays and a hand-drawn map as I found them in the Sheriff's Property Room. This evidence, referred to as the "homework evidence," was found along the East Area Rapist's escape route after a December 9, 1978, attack in Danville, California. (Paul Holes)

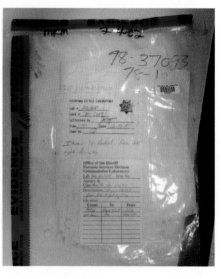

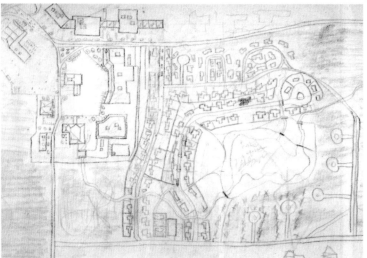

Hand-drawn map that was part of the homework evidence. I felt this map was unique enough that it could help identify the Golden State Killer and spent years pursuing leads from it. Michelle and I had an ongoing debate about whether it was related, but she agreed that if it was, it could be key to solving the case. (Paul Holes)

Exeter PD Officer Joseph DeAngelo circa 1974. At the time of this photo, DeAngelo was the Visalia Ransacker, committing numerous fetish burglaries and ultimately killing Claude Snelling during an abduction attempt of the victim's daughter, Beth. DeAngelo would soon be promoted to sergeant and head of the area's Anti-Burglary Task Force while he himself was committing that very type of crime. (Exeter Police Department)

Photo of me standing in front of DeAngelo's mugshot after the April 24, 2018, press conference. I had just finished several phone calls with living victims of DeAngelo and was trying to join Steve Kramer and the rest of the genealogy team when the media recognized me and started peppering me with requests for interviews and photographs. I was quite proud of the accomplishment of catching DeAngelo but very torn about my future, thinking I would be riding off into the sunset of retirement and not be in a position to work cases again. (MediaNews Group/*The Mercury News* via Getty Images)

Joseph DeAngelo in the interview room shortly after his arrest on April 23, 2018. DeAngelo sat unmoving in this position for an hour. (Paul Holes)

The law enforcement members of the genealogy team that worked with Barbara Rae Venter to identify Joseph DeAngelo as the Golden State Killer. This photo was taken right after the press conference announcing DeAngelo's arrest to the world. *From left:* Kirk Campbell, me, Steve Kramer, Melissa Parisot, and Monica Czajkowski. (Jay Czajkowski)

North entrance to the cattle culvert where seventeen-year-old Carla Walker's body was found on February 20, 1974, a few days after she had been abducted out of her boyfriend's car while in the Ridglea bowling alley parking lot in Fort Worth, Texas. (Fort Worth Police Department)

Campolindo High School 1970 yearbook portrait of fifteen-year-old sophomore Cosette Ellison.

Composite made from a witness who saw Cosette Ellison talking to a man wearing a hat after she got off the school bus on March 3, 1970. This photograph is the opening page of the binder of unsolved cases that still sits on my desk. (1970 case file)

Mary was as excited as I was. She referred me to Larry Pool, the lead detective at the Orange County Sheriff's Office. Pool is even-keeled like me, but I could hear the thrill in his voice. He briefed me on his offender. In addition to the four homicides linked by DNA, he said, he suspected that two other attacks were also related. In one, the couple had gotten away and were able to give details of the attack to investigators. Their account had EAR written all over it.

GOLETA IS A COMMUNITY IN SANTA BARBARA COUNTY in Southern California. It bleeds into Santa Barbara proper. Blanketed in agriculture until the 1950s, Goleta evolved into a hub of the aerospace and defense technology industries, instigating a housing boom and an influx of young professionals. There's a reason Goleta is nicknamed the Good Land. The mountains are tinted blue, and rocky bluffs speckled with wildflowers offer panoramic views of a slice of California's southern Pacific coast. Summer months hover around a sunny seventy degrees, and winter attracts migrating monarch butterflies to the town's butterfly preserve.

October 1, 1979. Paradise interrupted. A masked man stood at the foot of the bed of a sleeping couple in their home on Queen Ann Lane in Goleta. It was 2 A.M., and the house was dark except for the blinding ray of a flashlight in their eyes. They were a professional couple, both thirty-three and computer programmers. They'd lived at the address for two years, an upper-middle-class neighborhood with no crime to speak of. Until that night.

The woman awakened first when the intruder kicked the bed; then her boyfriend opened his eyes, blinded by the flashlight. "Don't move, motherfucker," the man said in a forged voice. "I'll kill you."

"Get on your stomachs. I gotta have money."

They complied.

"Tie him up," the intruder ordered, tossing strips of nylon twine and braided rope at the woman.

Her hands trembled as she bound her boyfriend's wrists and ankles, loosely at first.

"Tie it tight or I'll kill you!"

She obeyed, no doubt her life flashing before her eyes.

The woman was next. The intruder bound her wrists behind her back and tied her ankles. Once she was secured, he roamed through the house, rummaging through dresser drawers.

"Where's the money?" he growled when he returned to the bedroom. "One move, motherfucker."

The woman's purse and her boyfriend's wallet were in the kitchen on the counter, she said. The intruder loosened her foot bindings and yanked her off the bed. They would go to the kitchen together, he said.

He walked her into the living room, pushed her to the floor next to the coffee table, and retied her ankles. "Turn over," he said. "Faceup." I'm going to be raped, she thought. Once again, he left the room to stalk through the house. When he came back, he had a pair of her tennis shorts. He pulled them over her head, but she could still see enough that she knew he was scanning her body with the flashlight. Then he was kneeling at her left shoulder. "Now I'm going to kill you. Cut your throat," he said, before walking away.

She listened in horror as he rummaged around the kitchen, then paced back and forth in the hallway. "I'll kill 'em. I'll kill 'em. I'll kill 'em," she heard him say at least a dozen times.

The woman decided to run for it. They were going to die. She had to try to get away. As he paced nearby, she wiggled loose from her ankle restraints and ran screaming out the front door. Her boyfriend, still naked and bound in the bedroom, managed to slide off the bed and hop out the sliding glass doors and into the backyard. He saw the beam of the flashlight coming for him. Diving behind an orange tree, he stayed perfectly still until the light disappeared.

Out front, the attacker quickly caught up with the screaming woman. With her head covered, she was unable to find her way and had slammed into the side of the house. She was helpless. He pushed her down to her knees, pulled her head back, and pushed his thumb in her mouth. Holding a knife to her throat, he spoke through gritted teeth. "I told you to be quiet," he raged, pulling her back inside.

FBI Special Agent Stan Los and his wife jolted awake by the sound of screaming. "What was that?" his wife asked, sitting up in bed. Los couldn't see the neighboring house through the bushes separating the properties, but there was little doubt that whatever was happening was serious. He dialed the Sheriff's Department for help, pulled on his clothes, and handed his wife a gun, saying, "Lock the door behind me. Don't open it until I get back." Armed with his own handgun, the agent went out of his house and saw a man on a bicycle pedaling away from the driveway. "Hey!" he yelled. The bicyclist took off, ducking low and pushing the pedals harder. By the time Los was able to get his car started and give chase, the man on the bicycle had a good head start. Los caught the red reflector of the ten-speed in his headlights just as the offender dumped the bike and disappeared between houses. He was gone. The bicycle had been stolen from a nearby residence, the home of an unknowing parole officer.

The agent returned home at the same time a sheriff's officer was arriving. A naked woman ran down her driveway toward them. Her hands were still tied behind her back, and she was screaming. "They killed him! They killed him!" she cried, certain her boyfriend was dead.

Los and the sheriff's officer searched the house, then walked around the driveway to the wooden gate leading to the backyard. Los called the man's name. "It's me, your neighbor, Stan. I'm here with the deputy sheriff," he said, shining his flashlight from one end of the yard to the other.

The boyfriend was still hiding behind the orange tree. "Shine the flashlight on the sheriff's badge," he said.

There was little the couple could do to help identify the intruder. The house had been dark, and he'd been wearing a ski mask. All they could see was that he was a male, "possibly Caucasian and five ten or eleven." It wasn't much to go on, but it was more than the serial attacker's future victims would be able to offer. EAR had moved south, but his routine was the same as ONS's: the middle-of-the-night surprise. The ski mask. The gravelly whisper. Separating the couple and binding the male on the bed. And he'd placed dishes on the man's back. The Goleta attack was either a dress rehearsal or a botched attempt to up his game, but EAR was ready to kill. Two months later, and less than a half mile away from the Queen Ann Lane attack, the serial rapist successfully began his transition to serial killer. In the early morning hours of December 30, 1979, he broke into the home of Dr. Robert Offerman, an orthopedic surgeon, and bludgeoned Offerman and Dr. Debra Manning, a psychologist Offerman had recently begun dating, in the bedroom of the condo. None of his remaining victims would live to tell what they knew.

THE NEWS THAT THE EAST AREA RAPIST and the Original Nightstalker were one and the same was front-page news in 2001. In its story, the *Sacramento Bee* wrote: "He held eastern Sacramento County hostage from 1976 to 1978: Women feared nightfall; men were edgy in their own homes. . . . And now a criminalist in Contra Costa County, using long-shelved DNA evidence, has connected him to a series of Southern California murders— the killings of four couples and two women in Orange, Santa Barbara, and Ventura counties from 1979 to 1986."

The monster had a new name. He was EARONS, one of the most prolific and vicious serial predators in history.

I gathered up all of my case files, all the evidence, and other material and shipped it down to Pool in Orange County. I told him I would help in any way I could. I had moved into a support role. It was Orange County's ball game now. Pool had the murder cases, which had no statute of limitations. Up to that date in March 2001, he and the other Southern California investigators had been chasing a ghost. Their victims were dead, and all they had to go on was the vague description from the Goleta couple who had survived. Now they could use the fifty cases from Northern California, where the victims relayed all sorts of details about the offender—his size, his statements, his behaviors, his small penis. A long list of possible suspects had been compiled by the EAR task forces over the years. Pool now had all that information to cross-check against his homicide cases. Maybe a name in one of the EAR case files would match up to a name on his list of suspects.

I was confident that Orange County would solve the series. At least I'd had an impact, I thought, as I reluctantly put EAR out of my mind and started looking for the next challenge.

16

Postmortem

It was Tuesday, Tax Day, when I looked up and saw Giacomelli standing at the front counter at the Escobar lab. Seeing only half of the team seemed odd. I had never seen one without the other.

"How you doing, buddy?" Ray asked, removing his sunglasses and flashing a smile as I walked toward the counter.

"Doing good. What can I do for you, Ray?"

He told me that Conaty's mom had died unexpectedly, and Ray was left working a big case by himself that day. He had come over to ask for my input. It had been nearly four years since I'd bonded with Conaty and Giacomelli over the Pittsburg homicides. I felt honored to be accepted as their third wheel. We were so different—the reserved cold case enthusiast and the audacious super sleuths—but we had that unexplainable chemistry that happens between people. I was in awe of their investigative aptitude, and they deferred to me on the science of homicide. "Goddamn it,

Holes," Conaty would say. "We're just a couple of street cops. Talk to us like we're in kindergarten."

Those "street cops" offered to show me the ropes, and I jumped at the chance. They took me into the war zone to show me what the mucky side of detective work was all about. It was like being in a master class in homicide investigative techniques and attending a stand-up comedy act at the same time. Late at night or any chance I got to sneak out of the lab to ride with them, I did. Conaty drove the dark sedan with blacked-out windows, and Giacomelli rode shotgun. Picture the Blues Brothers in their dark suits and dark glasses up front and me hunched down in the back seat like the kid brother.

They loved, as Conaty said, "busting my balls." One day we were on our way back from a homicide reconstruction. Conaty was in storytelling mode. I watched as, in the middle of the narrative, he whipped his head around and did a wild U-turn on two wheels in the middle of busy Willow Pass Road. Now he was headed in the opposite direction. I felt like a bobblehead in the back seat. He turned right onto a side street and cruised to the curb, where a woman was leaning against a telephone pole, clearly waiting for a john. I saw Conaty's eyeballs looking over the top of his sunglasses in the rearview. "You recognize her?" he asked. Giacomelli nodded and rolled down the window. "Hey, Amanda!" he said. "We're looking for somebody. Do you know a Paul Holes?" I shrank into the back seat. The woman's eyes were half-mast and unfocused. "Uh-uh," she replied. "If you run across him, let him know we're looking for him," Giacomelli said. Conaty pulled off. While they had a good laugh, all I could think about was that now my name was out there on the street as some john that Pittsburg PD was looking for. "You pieces of shit," I said. "What are you doing to me?"

"Sorry, handsome," Conaty said.

Most of my work was done in the lab or at a desk. But Conaty and Giacomelli were out there in it, cruising forbidden neighborhoods, swapping clemency for information from dangerous felons and sex workers. Real-life homicide cops on the beat. I stuck to them like glue, watching how they related to people and how people responded to them. They were masterful at gaining people's trust and getting information—even from people who were involved in illegal activities and probably shouldn't have been talking to the cops. Investigative strategy is important, but they showed me firsthand how the interaction between an investigator and a source impacted a case. Talking to people like they're people and not animals gets a lot more traction than the arrogant-cop act we're all so used to seeing. Not that Conaty and Giacomelli weren't able to turn it up when it was necessary— especially Conaty—but their initial contact with people, whether it was a sex worker, a gang leader, or a killer, was always cordial and respectful.

Every trip I took with them was an education. I was learning from their cache of war stories and their experience with violent and adverse conditions. They could work their way into even the most dubious situations with their routine. Giacomelli's personality was more suited to the good cop, and Conaty was a master at playing bad cop, but their roles were interchangeable. They convincingly played off of each other and had an enviable record of cajoling confessions. I wasn't in the trenches the way they were, but watching how they used their different personalities to their benefit, I quickly realized that my own chameleonlike quality could suit me well in my cold case work. I wasn't someone who could go to a hard-core gang kingpin and speak his language the way they did, but I could get the most gun-shy victims to talk to me about the terrible trauma they'd suffered and wished they could forget. That was my strength. I could empathize and make them feel comfortable telling me their stories, and those stories were what drove me to turn over every stone in every case I took on.

That Tuesday when Giacomelli stopped by, I knew that they were in the process of cleaning up a patrol mess they'd inherited. Conaty had briefed me by telephone before he was called away. He said that a week earlier, the day shift had responded to a 911 call about a gravely injured man at a house on Abbott Avenue in Pittsburg. Patrol arrived to find a twenty-one-year-old male—Eric Louis Huffman—bleeding profusely from his head, fading in and out of consciousness. His sister's story was that he had shown up on her doorstep that way. She wasn't sure how he got there; maybe he walked, or maybe he was dropped off. He told her he'd been beaten in nearby Antioch. She led him inside, where he collapsed on the couch.

Conaty and Giacomelli were called in when the beating looked like it was about to turn into a homicide. The day was coming to an end, and they were preparing to go to the gym when the lieutenant came into their office. "I need you to roll out to this residence," their lieutenant told them. "We had a report of a beating, and now it looks like the victim won't survive." They arrived at the scene to find patrol standing inside the front door. He conveyed the story the sister had told him. You didn't have to be Sherlock Holmes to know it didn't make sense, Conaty said. The victim supposedly walked up to the house, his head oozing red, yet there wasn't a trace of blood outside. "No one walked up to the front of the house and didn't drop blood," Conaty said. But inside, the area around the living room couch looked like someone had slaughtered a cow there. Whatever had happened had happened inside that house.

Before the mortally wounded man succumbed to his injury, the hospital had x-rayed his skull. They determined that the head wound hadn't come from a beating. Someone had shot him in the eye. With that little detail, the sister's story fell apart. That made her a suspect or at the very least an accessory. Conaty and Giacomelli took her downtown for questioning. They appealed to her sense of loyalty to her brother. She wasn't having it. She was hard core and pregnant. "Either you did this, or you know who did," Giacomelli said. She knew only what her brother had told her, she said, sneering at them. When it became clear that the detectives weren't buying her version of what had happened to her brother, she grabbed her stomach and claimed she was going into labor. Clever. That was the end of that. Conaty called to the desk. "Call an ambulance," he said. They didn't have enough to get a warrant for her arrest.

Conaty decided the only way to prove the homicide had happened inside the house was to reconstruct the crime scene. He asked if I would do it. The goal was that the reconstruction would show the absence of blood at the front door. I would render my expert opinion, that the brother had been killed inside near the couch. That would dramatically reduce the pool of suspects and give the investigators probable cause to arrest his sister, incentive for her to tell what she knew.

The following morning, as the partners were in their office in Pittsburg plotting their next steps, Conaty's father called.

"Your mother died," he told him. That sent Conaty into a tailspin. His mother had been sick, but her death came as a complete surprise.

"What happened?" Giacomelli asked.

"My mom," he whispered, choking back disbelief. "She's gone."

Conaty came from a tight Italian family and was his mother's pride and joy. His routine had been to visit her every day, but he had been buried in work, and he hadn't made it the day before. Now she was gone, and he was overwhelmed with grief. Giacomelli was like another son to Patricia Conaty. He showered her with attention every time he saw her and danced with her at Conaty family gatherings.

"Go! Do what you have to do," Giacomelli ordered his partner.

WHEN GIACOMELLI ARRIVED, HE HAD A batch of photographs of the crime scene under his arm. He laid them out on the counter in front of me. He had already arranged with the homeowner to get back in the house to rein-spect it and had lined up the criminalists whose sophisticated equipment was capable of finding evidence that might have been missed during the initial processing. After the first inspection, the house had been scrubbed clean of the blood by the dead man's sister. All they had of the original scene were the photos, and they weren't clear enough to expose any trace amounts of blood that likely resulted from back spatter from the gunshot.

What could they do to resurrect what had been lost? Giacomelli asked. "Can we use luminol?" Luminol is used at crime scenes to detect imper-ceptible blood spatter. It could reveal the presence of hemoglobin, the protein found in red blood cells, long after blood has been washed away.

"We can," I said, "But first I would do a very intensive visual search before we consider spraying luminol. We need good photography of any of the visible blood patterns."

Giacomelli nodded. He was headed to the house to meet the Pittsburg crime scene investigators next, he said. CSIs from local agencies usually handled the less technically challenging cases.

"Once you get in there and do the search, get hold me of me, and we can figure out the next step," I said.

He stacked up his photos and held out his oversized mitt to shake my hand.

"Go get 'em," I said.

Giacomelli did his little nod, smiled, slid his sunglasses back on, and walked out.

"WE HAVE AN OFFICER DOWN." It was midday when my boss called to say that an officer had been shot, and we needed a criminalist at the scene. She gave me the address. Abbott Avenue in Pittsburg. *No, please.* "Who is the officer?" "His name is Giacomelli," she said.

The world stopped.

Giacomelli had gone to the crime house, as planned, to meet the CSIs. He had met with the homeowner, Earl Foster Sr., at a nearby gas station, and Foster Sr. had given him a key. The CSIs were late. Giacomelli got impatient. He called for backup. "On the way," the dispatcher said. Backup was a block away when the car was diverted to another call. Rather than wait, Giacomelli decided to go into the house himself. He was under the impression it was empty. It was dead quiet inside. He walked from the living room and down the hall to a bedroom. A killer was lying in wait behind the bedroom door. Ray never had a chance. He was ambushed, shot in the face. When he went down, the shooter stood over him and continued to fire until he was sure he was dead. Ambushed and executed. He never even had the chance to pull his gun.

The killer was career criminal Earl Foster Jr., the homeowner's son and the same person who had killed Eric Louis Huffman in the same house a week earlier. Huffman's sister was Foster Jr.'s girlfriend, and she'd lied about her brother's murder to cover for him. What a tangled web we weave.

Conaty was at the florist with his father and sister, choosing flowers for his mother's funeral, when he was told about the death of his partner. He broke down and drove a hundred miles per hour through city streets to Abbot Avenue. Giacomelli's body was gone by then, pulled out of the house by the first attending officers and transported to the morgue.

I arrived at the scene before Conaty and did a walk-through of the house. Blood stained the back bedroom. Ray's teeth had been shot out of his head and were scattered among bullet cartridge cases on the floor. I'd assigned my most experienced criminalist and made sure he had a full understanding of the significance of the case. I walked back outside and saw Conaty arrive. He'd been crying and was barely holding it together. "What happened?" he asked over and over. We hugged. I knew what Ray meant to him, and I couldn't imagine his pain. I loved those guys.

After dark, I had to peel away. Another massive case awaited. I had to be at the morgue early the next morning to attend to the remains of Laci and Conner Peterson, but I was in a fog.

I don't remember driving home that night.

IT WAS THE STORY FOLLOWED AROUND the world. Laci Peterson, a wholesomely pretty substitute teacher, eight months pregnant, went missing on Christmas Eve from her home in Modesto. Her husband, Scott Peterson, a thirty-year-old fertilizer salesman, told police that he had last seen his wife when he left home to go fishing at the Berkeley Marina. But Scott had a secret. Her name was Amber Frey, and he'd met her a month before his wife disappeared. He was the prime suspect. But another prevalent theory, one that Scott's defense would later use, was that Laci had been abducted while walking her golden retriever and held in captivity until sometime after she'd given birth to the son that they had planned to name Conner.

A day before Giacomelli was murdered, on Monday, April 14, the badly decomposed body of Laci had washed ashore in the East Bay after she'd been missing for nearly four months. Her eight-month-old fetus had surfaced a day earlier on the rocky shore a mile away. An initial autopsy shed little light on how or when Laci had been killed. Our pathologist speculated she might have been strangled or smothered, but it was impossible to be sure from the condition of her body. Her head and neck were missing, along with her legs and forearms.

I suggested we bring in Dr. Alison Galloway, a forensic anthropologist I'd worked with on another challenging homicide. Perhaps Dr. Galloway could determine the time of death from marine organisms on Laci's body. If we could pinpoint when she died, it would move the case forward.

I met Dr. Galloway at the morgue on Wednesday, April 16. She signed into the viewing room, where the coroner had positioned Laci and Conner on slabs next to each other. As she began her examination, I saw a somber progression of investigators I knew filing into the adjoining autopsy room. *Ray.* A window separated the two rooms, and I could see through the open blinds. Giacomelli was being rolled in. It's one thing to attend the autopsy of a stranger, but Ray was a dear friend. Only a week or so earlier, he and I had been in the morgue on a case, and he'd made the pathologist and me promise we would never allow him to be cut open.

As I stood there, remembering that conversation, Deputy District Attorney Bob Hole approached me. Hole was someone we all worked closely with. "Hey, Paul," he said. "I'm seeing some things on Ray. Can you come and take a look?" I walked in, and there was Ray, nude on the autopsy table. I did what I do best: compartmentalized it deep in my brain. I went into analytical mode. There was dead silence as I went about examining injuries on Ray's body, no small talk between the guys from Pittsburg PD. No dark humor. It was too close to home. I looked into Ray's eyes, the same eyes that the day before had been full of life. Now the energy was gone. I could hear his voice. "Promise me, Doc, you'll never do that to me." It was all I could do not to cry.

AS IT HAPPENED, THE PETERSON CASE turned on Dr. Galloway's findings. She couldn't get anything from Laci, but Conner's body told the story. The fetus had not been born before Laci's death. In fact, the doctor said, the fetus had been protected from the elements in the uterus. Because his body was in much better condition than his mother's, Dr. Galloway was able to use Conner's leg bone to determine the date of his death. Conner died on December 24, the same day Laci disappeared.

Scott Peterson murdered his wife and dumped her into the San Francisco Bay, where she lay for four months before their unborn child separated and washed ashore, alone.

17

Changes

2004

Lori and I had been split up for six years now. Sherrie and I had been dating on and off for most of that time—the off times being when she decided to see others because I was maddeningly indecisive about committing, and there were many of those times. The guilt I felt over the breakup of my family had eased over the two years since the day I'd gone to see the kids and found a red pickup parked in the driveway. "This is Jim," Lori said. "He's a friend from church." I was jealous, which I hadn't expected. Was I threatened that another man would be spending time with my kids, and I'd be pushed into the background? Was it simply a bruised ego? One of Lori's biggest issues with me had been that I had left the church. Now she had what she'd always wanted, something I couldn't be—a partner who was as committed to the faith as she was.

If anything, with the passage of time, I'd grown even more distant from the idea of religion. I'd been raised in a strict Catholic household with parents whose faith was unshakable. But I had never been a believer.

Growing up, I went through the motions of attending mass every Sunday and participating in all of the rituals—confession, catechism, confirmation—but I never really understood religion. My memories of church are of my brother, Dave, and I poking at each other and my father's hand reaching over the pew with a gesture of "Cut it off!" In high school, our church began offering Saturday evening services, which worked well because we always went out to dinner afterward. Dave and I got to choose the restaurant. The anticipation of good food afterward always made the homily more palatable. Once I started driving, I was allowed to take myself to mass. I purposely always chose the service my parents didn't. They'd watch me pull out of the driveway, their good Catholic son. What they never knew was that I'd skip mass and wander around cemeteries instead, wondering what had happened to the names on the headstones and feeling sad when there was a picture of someone who had died young. It isn't that I didn't marvel at Creation, but I'd always questioned anything that wasn't proven. To me, the book of Genesis read more like science fiction than historical record. In middle school, I became fascinated by archaeology, and I'd picked up a book from the library about archaeological expeditions attempting to recover Noah's ark. It didn't make sense to me that no one could ever find it. With something big enough to carry thousands of animals, how could there be no trace of it? Lori always bristled when I used the story of the ark as an example of why I had doubts. "Faith means you just have to believe," she'd say, echoing my parents. "When I see proof, I'll believe," I'd respond.

My line of work contributed to my misgivings about the Bible. I'd become even more cynical about the idea of an omnipotent, benevolent God after having witnessed more than twenty years of unimaginable tragedy. Laci and Conner Peterson side by side in the autopsy room at a time when she should have been celebrating her new child; the little girls from Antioch whose lives were taken at the hands of a father they adored;

eleven-year-old Cynthia Waxman, raped and strangled by a serial killer who should never have been released from prison. Sometimes I found myself driving away from an agonizing crime scene asking myself, *How does the God I'm supposed to believe in allow that to happen?*

Our views on religion were one of the things Sherrie and I had in common. My being a nonbeliever was not an issue with her. As a scientist, she tended to base her beliefs on verification of facts and proof. Having been raised in a nonreligious household as a nonpracticing Jew, she didn't worry about being judged for thinking independently. Religion was an intellectual discussion to be had. She didn't look at life through the filter of a particular faith, and that opened up a whole new world for me. I relaxed.

I was in my late thirties and finally felt free to be me. I talked about cases without worrying that she'd tire of listening. I ordered drinks with dinner if I felt like it. We'd be out to dinner, having animated conversations about semen and blood, and catch people at nearby tables eyeing us. For us, those topics were as stimulating as politics or fine art were to others. I understood why people's ears perked up when we were out in public. Having dinner out one night, we were discussing a homicide related to the Pittsburg sex workers series. A known sex worker, Christine Hubbard, had been shot twice in the head and dumped in the driveway of a junkyard in Pittsburg, in the same area where the other sex workers had been found five years earlier. Witnesses had seen Christine alive forty-five minutes prior to her body being found. Sherrie was assigned to process her sex kit. "I got oral semen, and the sperm still had tails on them," she said, excited to share her findings with me.

"So either she orally copulated the killer, or she gave her john a blow job, and then she was dropped off and killed right afterward," I said.

"I don't have enough to do a DNA analysis," Sherrie said, frustrated.

"You have to go back to the morgue and get more swabs out of her mouth," I said.

Who could blame the couple at the next table for asking to be moved?

Around Sherrie, I didn't feel like an imposter anymore. I felt lighter and more hopeful. Lori and I had two kids by the time we were twenty-five. Our lives had been all about obligation and responsibility. I'd gone from living at home with my parents to having my own family with no time in between to get to truly know myself. After the breakup of my marriage, I'd learned that there are times when I need to be alone. If I wanted to get on my mountain bike and explore rocky trails, I did. If I wanted to bounce along Pismo Beach in my Jeep, I could. Sherrie encouraged my alone time and took hers, too. We were together but independent, and that just felt right.

From early in our relationship, Sherrie felt like that soul mate I'd always thought about, but I was in no rush to marry again. There were times, well after my marriage to Lori was over, when I'd be visiting the kids and think, *This is where I should be.* I didn't even really understand it myself. Was it guilt over my kids not having their father present or my way of keeping Sherrie at bay? After my separation, I had allowed life to just sweep me along, and frankly, I was pretty content with the way things were. For the longest time, I just couldn't bring myself to formalize the divorce. After one of the many discussions where Sherrie would ask "Why?" and I would stutter and stammer without answering, she told me to forget it. She had decided to apply for a deputy sheriff's position. That meant six months away at the police academy. We broke up, and then she was gone. I knew how the academy worked. Students were stressed together and often found comfort in each other. I'd been there. So many nights I'd lie awake on my air mattress in my dingy studio wondering what she was doing, and who she was with. It was a tough time, but it became the sign that I needed to move out of my comfort zone. Lori and I agreed to file for divorce, and I was fortunate that Sherrie hadn't found someone else. She returned from the academy and took me back.

Sherrie and I made our relationship official, and I felt it was the right time for her to meet my kids. This was a significant step for me. The big meetup took place at a chain restaurant, Fuddruckers, in a shopping mall just up the road from my place in Walnut Creek. Renee was nine and Nathan was six, both of them still too young to make judgments or ask probing questions such as "When did you meet?" or "How long have you been dating?" It was a memorable meal in that Renee pretended to be a dog and scoffed the French fries on her plate the way a dog would. Yep, that's my girl. Considering that Sherrie didn't have kids, she adapted well. She rolled with the change of plans when visitation dates switched around and was understanding if I couldn't be with her on a meaningful day like her birthday or a holiday. My kids had to be my priority. She understood my commitment to Renee and Nathan and my need to be more than a visitor in their lives. I couldn't let them slip away. I think Sherrie was tolerant of a lot of things at that point in the relationship because after years of my indecision, we were finally planning a future together.

Lori was making her own plans for a new life. She had sold our house in Vacaville and bought another place in town, just a couple of miles from my parents. She and Jim, her friend with the red truck, were getting married. As clueless as I could be, I thought I would continue to act as I had in the old house, showing up in her new family room and playing with the kids for hours—but she put her foot down. Someone at her church had counseled her that it wasn't right that I'd involved myself in her new life in such an invasive way, especially now that she was starting over with a new partner. "You're not coming over and hanging out at *my house* anymore," she said firmly one day when I walked in and dropped onto the couch. "Why can't you take them out to a park or a restaurant? Your parents live a short distance away. Couldn't you visit them there?" "Oh . . . oh," I stuttered. It was a perfectly reasonable request. I'd been selfish, but I was still hurt, especially when it finally dawned on me that "Oh, I'm not going to be doing the typical dad things anymore." After that, my visits were at my parents' house. Occasionally, I brought them back to my dumpy apartment in Walnut Creek, the studio with the moldy shower, the appliances that didn't work, and the vomit-stained carpet from the previous tenant's cat. My kids put a hole in my air mattress when they used it as a trampoline. At night I'd have to blow it up before I went to sleep and again in the middle of the night when I'd wake up lying on the floor.

Sherri and I kept separate residences—I had my apartment, and she had bought a house near work in Martinez—but otherwise we were all in. When there was a lull in the lab, we sat together and chatted about cases or consulted on test results. We rode to crime scenes together in the crime scene van. Any free time we could steal we spent hiking local trails and taking quick trips to Las Vegas or the coast, just to get away. After a while, people at work began to whisper. The Sheriff's Office had a long-standing policy discouraging interoffice romance—especially when it involved people in supervisory and management positions dating subordinates. Sherrie had reported to me for three of the four years that we'd been seeing each other. We thought we'd done our due diligence to be professional at work and discreet about our outside lives, but as we got closer, it became obvious that we were sharing more than the lab.

Any doubt about our status was jettisoned when, one evening in early 2004, I was on my way home from visiting the kids and made a snap decision to stop by Sherrie's house. She'd given me a key a few weeks earlier. The lights were on, so I figured it was okay to drop in. I climbed the porch, turned the key in the lock, and went inside. By the time I heard voices, it was too late to sneak back out. "Paul!" Sherrie said, spotting me walking into the family room. All heads turned. A pair of work friends and their wives were sitting around chatting. "Oh," I stuttered, my face turning bloodred. Excuses rolled through my head. *I'm just dropping off work. We're being sent to a crime scene.* I felt like a trapped animal. Sherrie invited me to take a seat, and everyone babbled away, trying to avoid the elephant in the room. Sherrie kept her cool, but I was wringing my hands and trying to figure out a way to wipe the sweat from my upper lip without looking obvious. I kept the visit short, trying to steady myself as I walked out the door. There was no hiding after that. I could feel the eyes following me as I walked into my office the next morning. Sherrie felt the chill.

With the romance unofficially official, some of our colleagues began to resent us. We were breaking the rules, they said, and it wasn't fair to everyone else. Two criminalists in particular complained bitterly among themselves that Sherrie was getting preferential treatment. No one wanted to antagonize me, so Sherrie took the heat. She had to endure the knowing looks and the hushed whispers. There were times she came into my office, closed the door, and burst into tears because she'd caught a disapproving look or felt iced out of the group. It was a difficult time, especially for her. I, being me, the master of avoiding conflict, focused on my work. Hear no evil. See no evil. Conflict made me break out in hives.

At that point, in February 2004, I was ready to ask Sherrie to marry me. We'd been seriously dating for two years, and the timing felt right. *Let's go ahead and make this a formal thing,* I thought. I went to the jewelry store near my place in Walnut Creek before a trip we had planned to Yosemite. It was snowing when we got there. I put the diamond in my pocket as we prepared to hike around Mirror Lake. It seemed like we had been out for hours, and no place felt like the perfect spot. When we came upon a clearing, I decided to make my move. Turning to Sherrie and reaching into my pocket, I asked, "Will you marry me?" No one has ever accused me of being a romantic. I've made attempts—sending flowers, cooking a surprise dinner, the usual stuff—but I'm not the guy who's going to rent a plane and write things in the sky. The word "love" had always been uncomfortable for me to say out loud. It represents either too much of a commitment— the kind that locks you in—or the potential for gut-wrenching rejection.

I'd only said the words "I love you" a handful of times in my whole life. I just didn't feel confident putting myself out there that way. Sherrie was similarly reserved. She picked and chose her moments. But she did insist on a proper proposal. As I stood there, the ring sparkling in my shaking, outstretched hand, she looked at me and smiled. "Don't you think you'd better get on your knee?" she asked. I dropped to my knee in the snow and proposed again. She said yes and we continued our hike, me with a wet knee.

The first thing I did when we returned to work was tell my boss, Karen, the news. Better to put it out there, I thought, especially since Sherrie was returning to the lab wearing a diamond on her left hand. The working environment didn't improve much in the immediate aftermath of our engagement announcement. I ignored the tension until I couldn't anymore. That same month, I passed the conference room on the way to my office and saw a group of my staff gathered there, everyone except Sherrie. Karen was seated at the head of the table. I hadn't been invited. *This can't be good,* I thought. After the meeting, Karen came into my office and sat down across from me. I could tell from the pained expression on her face that she was dreading the conversation. "People think you're giving Sherrie preferential treatment," she said. Karen had once reprimanded me because Sherrie and I were chatting it up back in the lab. This was much more serious. I explained that my perception was that not only had I not shown Sherrie favoritism; I'd been tougher on her to avoid the perception of partiality. I sent her to crime scenes in the middle of the night when no one else wanted to go. I gave her the lab assignments no one else wanted. Karen held firm. There was a policy. "We have to separate you," she said, echoing orders from her commander.

Sherrie shrugged when she was told. "If this is the way it has to be," she said, but I knew she was hurt and unhappy. She continued to work in our lab, and I still assigned her work, but she reported to the head of a lab across town. I was bitter. I'd always had a good, friendly relationship with my staff, and I felt like they'd stabbed me in the back by going over my head. I'd ignored their sarcastic remarks and eye rolls, thinking that the gossip would die down and time would take care of things. It clearly hadn't, and now the person I was going to marry was suffering. I felt betrayed. I wished I could have responded to their complaints, but I was silenced by my position. I just had to grit my teeth and focus on the work.

IN MAY 2004, SHERRIE AND I GOT MARRIED in a small ceremony hosted by her parents at a country club near their home. We had planned to elope, but her parents wouldn't hear of it. It was Sherrie's first marriage, and they wanted it done right. The wedding was a small gathering of around thirty family members and close friends. Nathan wore a suit, and Renee, the quintessential tomboy, agreed to put on a dress for the occasion. With Sherrie, I felt like I had found a true partner. I was excited about our life together. When we returned from our honeymoon, she started looking for another job. We both agreed it was for the best. We didn't want the stress of being constantly scrutinized at work, and even if we did everything right, there would always be complainers—that was one of the early things I'd learned when I got into management. Within a year, Sherrie was working in the DNA lab at a private firm. And we were expecting our first child together.

18

Small Victories

There was a single moment when I realized that I had a gift. I can
pinpoint it with a case. October 15, 2005. I was at a homicide in
the gentrified hills of Lafayette, in an exclusive area with sweeping views of Walnut Creek and Mount Diablo. Even by Lafayette stan-
dards, the Italian villa being built on Hunsaker Canyon Road was wildly
elaborate. Attorney and TV pundit Daniel Horowitz and his movie pro-
ducer wife, Pamela Vitale, had been building their dream home. But the
dream ended with Pamela's murder. The homicide sent the community
reeling. Bad things weren't supposed to happen in Lafayette. And the *way*
Pamela died. She was killed in a savage, almost maniacal attack. After a vicious beating, her attacker carved what looked like a Gothic signature into
her back. Horowitz discovered her bludgeoned body when he returned
home after spending the day at his law office preparing for a murder trial.
The couple had been living in a trailer on their property during construction, and Vitale's body was just inside the door of the trailer. Pamela had
put up a hell of a fight. Furniture was overturned as she fought off her

attacker, until he finally got the upper hand. While she lay there, dazed and helpless, he struck her dozens of times in a frenzied act of overkill.

Standing inside that trailer, I could see the whole thing play out in front of me.

IT'S EASY TO GET OVERWHELMED WITH the number of moving parts in the early stages of a homicide investigation. On day one you're documenting the crime scene and collecting and preserving evidence in a certain order so as not to compromise other evidence. There is a lot to do and a lot at stake. You have to keep a cool head and know how to multitask. You are constantly being pulled in different directions, so it's easy to be distracted and miss critical clues. One of the more experienced criminalists on our staff would roll up to a big scene and immediately go into a panic. *Oh fuck,* he'd murmur under his breath. *Oh fuck.* He choked before he even started. "Break it down into small chunks," I'd say, following him around as he paced nervously, trying to calm him down.

I was comfortable in that environment and with that pressure. I had learned to break down the work into logical and manageable steps. I was fortunate to have expertise in crime scene reconstruction and wound pathology that gave me a leg up. Most investigators follow a standard routine and don't take the time to study what happened. They are off and running, tracking down witnesses and leads before they've ever assessed what happened and why. A lot of times, crime scene investigators follow the detective's lead without questioning whether the evidence matches the theory. I always stepped back and took the time to ask myself, "What does this crime scene tell me, and what can I glean about the victim and the offender from it?"

In the Vitale case, it was a combination of understanding the physical evidence and the blood patterns and then correlating those with Pamela's injuries. I saw it like a movie. She and her killer have their initial encounter. She's wearing a T-shirt and underwear, so I'm thinking he walked in and surprised her. The evidence shows that things moved quickly after that. Judging from the bloody handprints and smudges in every room, she moves through the trailer putting up quite a fight. She runs to the front door, which is closed. The inside of the door is smeared with bloody handprints. She was so close to getting out. Defensive wounds told me she was able to ward off dozens of devastating blows to her legs and hands, but she ultimately died just inside the door. She was already down when she was clubbed in the head. *You know what?* I thought. *This guy, if it was a male, really struggled to get her under control.*

I was already building a mental profile of the killer. It made sense that if the offender was a man—since women rarely kill by bludgeoning—he was likely on the small side. Anyone larger could have taken control much quicker than the chaotic crime scene suggested. "Whoever is responsible is not really strong," I told the lead detective. "This was not done by a large, robust male." That was speculation on my part, but it was based on practicality and experience. The detective responded with a shrug, as if it hadn't occurred to him, but it was the kind of clue I tucked in my pocket for later.

I had a similar reaction from the criminalist when I asked that he make sure to swab the bottom of Pamela's feet. I noticed she had a tear in her sock. On one hand, it could have been from wear, but in the scene in my head, the one where I re-create the crime as I suppose it happened, she is punching and kicking her attacker, and *that* is when the sock rips, exposing part of her bare foot. If that was the case, a speck of his blood or saliva could be hiding there. DNA.

It was those kinds of ancillary observations that sometimes provided peripheral but significant pieces to the bigger puzzle. At that point, I had accumulated enough small victories—predicting or doing things that played a role in solving so many homicides—that I'd learned to trust my instincts. With every win, my confidence grew. Sherrie and others in the lab called it "Sherlock Holmes magic." How many times had I been asked, "How did you come up with that?"

In my fifteen years on the job, I had worked in multiple forensic disciplines and been sent to the most complex and bizarre crime scenes. What I didn't know, I studied. My head was always in a book, whether it was about victimology, homicidal characteristics, or anything relating to the kind of crime I was interested in. I stuffed it all into my mental library to draw upon when a new case occurred or I was revisiting an old one. Conaty always said I had a file cabinet in my head, that it was as if I had alphabetical files in my brain and could pluck them at will.

I eventually had to concede that I had an innate ability to look at a case and have a fundamental understanding of what happened and what type of offender did it. I fostered that by combining science, art, and instinct to prove or disprove my gut. It was an unconventional approach to solving homicides, and it didn't always produce magic, but it had worked too often for me to question my process.

Finding offender DNA on Pamela Vitale's foot was a long shot, but I was willing to take the chance. One of the things I'd learned over the years was to never skip that extra step if your gut tells you to take it, even if it seems unlikely to produce anything of significance. You owe the victim that consideration. The mindset of most criminalists is that anything beyond by-the-book procedures probably isn't worth attempting. It's a waste of time and effort. They tell themselves, "This is the lane I have to stay in," and in some ways they are right to do that, but it's limiting. I had decided that all lanes were open to me. If I went out on a limb to prove or disprove a theory, and it turned out to be wrong, well, at least I could eliminate it and move on to the next idea.

The Vitale case was pivotal for me in that I realized I was making observations others were not. *I am approaching this differently than others,* I thought. *They don't look at a case as comprehensively as I do.* They don't do the deep dive. I say it over and over: "You don't know until you look."

FOUR DAYS AFTER PAMELA VITALE WAS KILLED, her teenage neighbor was arrested and charged with her murder. Scott Dyleski was just shy of his seventeenth birthday. Small and slight at five feet five inches and 110 pounds, Dyleski painted his fingernails with black nail polish and self-identified as goth. The theme of the art found in his bedroom was violence and death: a man holding a severed head and a knife with blood; a face with the mouth stitched with Xs; a figure in a long coat with a knife and the words "Guns don't kill people. I kill people." Dyleski's conversations with friends were dark. When the subject of Vitale's murder came up—which it did all over Lafayette—he speculated that she had been chosen because her husband was a prominent figure. If you wanted to kill someone, shooting them was the most merciful way, he said. You'd bludgeon them if you wanted to cause pain. He recited a nursery rhyme: "*Lizzie Borden took an axe and gave her mother forty whacks. When she saw what she'd done, she gave her father forty-one.*"

Dyleski had changed dramatically from a quiet kid to a troubled teen, but not so troubled that anyone thought he was capable of what he did to Pamela Vitale. Not his mother. Not his father. Not his best friend. But his friend was able to tell police how he thought Dyleski ended up at Vitale's trailer. The pair had decided to grow marijuana and bought growing equipment online using a stolen credit card. Dyleski believed the purchase was delivered to Vitale's address by mistake and went there to retrieve it.

What happened after that is speculation. Had he gone there with the intention to kill? He had worn gloves. Had he tried to sexually assault her? Rob her? She fought him off. Things escalated. He couldn't dominate her, so he resorted to bludgeoning her?

On September 6, 2006, Dyleski was found guilty of first-degree murder at trial and sentenced to life without parole. When I heard, I sat back in my office chair and collected my thoughts. My involvement in the case had ended after that first day at the crime scene, but I was satisfied that I had brought value in the limited time I was there.

Dyleski has consistently denied any role in killing Pamela Vitale. In 2017, he asked a judge to reduce his sentence. "I did not kill Pamela Vitale," he said. "There is no blood on my hands."

But DNA doesn't lie. And his was on the bottom of her foot.

19

Hurricane Holes

In 2009, the position of chief of forensics opened up, an administrative position overseeing seventy-two employees and a $12 million budget. "Not interested," I said when I was encouraged by the higher-ups to apply. I'd learned my lesson about desk jobs when I was promoted the last time, and it was only luck that Karen had allowed me to take on EAR using the grant we'd received. I thought I dodged a bullet when I turned down the invitation to apply for chief, but then word came down from the top. The sheriff himself wanted me to apply. That put me in an awkward position. The top guy was asking me to promote up. It wasn't good form, or a career booster, to ignore what the boss wanted. Sensing my continued reluctance, the commander I would be reporting to approached me with a pitch. "C'mon Paul," he said. "Take the job, and you can work cold cases." Hearing that, how could I not take the job? I was supporting Lori and the kids every month, and Sherrie had left her job to stay home with our two kids. I needed to make up that income, and the promotion came with a healthy pay increase and a path to earn significantly more. When the opportunity first arose, I worried that I would feel trapped into taking the job because I needed to support my family. But now I had the boss's blessing to do cold cases as well. Against my better judgment, I was sold. "Okay, I'll apply," I said.

And there I was, in management again. My orders were to change the foundation of the lab so that it could expand and grow. That meant revising job descriptions, lobbying for a new, updated facility, and getting us out from under old, antiquated procedures. At the same time that we were growing the lab, we were ramping up our efforts to earn accreditation from the International Organization for Standardization (ISO). That in itself was a full-time effort, and stifling. With that overarching agenda, I was constantly being pulled by the Sheriff's Office and the forensic lab accreditation oversight body, each of which thought they should be the priority. My days were spent pushing paper, listening to employee grievances, and trudging through layers of bureaucracy. I called it weary work, and my anxiety kicked in again after having been in remission for quite a while. I tried to work out my frustration in the gym or by jogging the hills of Martinez. I was miserable and mad at myself for not listening to that inner voice that had told me not to take the job. The promise of cold case work was the only thing that sustained me. Except, as the saying goes, a promise is only as good as the person who makes it, and within months, the commander who had dangled the carrot in front of me sustained an injury and decided to retire early.

But life works in mysterious ways, because just as I was beginning to question this new job, one of the most notorious kidnapping cases in contemporary history showed up at my door. I felt like I had been born again.

JAYCEE DUGARD WAS ELEVEN YEARS OLD on June 10, 1991, when she was snatched while walking to the bus stop in a rural community outside of South Lake Tahoe. For the next eighteen years, the world wondered what had become of the missing little girl. And all that time, she was hidden under our noses on Walnut Avenue in Antioch in Contra Costa County, 170 miles from her home, in a series of tents and sheds in the obscured backyard of her abductors, convicted sex offender Phillip Garrido and his wife, Nancy. The hair-raising case had all of the elements of a Stephen King novel. During her captivity, Jaycee gave birth to two daughters— Garrido's children—who she was raising in the makeshift quarters behind the house. It was not until Garrido took Jaycee's daughters, by then eleven and fifteen, to visit the University of California, Berkeley, to inquire about holding a religious event on campus that her whereabouts were discovered. When the case was cracked in late August 2009, the law enforcement community was incredulous (and embarrassed) that no one had had a clue that Jaycee was in our jurisdiction.

Garrido was an odd man, tall and lanky with blue saucer eyes and hollow cheeks, a Lurch-like figure who said he had founded his own church and claimed to have extraordinary powers granted to him by God Himself. Two alert members of campus security were alarmed by his strange behavior and ramblings about superpowers and government conspiracies, but they focused even more on the peculiar young girls with grayish skin and blank stares. One of the officers recalled that the youngest child was spooky and had penetrating eyes that looked into your soul. The officers did a background check on Garrido and discovered his criminal past. He had served time for a violent rape. He was a convicted sex offender on parole. They contacted his parole officer. "He doesn't have daughters," he said. Garrido was ordered to show up at the parole office the next morning. The whole family arrived for the meeting: Garrido; his wife, Nancy; a younger woman they called Alissa; and the two girls. Twenty-nine-year-old Alissa was ultimately identified as Jaycee, the eleven-year-old who had been kidnapped from South Lake Tahoe eighteen years before. The story made headlines around the world.

Garrido was a dangerous sexual predator with a rap sheet. I wondered if he might be culpable in any of our unsolved cases and started to investigate him. He certainly fit the profile of a sadistic stalker, and his geographic profile put him right in the heart of the industrial area where the bodies of Lisa Norrell and the bludgeoned Pittsburg sex workers were found. He ran a printing business there, and he was closely associated with the sketchy owner of the automotive salvage lot where one of the sex workers had been dumped. In 1972, Garrido had drugged and repeatedly raped a fourteen-year-old girl but escaped punishment when she refused to testify against him. Four years later, he was convicted of kidnapping and raping a twenty-five-year-old woman. During his trial, a psychiatrist who conducted a court-ordered psychiatric evaluation of Garrido diagnosed him as a chronic drug abuser and sexual deviant. He was sentenced to fifty years but served only eleven before being released and turned over to parole officials in his home county. Our home county. Three years later, Jaycee was abducted.

I called Conaty and said I thought we should search Garrido's property for any evidence that could link him to the Pittsburg cases. Once the FBI cleared out, we got a search warrant and went in. Seeing the way Jaycee and her daughters lived was shocking. She and her girls slept in a cluster of sheds and tents and tarpaulins in a cordoned-off area at the back of the two-acre lot, behind the backyard proper and hidden by a tall fence and a barrier of shrubbery. The land looked like a junkyard, with abandoned cars and old, deserted horse stables. The living quarters were cluttered with garbage. Clothes hung over lawn chairs, and food containers sat on top of a dresser. Holes in the ground had been used as toilets, and a power cord from the house provided the only crude electricity. Being there, I better understood how Jaycee and her kids had been kept hidden for so long. The enclave was hidden from plain sight. My youngest children, Ben and Juliette, were toddlers, and I couldn't even conjure up an image of them running around in that filthy, uncontrolled environment. How did that poor girl do it, I wondered, raise two babies fathered by her kidnapper and rapist in what amounted to a ramshackle encampment with no plumbing—and starting when she was just a kid herself?

Standing in the midst of it all, I looked over at Conaty. I had never seen him at a loss for words, but he was unable to speak. For the longest time, we stood there in silence, incredulous at what we were witnessing, the tragedy of stolen childhood. Conaty and I both had daughters. I knew he was feeling the same sense of helplessness and rage I did. "This is fucking unbelievable," he said, finally. The revulsion I saw on his face matched what I felt in my gut. We'd both encountered devilish characters in our work, but Garrido's depravity was staggering.

I lay awake that first night, trying to swat away involuntary images of my kids being snatched by a psychopath. Nighttime was always my enemy, a time when there were too few distractions to focus on, and my fears went into overdrive. Parental paranoia was a side effect of my line of work, and I'd just come away from every parent's nightmare scenario. I was admittedly overly protective of my kids. When I was home, I hovered around them. They couldn't play in the backyard unless they were in my line of sight. Ice-cream trucks were off-limits. Child predators were always looking for opportunities to be where kids were.

A team of us from multiple agencies stayed at the Garrido property for the next few weeks, searching every inch of the compound. He was bound to have had other victims, and if we could nail him on any of our unsolved homicides, all the better. We bulldozed the backyard down to the rock ledge and brought in police dogs and ground-penetrating radar, looking for human remains. No soil was left unturned. Teams came and went. I only went home to sleep. Just when it seemed like there was no place left for anything to hide, I opened a metal trash can and discovered it was packed with VHS tapes. The tapes turned out to be graphic evidence of illegal sexual encounters, which would later play an important role in Garrido's trial. What else had we missed? I wondered.

I continued to go out to the scene every day until my boss stepped in.

"Paul, this is not your job," he said. "You are chief of forensics. You're a manager now."

It wasn't hard to read the writing on the wall. The promise that I could do my job and still involve myself in cases in an investigative capacity was off the table. I was a manager now, the commander was right, and I had specific goals I was committed to, so I went back to pushing papers and writing reports. Ultimately, the Garrido search turned up nothing of value in the unsolved Pittsburg homicides. But I continued to dip into those and other cold cases on my own time, and with my boss's office in a separate building, I still had enough independence to use the lab as I wished.

In January 2011, a newly elected sheriff was sworn in. My commander was promoted, and I got my third new supervisor in two years, a former peer from the lab. He was a good administrator; he talked to my staff about working conditions, what worked, what didn't. And since my reputation for chasing cold cases was well known in the lab, he knew it, too. I'd been assigning DNA testing on old evidence for years. What I hadn't realized was that not everyone was as invested in solving cold cases as I was. Staff members complained to the new guy that they were overworked and stressed out. They had their regular cases to do, and I often came into the lab, excited about a cold case, and interrupted the flow of work. They had nicknamed me Hurricane Holes.

Armed with the complaints from my staff, the new boss summoned me to a meeting via video chat. "You can't pepper the lab with your cold cases," he said. Then he issued an edict: the lab was to stop all cold case processing. I wondered how much thought he had given to his decision. Had he given no consideration to the fact that evolving DNA technology would likely close out at least some of those old homicides? Did he think about the public safety aspect of closing cold cases, and that dangerous offenders had gone free, some of whom were surely still out there, ticking time bombs whose compulsion to kill would one day have to be satisfied again? To him, there was no room for compromise. He'd decided that Holes was off the rails.

A few months after the new boss put me in my place, I was approached by one of our agencies asking for help. They had a rash of fetish burglaries, an offender who was starting to enter houses when people were obviously inside. It was a dangerous change of behavior that was likely going to escalate. The agency requested that we do a rush DNA analysis to assist them in catching the offender before someone was hurt. In the past, I would have just done it, but I was skating on thin ice. Rush orders were normally extended only for homicides and sexual assaults, and this was neither, at least not yet. I made the decision to pass the request by my commander. "This is a public safety matter," I said. He denied the request. It didn't fit within agency guidelines.

My future is not here, I thought. *The red tape of bureaucracy is choking me.* It felt like a turning point in my career, a wake-up call. With twenty years of experience in various aspects of crime solving, I had evolved into a unique hybrid in the world of criminal investigations. The science of murder continued to challenge me, but I was also a capable investigator. Sitting behind a desk was a waste of my talents. I could be much more useful getting out there and helping to solve homicides.

Sitting back in my office chair, my attention wandered to the metal file cabinet that still stood in the corner. My eyes dropped to the bottom drawer, labeled "EAR." It had been eight years since I'd turned the case over to Larry Pool in Orange County. I'd been so sure back then that it was only a matter of time before Orange County made an arrest that EAR had become buried in my subconscious under all of the other homicides I'd worked since then. Now I thought, *Wait a minute. That case still isn't solved.*

Taking up a cold case after just being reprimanded was risky. I had a family to think about. Financial commitments. I stopped myself from getting up and going to the drawer. Glancing at the camera on my computer monitor, the one I used for video conferences with the boss, I wondered, *Is he watching? If I do this, will he know?* The file drawer was just sitting there, tempting me. Tapping my fingers on my shiny faux cherry desk, I went back and forth in my head. In 1994, when I had first discovered the EAR files in the crime library, my ambition had been to look at what I could do as a forensic scientist. Now, with complex investigations like Abernathy, Pittsburg, and Phil Hughes under my belt, I wondered what I might contribute using my investigative skills. *Should I?* I wondered, looking from the file cabinet to my computer screen and the camera mounted on top. I stood up from my desk, then sat down again. *Nope. Yup. Nope. What's the worst that can happen? You can be fired. But what if . . . ?*

What if I could solve the case?

Fuck it. I stood up, walked around my desk to the metal file cabinet, and pulled open the bottom drawer.

20

EAR Revisited

I hibernated in my office for weeks getting reacquainted with the EAR files. At that point in my career and life, I had too many other responsibilities, so my intention was to fit my EAR work in between family time and white paper assignments for the lab. But the details in the files were so thrilling that I almost instantly felt myself being sucked back into the case. I couldn't stop turning from one attack to the next. EAR was thought to have struck at least fifty times between 1976 and the end of his ten-year spree. He had outsmarted first-class investigators over the years, but I was now confident enough in my crime-solving skills to believe I could unmask the predator. My whole career, the lab jobs, the crime scene analyses, even the administrative work, had been preparing me for this, and nothing could deter me from pursuing it, not even the threat of losing my job. That meant I was back to sneaking around.

Hidden in those thousands of case-file pages were the details that I needed to begin building a profile of the offender. A checklist almost, something I could use to whittle down the roster of suspects from over the years to those I thought deserved another look. I keyed in on the summary sheets for every person who had ever been looked at. There were hundreds, and the process was time consuming. My assistant covered for me. "He's in a meeting," she'd say when someone asked about my closed office door. I immersed myself in thick case files, remembering details I hadn't thought about in years and learning things I hadn't gotten the chance to know before turning the case over to Orange County eight years earlier. A lot of investigators find that part of the job tedious, studying the voluminous files with comprehensive accounts from every person who might possibly contribute something about a particular investigation, but for me it was thrilling. You can't finish a puzzle without all of the pieces. So much of the detail in the EAR files had been dissected and discounted over the years, but I didn't trust the previous findings. I needed to look at everything myself, which meant duplicating previous efforts to see if I came to the same conclusions. Some people will see that as arrogant, and aggravating. For me, it was an uncontrollable response. I think that's one of the things that makes me good at what I do. I'm thorough to the point of obsession. It's part of the obsessive gene that runs through my family, Mom with an eating disorder and my brother, Dave, with OCD.

Scrutinizing every page in the EAR files gave me a partially exposed picture of who he was. The devil was in the details. His swath of harm was vast. It had taken eight attacks after his June 1976 debut in the east area of Sacramento County for authorities there to recognize that the same dangerous predator was likely responsible for all of them. EAR wasn't the only serial predator working in the area back then. The Early Bird Rapist, who struck between the hours of midnight and dawn, the Wooly Rapist, who got his name because he wore woolen gloves during his assaults on women, and the Vampire Killer, whose name says it all, were all active when EAR crept onto the scene. The others were caught. Not EAR. It wasn't for lack of trying.

The EAR was a challenging and complex adversary, stalking sleeping neighborhoods, masked and well armed with bindings and weapons, stealthily breaking into homes and surprising his victims with the piercing beam of a flashlight in their drowsy eyes. Dozens of skilled investigators had hunted him before me. I tried to visualize him. What he looked like. Victims had described him every which way. Tall. Medium height. Muscular build. Fat. Average weight. Thin legs. Chunky thighs. Blond. Brown hair. Some guessed at his hair color. Others only saw the skin between his glove and his sleeve. He's attacking in the middle of the night, with a mask on, wearing loose clothing. His victims are scared. Not ideal circumstances for trying to describe someone. I developed a spreadsheet of all the characterizations. The bottom line was that what we had was an average white male. Not much to go on.

He had the gift of blending in. I wondered if he was the guy next door, out there mowing his lawn every Saturday. Did he have a wife and kids who were oblivious to his dark side? Was he ominous, a devil with beady eyes and an evil aura, like Phil Hughes? Maybe he was a professional, a businessman or accountant who wore a tie to work every day. Or a construction worker who moved from job to job and hunted local prey. How did he choose his victims? Most of his attacks appeared to be well thought out. Except for a couple of close calls, his getaways were impeccable.

A psychological sadist, he seemed to revel in brandishing control, tying up and blindfolding his victims, before ordering them to sexually satisfy him. He talked through clenched teeth in a forced high-pitched voice, using vulgarisms and repeated threats to kill. He left victims bound and trembling in their beds while he took breaks to ransack their homes, rifling through dresser drawers and stealing cash, coins, jewelry, and photographs, or sit in their kitchen, eating their food and drinking their beer. He put dishes on his victims' backs and promised certain death if he heard them clatter. In some cases, he cried, and some victims were of the opinion it was sincere. After one attack, he was heard whimpering for his "Mommy." *I'm sorry, Mommy. Please help me. I don't want to do this, Mommy. . . . It scares my mommy when it's in the news.* Another time, he crouched in a corner and sobbed following the sexual attack. Bizarre, for sure, especially coming from such depravity. The tears, it seemed to me, were for himself.

As I went about gathering information and keeping a log of his behavioral traits, it occurred to me that he, although a monster, fell short of the clinical definition of a psychopath. I branded him more of a sociopath, someone who has a conscience, albeit a weak one. I noticed a thread through some of his attacks that suggested he was at least capable of feeling guilt. Typically, when a victim tried to personalize herself in any way, he angrily ordered them to "Shut up!" The woman who confided to him that she was pregnant. "Shut up! Shut up!" The woman who told him she was Christian and forgave him for what he was about to do. "Shut up! Shut up or I'll kill you!" Was he shutting them down because a feeling of guilt was creeping in, interfering with his malicious intentions? This evolving portrait was key to eliminating some of the names on the list and investigating others.

As with sociopaths and psychopaths, empathy was alien to EAR. His callousness extended even to children. What struck me was his seeming disregard for their presence. If he didn't know they were there when he chose his victims, he didn't hesitate to carry out his activities when he realized that kids were home. In one case, a seven-year-old girl encountered him in the middle of the night on her way to the bathroom. He was standing at the far end of the hallway, in the doorway to the kitchen, masked and wearing woolen mittens but naked from the waist down. "I'm playing tricks with your mom and dad," he said. "Come watch me." The girl returned to her bedroom. In another, he tied up a ten-year-old boy and covered him with a blanket while he sexually assaulted his mother. "Every time you move a muscle, it will take a second off your mother's life," he promised. The boy stayed silent for several hours. I wondered what his life looked like after that. I couldn't imagine that anyone who survived an EAR attack came out of it unscathed.

EAR used children to manipulate their parents into doing what he wanted. "If you don't behave, I'll cut off their ears and bring them back to you. I'll chop up the kids," he threatened during one attack. In another, he stormed a mother who was cradling her three-year-old in her bed and ripped the child from her arms. He tied the boy's hands and feet and ordered the frantic mom to "keep him quiet" while he raped her. If she didn't comply, he said, "I will kill your kid." They both survived, physically, but the psychological damage was terminal.

Reading the files, I made a note to myself: "Need for self-preservation." EAR did not want to be caught. He went above and beyond to protect his identity. His face was always covered, and he blinded his victims with his flashlight. He threatened to kill if someone looked at him. He disguised his voice with a harsh whisper, and he wore gloves to make sure no prints were left behind. He moved about with the dexterity of a cat burglar, quietly prowling from room to room. His victims never quite knew where he was or when he was about to pounce. He wanted to keep them guessing, to keep them on edge. I concluded that his silence was part of his escape plan. It gave him time to get away because people were too afraid to move, terrified that he was still there.

Sometimes he was.

AT 6 A.M. ON FEBRUARY 7, 1977, Heathcliff Drive in Carmichael was just beginning to wake up. Number 6269 was one of the newest homes in the development, a two-year-old ranch with a pitched roof and sliding glass doors that bordered on a park. The thirty-year-old homeowner inside was waking her husband for work at that hour. His habit was to leave for his job at a glass company by 6:45 for the twenty-minute commute. While he dressed, she made him breakfast and packed his lunch. Their six-year-old daughter was still asleep in her room down the hall.

The couple talked while he ate breakfast; then the woman walked him to the front door and kissed him goodbye. She was closing the door when he called out to her. "Karen!" A suspicious-looking van was parked nearby, George said. Both of them had been on edge since the house was burglarized a month earlier. Lock the house up tight, he said.

When George pulled off, Karen shuffled through the house, locking all of the doors. She'd been in the kitchen doing chores for ten minutes or so when she had a sensation that someone was with her. *George is back,* she thought. He must have forgotten something. Turning around, she came face-to-face across the breakfast counter with a man wearing a ski mask, and she was looking down the barrel of his gun.

"Don't scream or I'll shoot," he said in a menacing voice. "I just want your money. I don't want to hurt you."

Panic struck and she began to shake uncontrollably. Her first thought was that he was going to shoot her, and her little girl would have no one to protect her. What should she do, she wondered. Fight? Comply?

The masked man led her into the living room and ordered her to sit in a chair. "I'm going to tie you up," he said. "Do what I say or I'll kill you."

He tied her trembling hands with some kind of ties. They felt like shoelaces to her. Once she was bound, he put a knife to her throat. She started to speak.

"Shut up or I'll kill you," he said. "Get up."

"No," she replied.

"I have a gun; do what I say. I want to tie you to the bed."

She did as he said, and he led her past her daughter's bedroom to the master bedroom. Her daughter's door was closed, something the intruder must have done earlier, she thought. Her daughter always kept her bedroom door open. Once they were in the master bedroom, he told her to lay facedown on the bed. He was going to tie her feet.

She resisted. She could feel her racing heart in her throat. "No," she said again.

Forcing her facedown on the bed, he tied her feet with a shoelace and placed a pillow over her head. She couldn't breathe and flipped the pillow off. She could hear him in the dressing room, tearing strips of towel. She tried talking to him. "Shut up!" he said whenever she attempted to speak. "Shut up or I'll kill you."

"I'm going to cover your face," he said when he returned.

"No!" she cried. "Get the fuck out of here!"

She was a fighter. Her hands still tied behind her back, she tried to shimmy off the bed, but he was too fast for her. She felt the full weight of him on her back. His gloved hand covered her mouth. She called to her dog. "Get him!" she screamed. "GET HIM!"

"Shut up!" he said. "Shut up!"

She continued to scream. She was a mother first, hardwired to protect her child. Above all else to protect her child. No matter what it cost her. Discreetly, she worked her bound hands to one side and felt the gun in the intruder's right front pants pocket. She continued to scream to distract him, then pulled the gun out of his pocket. It was too little, too late. He reached for the gun, and they struggled. Before she could find the trigger to pull it, he grabbed it back. Seizing with rage, he hit her in the head several times.

"Do what I say! Shut up or I'll kill your daughter," he said through gritted teeth. "If you don't believe me, I will bring back a piece of her. I'll go down and cut her ear off and bring it back to you."

She believed him.

The man then wrapped a strip of towel around her eyes. She heard his footsteps and then more towels being ripped. Returning to her bedside, he stuffed a towel in her mouth and poked his knife next to her on the mattress. She was certain he was about to stab her, but then everything went still. He seemed to have left.

Moments went by. "Can you hear me?" he asked.

She shook her head yes.

He tied another towel around her head, covering her ears, but she was able to hear the opening and closing of the bedroom sliding glass door. This was her chance. She slid along the bed. If she could just get to her daughter, they could run to the neighbor's house. She made it to the edge of the bed when she felt the blade of his knife on her face. "If you make one move, I'll kill you," he said through clenched teeth. "If you move or say anything, I'll cut off your toes. I'll cut one off each time you move."

He rolled her onto her back, unzipped her jeans, and pulled them off. It had to be ten or fifteen minutes of gut-wrenching anticipation. She could hear him masturbating at the side of the bed; then he raped her. It happened fast, and Karen remembered that her attacker's penis was very small. He stayed on top of her, moving up and down.

He stopped suddenly, and the room was very, very quiet. She sensed her daughter's presence.

"You're going into the bathroom, and I'm going to tie you up," he said to the seven-year-old.

The child started to cry. "No-no-no!" she said. "You're going to kill us! You're going to kill us!"

"I'm not going to hurt you," the man said, but she continued to scream.

"Leave my daughter alone!" The woman screamed through her gag.

EAR brought the girl over to the bed and placed her next to her mother.

He retied the mother's ankles, then went through the house ripping the phone cords out of the wall. When he returned, he tied the girl's hands behind her back and covered mother and daughter with a blanket.

"I'm just going to tie you up and take the money and leave," he said. "I promise. I promise."

They thought they heard him leave the room and walk through the house. They listened as everything went quiet. *Please, God.* Five minutes passed. Ten minutes. Nothing.

"Are you okay?" the mother whispered to her daughter.

"Shhhh. Momma. Be quiet," the girl whispered back.

Karen felt someone push down abruptly on the mattress. The only sound was his breathing. EAR had been there the whole time.

21

Him

I was cruising past the wind turbines on Highway 12, headed home after shadowing the East Area Rapist's movements in the late '70s in the Central Valley, when my new supervisor called my cell phone. *Oh shit.* "Hi, Paul," she said. "I have the undersheriff with me on speaker phone. Do you have a few minutes?" *Double oh shit. I've been caught. Somehow they know I'm on an illicit EAR mission.* "Hello!" I said in my cheeriest voice, waiting for the hammer to drop. "Do we have a plan in place for urgent forensic exams during the lab transition?" the undersheriff asked. I breathed a huge sigh of relief. At the time, the lab was scheduled to move from the Escobar location to a bigger, renovated facility in town. We'd notified our agencies that once the move commenced, we wouldn't be in a position to do evidence testing for several weeks, which is what the undersheriff had called to discuss. The higher-ups assumed I was in my office, and I did nothing to discourage that assumption. I couldn't have them hear the traffic whizzing past, so I pulled off the freeway onto a levy road. I threw the car in park and recited the plan. The beauty of the administrative offices being across town from the lab was the freedom it gave me to sneak out to chase the East Area Rapist on the pretense of traveling between buildings. I routinely left my office in the lab to visit people and places where he'd struck, which is what I'd been doing that day.

My trips to EAR's attack locations were part of my desire to know him. I wanted to see what he saw when he selected a victim or a neighborhood, to feel the adrenaline he felt as he jumped fences and jimmied locks to sneak into a house in the dark of night and surprise sleeping women and men. I'd put myself in his shoes, trying to figure out what he was thinking when he chose a particular person or place. By then, I felt as if I'd come to know him well enough to get in his head when I needed to. Sometimes it worried me how easy it was for me to feel what I thought he was feeling when he was plotting and carrying out his evilness. I had become so good at getting into the minds of serial predators that when I lay awake at night, thinking about cases, I wondered if I'd crossed some kind of boundary. If cops were only a fine line away from criminals, how close was I to the monsters I had spent my life following?

As even-keeled as I was, there were times when I was shaken by the darkness I'd invited myself into. In those moments when reason got away from me, sweating, heart pounding, on the verge of another panic attack, I brought myself back with the mindfulness that I didn't have a compulsion to commit their vile crimes. When you spend your life in the trenches with madness, it can really play tricks with your mind.

My process of getting into an offender's head had begun with the Pittsburg sex workers case while I was investigating one of the more gruesome of those homicides. Valerie Schultz was mutilated before she was killed, her body dumped like trash along the industrial strip where the other victims in the series had been left. The grisly crime scene photos led me into the killer's psyche. Studying each one, I put myself in his place. I feel him on top of her, one hand around her neck, the other holding a knife. He carves deep crevices in her face while she is still conscious. She is suffering, begging him to spare her. He watches her wounds spurt blood. His heart pumps faster and his breathing hastens. In his final act of cruelty, as she fades toward death, he plunges his knife up under her chin, then deep into her stomach, like a hunter gutting a deer. I feel his release and know he's finished. This is not an anger killing. This is the killer's fantasy playing out. He likes watching his victim writhe and scream. He's turned on by her pain. I believe I have a clear understanding of who he is, but I'm shaken to the core for having resided in his mind, even for a moment.

It's a hazard of my investigative process, putting myself in the role of the killer. After spending so much time in EAR's head, I had an unsettling thought: what if I got stuck there?

BY THE TIME I'D TAKEN THE TRIP to the Central Valley that day in 2012, I had managed to keep my EAR investigation under wraps for almost three years. I don't know how I did it. I think what saved me in the lab was my ability to finish a day's worth of quality administrative work by midmorning so that I could then take up my EAR work.

What started with organizing the six hundred summary sheets from the original task force files graduated to a herculean investigative process to generate a list of names I thought were significant enough for further study: twenty-four. I'd spent the two previous years researching all the suspects to find out who they were and what they had been up to for the last thirty years. I started by running each name through databases for basic information, like driver's license numbers and address histories, that allowed me to dig deeper. Common names took longer. Once I'd completed the first phase, I could graduate to the next level of detective work—the tangled web of criminal histories and DNA profiles. So many times I'd heard investigators grouse about how tedious laying the ground-work for cases was, but I liked the process of taking it in steps. I compared it to woodworking. You start sanding with coarse sandpaper, follow up with medium grade, and use fine grade to finish. For me, that was the part where I was out in the field doing the gumshoe detective work: visiting towns, neighborhoods, and houses where EAR attacked; tracking down relatives and friends; talking to witnesses from the case files; commiserat-ing with victims—both women and men—still traumatized decades after their encounters with him. So many agencies had spent so much man-power trying to catch EAR that it seemed likely to me that at some point law enforcement had made contact with him. That was a criterion I used when I was ranking my chiseled-down list of two dozen. One name bub-bled to the top. I'll call him Robert Lewis Potts.

I BEGAN MY DEEP DIVE INTO Potts in early 2011 and quickly came up with what read like a précis on the East Area Rapist. The similarities were uncanny. Potts grew up in Sacramento County, EAR's home base, and lived there for most of his life. His job as a railroad brakeman took him along the same protracted route—to the same locales and across the same jurisdictions—and within the same time frame when EAR was attacking in each. The geographic profile I developed for Potts was so close to EAR's that the crisscross of the map's yellow data points looked like they'd been drawn with tracing paper over the rapist's movements around Northern California. *How could he not be EAR?* I thought as I studied the fifteen-page timeline.

Besides the undeniable similarity in travel, a litany of other correlations solidified my hunch that Potts was our guy. Potts, like EAR, had a pecu-liar attachment to his mother. His history of violence, which included a domestic violence arrest for beating his common-law wife, matched a prediction in an early profile by criminal profiler Leslie D'Ambrosia that the offender "would have a history of assaultive or abusive behavior towards partners." And there was the detail that two of EAR's attacks were in a neighborhood adjacent to where Potts had attended school only a few years earlier.

Potts was no stranger to East Area Rapist inquiries. He had come to the attention of the original Contra Costa County task force shortly after EAR moved eighty miles from the Sacramento area to begin attacking in the East Bay in 1978. In December of that year, a thirty-two-year-old Danville woman awakened to a masked man straddling her and holding a knife to her neck. The attack was typical EAR. He bound her at the wrists and ankles, blindfolded her, and threatened to kill her if she made a sound. "Do you like to fuck?" he asked. "No," she said. "Do you like to raise dicks?" "No," she said again. "Then why do you raise mine every time I see you?" he asked, before raping her twice. Potts was arrested in that same area two months later.

In the early morning hours of February 3, 1979, Contra Costa deputy sheriff Carl Fabbri was patrolling Danville when he spotted a suspicious car parked on the side of the road a half mile from Liberta Court, where EAR had attacked in December. The primered 1968 Pontiac LeMans hadn't been there an hour earlier when Fabbri passed. It was an awkward spot to pull over, he thought. Something didn't feel right. Fabbri was already on high alert. The night before, he'd chased a masked man near there but had lost the prowler when he'd hopped a tall fence. Fabbri suspected the rapist was back.

He radioed in, then pulled up behind what looked like an empty car. Walking cautiously to the passenger-side door, he lit up the car with his flashlight. A man appeared to be sleeping in the back seat—Potts. Fabbri tapped on the window, and the man startled awake. "Step out of the car," the officer said. He thought the man fit the general description of the East Area Rapist—five feet ten, 150 pounds—but what really got his attention was the address on his license. The guy lived up in Carmichael, in the heart of EAR's Sacramento County attacks. What are you doing all the way down here in Danville? Fabbri asked. Potts said he was on his way home from his railroad job at the Fremont rail yard. He was tired and jumped off the interstate to nap before driving the rest of the one-hundred-mile commute. The story didn't fly with Fabbri. The freeway was a couple of miles up the road. Why would this guy drive so far out of his way when there were closer, more convenient spots to pull over?

Things were about to get worse for the young railroad brakeman. Fabbri told Potts to hold tight while he ran his history. Turned out he had an open warrant—nothing major, some motor vehicle offense—but enough to allow Fabbri to take him into custody. The officer returned to Potts's car. "You're under arrest," he said.

Backup arrived with flashing overhead lights and blaring sirens. Up until then, Potts had been relatively calm. He'd grumbled and grimaced, but nothing unusual for someone in his tenuous position. Strangely, the panic came out when one of the officers pulled out a camera and prepared to take his mug shot. Potts went berserk. He did not want his picture taken. *No! Get the fuck out of my face!* Kicking and flailing, he shouted that he was being treated like shit, goddammit, and for no good reason. He had been sleepy on the drive home and had stopped to nap. He just wanted to go the hell home!

The officers had to subdue Potts to cuff him and get him into the back of the police car. During the twenty-minute drive to jail, he held a conversation with himself. "If anyone fools with me, I'll poke his eyes out. I'll bite his tongue off." . . . "Would you shoot me if I try to escape?" . . . "Nobody ever catches the real criminals; they always get away." Fabbri recorded it and turned it over to the task force.

Potts was taken to the old jail in Martinez. At 7 A.M., he requested that he be allowed to call his mother. She came to the jail and posted $115 cash bail, and he was released at 1:45 P.M. that same afternoon. He went back to his normal life, toggling back and forth from home to work, up and down the Interstate 80 and 680 freeways, passing the same exits that EAR took for attacks from Davis all the way down to San Jose.

FOUR MONTHS AFTER POTTS'S ENCOUNTER WITH police in Danville, and after EAR had attacked a couple in Fremont and two teenagers in Walnut Creek, the predator was back in Danville, terrorizing a couple in June on Allegheny Drive just off Interstate 680. It was consistent with his pattern of returning to places where he'd already attacked.

He struck again on July 5, this time a husband and wife on Sycamore Hill Court, a half mile from the spot where Potts had been napping. At 4 A.M., the husband was stirred awake by a rustling sound. When he opened his eyes, he saw the reflection of a man pulling on a mask in the bedroom mirror. The husband pitched up in bed, and their eyes met. "Who the fuck do you think you are?" he shouted at the intruder. "What the fuck are you doing here?" The masked man stepped back, as if stunned, and the husband lunged. He was bigger and stronger and managed to trap the intruder in a corner of the room. Now awake, the wife bolted out of the room, down the stairs, and outside, screaming for help. The husband suspected that his opponent was the dreaded East Area Rapist. "If you leave now, you can leave," he told the intruder, hoping to save his own life. The husband turned and ran, and the intruder retreated into the dark.

Isn't that just like him, I thought, as I attempted to match EAR's MO to Potts. He's here a few months earlier. He's arrested, but that doesn't scare him off. Now he's thumbing his nose at the patrols that were set up to trap him, just as he had done so many times in Sacramento. Except this time, things went sideways. It was EAR's last attack in Danville.

The East Area Rapist was quiet after that. From July to October, people held their breath, hoping he was gone for good. In a way, he was. The next time he was heard from, he was four hundred miles south and about to graduate to murder. The East Area Rapist would soon be known as the Original Nightstalker.

HAL FRANKLIN, AN INVESTIGATOR WITH the Contra Costa County District Attorney's Office while EAR was active, wrote an eight-page summary of the Danville attacks to the original EAR task force commander. The summary, with an addendum from Fabbri's encounter with Potts, concluded that there was enough circumstantial evidence to consider Potts as the East Area Rapist. Franklin was certain it was him. On August 8, 1979, after months of dodging authorities, Potts finally agreed to a saliva test. Two days later, he was eliminated as a suspect based on the results of that test. Four months after that, the Original Nightstalker started killing in the southern part of the state. My first thought was "Oh boy, did they arrest EAR and then let him go?" Potts's saliva sample was brought to the Contra Costa County Sheriff's Crime Lab and subjected to a secretor status test. A secretor is someone who secretes their blood type antigens into bodily fluids, such as saliva or semen. Little or no blood type antigens are found in the bodily fluids of a nonsecretor. Only about 10 percent of the population are nonsecretors.

Potts's saliva typed A and was determined to be a secretor, indicating he secreted the ABO substances into his saliva and other physiological fluids. Since Potts was determined to be a secretor, and EAR was a nonsecretor, he was eliminated as an EAR suspect at that time. In my opinion, eliminating him based on that test had been a big mistake. Multiple studies had demonstrated the existence of individuals with aberrant secretion of ABH substances between body fluids, which meant the tests were unreliable. I couldn't trust any elimination based on secretor status.

I consulted with Brian Wraxall, a noted serologist from Britain and lab director from the Serological Research Institute. Wraxall had published many studies on old serology methods and was considered an expert in the field. He reviewed the procedure done by the Contra Costa lab for absorption inhibition from saliva samples obtained from suspects and determined that the procedure had been done incorrectly. After litera-ture reviews and consultation with Wraxall, I concluded that any suspect elimination done on secretor status from the Contra Costa lab was prob-lematic, and otherwise strong suspects who were eliminated on secretor testing should be reconsidered. Potts was not a valid elimination.

But I would have to find a different way to prove he was EAR.

22

Roller Coaster

The DNA profile for the East Area Rapist had been on file for ten years without a hit. All I had to do was get DNA from Potts to prove he was the guy. Except that he was in the wind. I was able to track him until 2004, when he finished serving time after his domestic violence conviction. And then he dropped off the map. In the seven years since, he hadn't applied for a credit card or renewed his driver's license or updated his mailing address. He hadn't held a job that I could find or applied for welfare. Remarkably, there was no record of any contact with law enforcement, a break from the typical. "All of this suggests Potts is either dead or making a concerted effort not to be found," I wrote in my notes. "His continued viability as a suspect justifies efforts to get a direct DNA sample."

My gut feeling was that Potts had gone into hiding. The same year he disappeared, California passed Proposition 69, which overhauled the state's DNA system and broadened the types of crimes that allowed for genetic testing. Under the new law, convicted felons and suspects arrested on suspicion of committing a felony could be DNA tested and the results uploaded in CODIS in the state's DNA databank. Potts's domestic violence conviction made him vulnerable under the new law. Had he disappeared to avoid having to submit to a DNA test because it would identify him as the serial predator? Ironically, the legislation passed in part due to a campaign driven and funded by the brother of one of EAR's victims. Keith Harrington and his wife had been bludgeoned in their Orange County home in August 1980. The Harringtons were among the six Original Nightstalker attacks between 1979 and 1986 that we'd been able to connect by DNA to EAR.

MY WORK ON POTTS COINCIDED WITH Sherrie's decision that she needed more personal time to be able to pursue things other than being a mom. Our kids were six and seven and becoming more self-sufficient. Sherrie's very crafty, and she took an interest in sewing. I helped turn our multipurpose room into a sewing room and bought her a nice new sewing machine. As time went on, instead of spending evenings curled up on the couch together watching TV after the kids were in bed, she sewed, and I buried myself in my laptop, following the next lead.

It was during one of those late-night searches that I found a footnote in a report from the original task force that made me do a double take. In 1979, when Potts was under active investigation, detectives had collected a black ski mask he'd left behind at a friend's house. *Wait!* I thought, as the sewing machine whirred in the next room. *A ski mask?* That was the first I'd heard of it. EAR wore a ski mask during every one of his attacks. The report noted that hairs had been picked off the knit mask to preserve as evidence should there be a need for future hair comparisons, but none had ever been requested. Nothing had ever been done with the mask. Was it possible it had been preserved? I wondered. Had we had Potts's DNA all along? The mask had the potential to solve the case. If it still existed, biological material was likely still in place. *My God,* I thought, the East Area Rapist's identity could be hiding in that ski mask.

I was so excited. I wanted to tell someone, but Sherrie had gotten to the point by then that the times I did mention the case she usually rolled her eyes. That night, I barely slept. I watched the clock until it was reasonable to get up and go to the lab. All the way to Martinez I talked to myself. *I've solved the case. I've solved the case. I've solved the case.*

I was barely able to keep my composure as I made my way from my office to the Evidence Room. I carefully thumbed through the old property cards. When I pulled the three-by-five-inch card with "ski mask" written on it, I felt like I was holding a winning lottery ticket. Rich Wara, the new Property Room manager, retrieved the evidence box. I knew there was no guarantee the mask would be there. It could have been destroyed at any point over the last thirty years.

Wara brought out the box and placed it on the counter. He couldn't have known what that moment meant to me. I was so anxious and excited I could feel my heart pounding in my throat. I tore into the box. There it was, carefully wrapped in plastic and secured with a metal tie. *I've got him,* I thought. I don't know where Potts is, but I've got his DNA.

I took the box back to my office to study the contents more closely. At the bottom was a plastic baggie with folded pieces of paper inside. The label read, "Collected from RR Right of Way." I was investigating a railroad guy, so that got my attention. Three sheets of lined paper torn from a spiral binder were folded together inside the baggie. According to the Evidence Log, the papers were collected by John Patty, a criminalist with the county, from the scene of EAR's 1979 attack on the thirty-two-year-old woman from Danville. I'd met John when I was in my early twenties and just starting out at the lab. He was a seasoned criminalist, and he'd poked his head in to introduce himself. I never saw him after that. A few months later, he died after a battle with cancer. Ironically, it was his crime scene jumpsuit I subsequently inherited. *Was there a message somewhere in that connection?* Patty's reputation as a maverick preceded him. We were of the same ilk. I felt like I was in good company when I realized he had been on the case. Patty had been there when bloodhounds tracked EAR's scent from the Danville woman's house through her backyard to the railroad tracks beyond. He'd picked up the papers from the side of the tracks. I was certain he—like me—figured it was entirely possible that EAR had dropped them, probably when he was stuffing his mask and weapon into a backpack during his getaway.

I took the papers out and unfolded them. The first appeared to be a high school history assignment on General Custer. Aside from the poor spelling and grammar, there didn't seem to be anything remarkable about it. The second sheet was more intriguing. It appeared to be the grumblings of someone who was holding a grudge about something that had happened in elementary school. *"Mad is the word,"* it began. *"The word that reminds me of 6th grade. I hated that year."* The writer went on to complain bitterly about the teacher who made him write sentences as punishment for talking. *"Those awful sentences that my teacher made me write, hours and hours I'd sit and write 50–100–150 sentences day and night. . . . It made me ashamed of myself which in turn, deep down inside made me realize that . . . it wasn't fair to make me suffer like that."*

The last was a penciled diagram resembling a map. It was indecipherable, at least at first look. I put it aside for later.

That same day, April 4, 2011, I sent the ski mask to the lab for DNA testing, knowing it would take time to get the results. The irony. Here I was in charge of the lab, but the moratorium on cold cases, prompted by my own reputation for pushing cold case work, meant my request was pushed to the bottom of the pile. I didn't dare undermine my boss by pushing it to the top when the lab was overwhelmed with work on active cases. I would have to make peace with the fact that I had to wait my turn. I had plenty of other tasks to follow up on.

I started with the sixth-grade rant. Potts had attended elementary school in West Pittsburg, which is now called Bay Point. I was relieved when I was able to convince the school to release his records to me. I looked at the name of the teacher on his sixth-grade report card. The man had retired years earlier, but I found him living in Orinda. I called him on the off chance he had any insight on the note.

The teacher was a crusty old guy. "So now I'm to blame for one of my students becoming a serial killer?" he asked when I explained why I was calling. He didn't remember Potts, but he did recall doling out repetitive sentence assignments as punishment for his sixth graders. Oh, and by the way, he told me, he'd received a strange phone call back in 2001. The caller sang a song the teacher used to make Potts's class sing for punishment. He sang it to me. "*Freedom isn't free. Freedom isn't free. You got to pay a price. You got to sacrifice. For your liberty.* Remember that?" the caller asked and hung up. The teacher was so rattled he had his number changed and unlisted. It was right around the same time in 2001 that the Sacramento woman who'd been attacked by EAR twenty-four years earlier got the call asking, "Remember when we played?"

Score. I had one more box checked on the Potts checklist.

My investigation continued in earnest. An updated rap sheet revealed that Potts had continued to have scrapes with the law in the years following his elimination as a suspect. He had a violent streak. A body search during a traffic stop in San Jose turned up two steak knives in a duct-taped sheath in his waistband. EAR was known to use steak knives during some of his attacks. Potts claimed he had them because his neighbor was ruining his life, but the neighbor was a disabled woman who posed no threat to him.

In 2002, he was arrested for beating his common-law wife and threatening to "cut her up into little pieces." EAR's file was rife with similar threats. "I'll just cut you up." . . . "Be quiet, or else I'll cut you up." . . . "I'll cut your daughter's ear off and bring it to you." . . . "If I hear this move, I'll slit her throat, cut off her ear, and bring it back to you."

Coincidence? I didn't think so.

I believed Potts had gotten away with murder.

I WAS CONFIDENT ENOUGH AT THAT point to share my conviction about Potts with Anne Marie Schubert, a Sacramento County assistant district attorney. Schubert had formed the Cold Case Prosecution Unit in her office two years before. I'd met her ten years earlier over the phone when I had linked the East Area Rapist and the Original Nightstalker with DNA. She told me she was interested in pursuing cold cases and that she had a vested interest in EAR. She'd grown up in Sacramento during the attacks and had vivid memories of the terror that had paralyzed her city. After our introductory call, Schubert pitched the idea of bringing all of the relevant agencies together to share information, but interagency bickering interfered, and the meeting never materialized.

We'd met again by chance a few years later at a conference in Santa Barbara. Hanging out after hours, I got to know her better, and a professional friendship grew. I was sure she would be interested in the work I'd done on EAR since then.

I called Anne Marie that May. After a few minutes of catching up, I got to the point.

"I've got this guy," I said, giving her a rundown on Potts.

I was flabbergasted by her response. Ken Clark, a detective with the Sacramento County Sheriff's Office, had also come up with interesting leads in the case, she said. He had been sharing information with Santa Barbara, the agency that had stonewalled Larry Pool and me in 2001 when we were trying to connect their three homicides to Orange County's and EAR. *What? Someone else in Northern California is working on this case?* All that time I thought I was the only one who cared about trying to find the monster, others had been looking, too. Counties were putting resources into solving the case, but no one knew what the other was doing. Had I not made that call to Anne Marie Schubert, I might have never known what the others were doing, and they wouldn't have known about my work in Contra Costa County.

The good news was that Anne Marie was as interested in finding the East Area Rapist as she had been ten years earlier. "I think it's time we got everyone together in one room," Schubert said. And this time, she said, she would make it happen.

I was looking forward to having company.

The first new East Area Rapist task force meeting was scheduled for June 2011. I had to finesse it with my commander to be able to attend. I had valuable information to contribute, having had eyes on the case for so long, I said. I'd been invited by the Sacramento district attorney to present the EAR cases in our county. All of the other counties with cases would be represented, I said. It was important that we were, too.

In anticipation of introducing Potts as a promising suspect, I walked back to the beginning of my research. Days, nights, and weekends, I picked through police reports and task force minutes and studied my spreadsheets and geographic profiles. I drove to Potts's previous addresses and knocked on doors. I surveilled his last known address and staked out the home of his brother.

On June 14, we gathered in a conference room in a police training facility in Santa Barbara. Representatives from four counties attended. We all sat at an oblong table and introduced ourselves. It was the first time investigators from the East Area Rapist cases and the Original Nightstalker murders were seated at the same table, and the only time any of us had ever seen each other. Ken Clark, the detective with Sacramento County's Sheriff Office, started the meeting with an overview of the Sacramento County cases. Greg Hayes, the investigator from Ventura, brought his elderly dad, Russ, who'd worked the brutal bludgeoning murders of Lyman and Charlene Smith in 1980. Larry Pool was brought into the fold to present his overview of the Orange County cases. Unbeknownst to me, he had been transferred out of Homicide to another assignment right after I'd turned my EAR files over to him. Santa Barbara Sheriff's detectives Gary Kitzmann and Jeff Klapakis were our hosts. I was surprised to hear they were still skeptical that their cases—the murders of Dr. Robert Offerman and his girlfriend, Dr. Debra Manning, in 1979, and Greg Sanchez and Cheri Domingo in 1981, were linked to the series. They were still focused on the theory that their cases were somehow related to a local drug cartel.

I presented Contra Costa County's cases, then launched into my theory about the identity of EAR. "I've got this guy, Robert Lewis Potts," I said, reciting all of the similarities I'd found between the two. "The lab is attempting to get his DNA from a ski mask that was saved to evidence," I said.

As I spoke, I saw what I thought was a knowing look or two. At one time or another, nearly everyone on the task force thought they had solved the case, only to be slapped down by that damn DNA.

We all gathered for drinks after the first day of the two-day meeting. Sitting at the bar between Ken Clark and Larry Pool, I remembered a funny story from earlier in my career. I was attending a law enforcement course in San Juan Capistrano, and a few of us went out to a bar afterward. I was sitting next to a homicide cop from Oakland PD. I ordered first, some fruity drink. "Hoooohhhhh nooooo!" he said, with more than a little disdain. "That ain't gonna fly." He ordered me a Ketel One martini, dirty.

Two sips and my tongue went numb. I was embarrassed for coming across as a lightweight and made a note to order manly drinks whenever I was around law enforcement.

"What'll you have?" the bartender in Santa Barbara asked.

"I'll have a bourbon," I said.

We spent the evening telling stories about our failures in the case and all the wasted hours spent on suspects who turned out to be duds. It was obvious to me that all of the agencies were still invested in or reinvesting in the case. And I was just as certain that the Northern California cases, my cases, would provide the proof we needed to identify EAR.

Going into that first task force meeting, I was completely convinced about Potts, but after listening to everyone else—about their theories and their misses—I started to have doubts. Ken Clark and Larry Pool were so experienced, and I respected their knowledge and their know-how. After the meeting, my confidence was a little shaken about what I had done to that point. It reminded me of the way it always was with Conaty and Giacomelli. Their input made me want to reassess my conclusions.

Six hours is a lot of time to think when you're cruising up the 101 freeway alone, and I thought about every detail that had led me to the conclusion that Potts was the East Area Rapist. It was right around Silicon Valley when I reassured myself that I had the right guy. "Now I need to double down and find him to prove it with his DNA."

After months of waiting for lab results, I was frustrated to learn that my request was no closer to being fulfilled than it had been the day I submitted it. By August, I was fed up. I couldn't wait any longer. I called down to Orange County and asked the lab director for a favor. Send it down, she said. They were backed up down there, too, but would get to it as soon as they could. I sent the mask and returned to my investigation, adding daily updates to my 157-page single-spaced rolling narrative on Potts. Every day for the next eight months had notations. Every phone call. Every email. Every personal contact and road trip. Everything depended on that mask.

The call came in April 2012 from the Orange County lab. "We can't get anything from the ski mask," the analyst said.

I felt sick. There was only one thing left to do.

I had to find him.

A BOLO WAS ISSUED—A BLANKET BROADCAST to law enforcement agencies with information about a wanted suspect. If Potts or anyone related to him came to the attention of any agency in the area, they would be stopped and scrutinized.

In August, Paige Kneeland, a detective with the Sacramento Sheriff's Office who worked with Ken Clark, called with news. "We located Potts's brother," she said. He was homeless and living in his car behind a Union 76 gas station in Antelope. That didn't match up with the information I had on Potts's brother. I knew that the brother had inherited his parents' house in Antelope and that it was paid for. Only recently, I'd driven past the house and seen his car parked outside. "Are you sure it's the brother?" I asked. A patrol unit with a mobile fingerprint ID device was sent to the gas station. They started the process of taking his prints, and he came clean. He was Robert Lewis Potts. Potts was arrested on his outstanding domestic violence warrant.

Every complex investigation is a roller coaster ride, and this one had just gained speed again. I was giddy.

Ken Clark was waiting for Potts at Sacramento headquarters. He sent me Potts's mugshot. He looked like a wild man, with uncombed, shoulder-length brown hair and a scruffy, full gray beard. But those were his eyes. Penetrating. Crazy. Clark told Potts he was a suspect in the East

Area Rapist cases. He'd been questioned so many times during the initial investigation and now thought he was free and clear.

"We need a DNA sample," Clark said.

"You've got to be kidding," Potts said.

The oral swab was delivered to our lab, and I assigned it to Johanna Estrada, one of my most-trusted DNA analysts, to compare it to EAR's. It took a day for her to run it through the multistep process of extracting the DNA from the Q-tip like instrument, separating the DNA from cellular debris, then mixing it with various components into a test tube for DNA typing. From there, she produced an electropherogram—a chart with a series of colorful lines and spikes—that she would compare to EAR's. The data was on Estrada's computer screen when I checked in at the end of the day. "I've got the results," she said, studying the charts on her screen. Standing behind her, I moved closer. "EAR has these markers at this location, and Potts doesn't," she said, pointing at her screen. "Over here it's the same thing. It's not matching up. It's not him."

My throat tightened, and I turned and walked back to my office. Dropping into my chair, I didn't have the energy to move. After staring at the wall for several minutes, I walked out to my car to head home. Driving out on Marina Vista, through the Shell refinery, I had that pit in the stomach feeling. I was in a tailspin, my mind churning over all the things that had led me to Potts. *How could it not be him? Did they give me the right sample? Of course they did.*

I had spent nearly two years of my life pursuing the wrong person. Two years of putting the case before everything. My obsession had impacted every aspect of my life. I'd set aside work assignments to pursue leads, certain I was on the right track. At home, I'd become emotionally and mentally absent. I thought back to all the times Sherrie was trying to tell me something, and I'd excused myself in the middle of what she was saying because I had to get on the computer. I'd given up those intimate moments with Sherrie on the couch after the kids had gone to bed. I'd welcomed her interest in sewing because it gave me the freedom to get on my laptop for the night. Sherrie had once been so interested in my work, my best sounding board. But lately she had lost interest in listening to my investigation reports. Her eye rolls had replaced that excitement I used to see when we talked about cases over the dinner table. Those two years had damaged my family. They'd damaged me. I was drinking more to soothe my frustration. I had stopped working out to give myself more time to work on the case. I'd spent valuable family time on weekends chasing this lead or that. And for what? A false lead.

Despondent, I collapsed onto the couch that night and poured a bourbon. I just wanted to feel numb—the same way my tongue felt when I'd drunk my first martini.

I never wanted to hear the words "East Area Rapist" again.

23

Michelle

I feel sad when I realize that my memories of Michelle McNamara are starting to fade. For nearly four years, she was my friend, my professional confidante, and my investigative partner. She filled a hole in me that was so deep at the time, I feared I might never feel anything again but emptiness. She called sometime in late 2012—two months after the Potts lead had dried up—as I was leaving the lab. I didn't recognize the number and let it go to voicemail. It had been a bear of a day. I'd had to give notice of termination to a fingerprint technician who chronically fell asleep on the job. The technician had seven kids, and I was loath to let her go. I hated that kind of thing. I hadn't slept the night before, which was always what happened when I knew I had to counsel an employee the next morning. It caused me high anxiety. This was not why I got into this work.

That's what was on my mind when I pulled off the road to listen to the message. "Hi. My name is Michelle McNamara. I think Larry Pool said I'd be calling. . . ." The voice was professional and pleasant. I'd been expecting the call. Pool announced at one of our task force meetings that he'd been talking to a woman who was writing a story about our case for

Los Angeles magazine. She'd asked him to pass her name on to the other task force members. She seemed legitimate. Would we be willing to talk to her? We all decided it couldn't hurt to rouse some renewed public interest in our case.

I was coming off of a major depression after the Potts setback. My enthusiasm about pretty much everything, including the East Area Rapist, had waned, and I was struggling to climb out of the abyss. My work with the task force was a constant source of friction with my captain. He'd gone out of his way to let me know that he disapproved. "By the way, I have another meeting coming up," I said one day, attempting to soften the impact by tagging it at the end of another conversation. "I'll put in a travel request." He pursed his lips and ran his fingers through his hair. "I don't think that's a good idea right now," he said. What was the point? he asked. Even if we were able to crack the case, all of our attacks were sexual assaults and past the statute of limitations. "I have a whole presentation prepared," I lied. "I'm on the agenda." Okay, he said. Just this time.

It was a dark period for me. I couldn't find joy in anything. I felt iced out at work and alone at home. I didn't feel like there was anyone I could talk to. Sherrie had stopped listening. She was done hearing about EAR after Potts didn't work out. She'd distanced herself from me. The lack of intimacy between us bothered me, but I didn't say anything. I have a tendency to go quiet when something is troubling me. Sherrie is similar in that way. Nonconfrontational. Reticent when it comes to personal feelings. Who knew what was going through her head? How could she know what was going through mine? I had encouraged Sherrie to pursue sewing, I'd told myself, because that was what she wanted. Maybe she took up the hobby because I had withdrawn from our life together. Maybe I was relieved because I'd been getting more out of the case than sitting on the couch watching *The Sopranos* together, and it had been an excuse to dig into my laptop at night. Now, while Sherrie sewed, I drank bourbon and stared at the TV, not even aware of what was on the screen. I was questioning my career, my abilities, my marriage. My whole life. That was the Paul Holes that Michelle got the first time she called.

I listened to the voicemail and pulled my silver Taurus into a parking lot in downtown Martinez to return Michelle's call. My experience with reporters was often a one-way street. *What can you do for me? What can you do for me again? What have you done for me lately?* I wasn't sure I had the energy to participate in that draining game. "Thanks for getting back to me," Michelle said, before giving me a quick overview of why she was getting involved in our case. She'd first learned about the East Area Rapist in 2010, she said, and picked up a self-published book by Larry Crompton, one of the former investigators. Her interest led her to a message board of amateur sleuths who were obsessed with the case. Soon, she was hooked, too. She'd referenced the East Area Rapist on her blog, *True Crime Diary*. Now she was writing a story for *Los Angeles* magazine and reaching out to all the key players. She hoped I'd be open to having further discussions.

I launched into my "talking to the media" mode. Just the basic facts, nothing extra. Michelle seemed truly interested in my involvement. I was a pretty good judge of people, and she sounded sincere. Still, I didn't know her. My guard was up. I gave her an abbreviated version of my work on the case. My concern was always that I'd say something that could hurt the investigation. And I certainly didn't want to exploit my self-inflicted involvement when I was already on shaky ground with the sheriff's department. Our conversation lasted a few minutes and ended politely. Michelle promised she'd be back in touch, and I thanked her for her interest.

MAYBE IT WAS THE CALL, or maybe enough time had passed since my Potts failure, but after weeks away from the case, I decided to take another look to evaluate where I had gone wrong. For the next few days, I pondered the decisions I'd made. I came across an article in a law enforcement journal by Dr. Kim Rossmo. Dr. Rossmo was highly regarded in my world. I'd read his book about geographic profiling and often referred to it in my work. The article was about criminal investigation failures. Reading it was like watching myself in the Potts probe. I realized I'd made a critical mistake in the way I'd gone about it. Rossmo talks about how even the best investigators fall into the trap of using inductive rather than deductive reasoning. You home in on a particular suspect and try to make things fit rather than allowing the investigation to take you to the truth. That's what amateur sleuths do. They make certain assumptions and only see the things that bolster their conclusions—oftentimes details that are so ordinary they're meaningless. I'd fallen into the same trap. I had been so gung-ho on Potts that I hadn't allowed myself to notice the warning signs that I could be on the wrong track. Instead, I had picked things across the case files that I could make fit and made excuses for the pieces that didn't. I'd made reckless connections. I remembered one weekend when I was in my in-laws' backyard picking the brain of a neighbor who was a retired railroad worker. He told me that during the 1970s recession, railroad workers flowed down to Southern California, where the work was. Before that, I hadn't been able to place Potts down south. "That's it!" I said. Without any documentation, I had linked him to the attacks there using that bit of railroad history from the neighbor. There were other nibbles of things I'd excused away—things that seemed flimsy in comparison to the strong connections I did have. I told myself, *Maybe someone wrote down the wrong date,* or *Maybe the witness got the description wrong.* If I were to revisit the case, I needed to beware of making connections that weren't there. I would have to refocus on the evidence and let it take me where the investigation needed to go, rather than pick and choose details to guide it where I wanted it to go. I should have known better. I did know better, but I'd let tunnel vision get in the way of good investigative practice. As much as it hurt to acknowledge that I'd made an amateurish mistake, I was determined to use it to make me a better investigator.

MY CONTACT WITH MICHELLE RESUMED OVER the next few months with sporadic emails and phone calls. It was usually her asking questions or fact-checking for her magazine story. Our conversations were almost exclusively about the case. We didn't tend toward small talk or the personal. She did mention that she was married to an actor and comedian and that they had a young daughter. Her husband's name was Patton Oswalt. My silence gave me away. I didn't know the name. "He's the voice of Remi in the movie *Ratatouille*," she said. It was an animated film about a rat that wants to become a chef. Ah, I said, that sounded vaguely familiar.

"In the Footsteps of a Killer" was published in the March 2013 issue of *Los Angeles* magazine. I was apprehensive about it coming out. When it did, I was reluctant to read it, fearful that Michelle had betrayed my trust and used off-the-record information that could cost me my job or jeopardize my relationships with the other task force members. And it wasn't just about that. I saw myself as a good judge of people. If she turned out to be someone other than the genuine person I thought she was, I would have to question my own judgment—and I'd only just begun to regain my confidence as an investigator. But my curiosity got the better of me, and I finally found the courage to dig in.

"I think I found him," I said, a little punchy from lack of sleep. My husband, a professional comedian, didn't have to ask who "him" was. . . . By day I'm a 42-year-old stay-at-home mom with a sensible haircut and Goldfish crackers lining my purse. In the evening, however, I'm something of a DIY detective. I delve into cold cases by scouring the Internet for any digital crumbs authorities may have overlooked, then share my theories with the 8,000 or so mystery buffs who visit my blog regularly. When my family goes to sleep, I start clicking, combing through digitized phone books, school yearbooks, and Google Earth views of crime scenes: a bottomless pit of potential leads for the laptop investigator who now exists in the virtual world.

After reading the 7,500-word piece, I no longer doubted Michelle's motivation or her commitment to seeing the case solved. She had done her research and presented it with compelling storytelling, and she hadn't betrayed my trust. She'd also given the monster a new handle that was catchier than EARONS. From that day on, the East Area Rapist and the Original Nightstalker would be known as the Golden State Killer.

Michelle went silent for a time after the magazine story was published. The next time I heard from her, she cold-called me, which was unusual. "Paul, I need to ask you something," she said. "I value what you think." She had been contacted about writing a book on the Golden State Killer. "Are you okay with that?" she asked. "Will the task force be okay with it?" Two books had already been written but not by professional writers, and they were rough reads. Michelle's idea was for a narrative that provided details about the crimes and the dogged investigators who had worked the case but also her personal hunt for the serial killer. Based on what I'd seen of Michelle's work, her book would be different from the others. "I think it's great," I said. "This case could use that type of exposure."

A few weeks later, she called again. She wanted to see the boots on the ground aspect of the case, she said. She didn't want to write the book from her perch in Los Angeles without seeing the places she was writing about. I offered to take her on a tour of the attack sites across Contra Costa County. "Yes!" she said.

I picked her up at her hotel in Concord on a warm morning that July. We'd been corresponding for nearly a year by then, but it was our first face-to-face meeting. We spent the day driving to crime scene locations. Neither of us were keen on small talk. There was so much to mull over about the case. She asked why I thought EAR had taken his spree from Sacramento to the East Bay. My feeling was that something had changed in his life. "Maybe he was still living in Sacramento and got a job here. He's taking advantage of the drive up and down the north-south Interstate 680 corridor, dropping off at exits in the East Bay. Most of our attacks were close to the freeway. You'll see as we go." Danville was a perfect example. "Do you want to see?" I asked. "Absolutely," she said.

I'd told Michelle about the "homework" evidence that John Patty had found beside the railroad tracks in 1979 after the first Danville attack. She'd referred to it in her magazine story and wanted to see the place where it was dropped. We parked near the Iron Horse Regional Trail— the old Southern Pacific Railroad accessway—now a paved footpath. "The homework evidence was found down there," I said, pointing down the track. "Want to go?" I asked. "Yes!" she said. Her enthusiasm was contagious. It was exhilarating for me to be able to share the same places I'd been to countless times and see them through fresh, eager eyes. "What about your shoes?" I asked, looking at her platform sandals. "What about them?" she shrugged. We trekked the four hundred yards to the unremarkable spot where the homework had been dropped forty-four years earlier.

Eight hours in a car together can make or break a friendship. That day solidified ours. From Danville, we traveled to attack sites from Concord to San Ramon to Walnut Creek and Davis, covering 130 miles of the county. The conversation was easy and the pauses comfortable. I take pride in my ability to read people, and I read Michelle as genuine and someone who was looking into the case with the best of intentions. I did not get the sense that I was dealing with an opportunist, which had been my experience with other journalists. She had married into Hollywood, but she wasn't a diva. She confessed that she wasn't comfortable living a celebrity lifestyle. She was proud of her husband and his success, but stepping into his professional bubble made her anxious. She'd grown up in the unpretentious Midwest. Dressing up and attending movie premieres was not her idea of a good time. Sharing space with crime solvers kept her grounded, she said.

I suspected that Michelle and I had similar souls in many ways. I appreciated her sense of empathy toward the victims—regular people living predictable lives until the masked phantom broke into their homes and stole from them their ordinariness. Nothing was the same for any of them after he attacked. Not for the young woman who hadn't been able to return to her house after he'd been there; or the couple whose trauma from the attack tore them apart; or the husband who was still trying to reclaim his masculinity more than forty years after he was bound helpless while his wife was raped and terrorized in the next room; or the victim who regularly called me in the middle of the night, drunk and fearful that he was still watching her four decades later. And certainly not for those whose loved ones were stolen from them under the most gruesome of circumstances, and for no better reason than the whim of a madman.

Our day together ended in Martinez in the lab. Michelle wanted to see where I worked. Seated across from her, I saw the tough negotiator emerge. It takes more than charm and the twinkle of an eye to get toughened homicide investigators eating out of your hand. "I've got to ask," she said. "This is the other side of me, the journalist. I need inside information, and you have that. And I have things that you don't." Was I willing to swap certain information? She had autopsy reports and crime scene photos from other jurisdictions that I didn't have. It would aid my work on the case. I pushed back from my desk and looked at her. She held my gaze.

"Okay," I said.

MICHELLE AND I SPOKE REGULARLY AFTER that, and it made me feel alive again. We shared information and ideas. I was still holding back but slowly loosening up. I confided in her that the nights were not good to me. I had trouble stopping the data bank in my head from spitting out unfinished business. When I did sleep, I was often awakened by vivid nightmares. Michelle revealed her habit of staying up all night on her laptop after her husband and daughter went to bed. I noticed her emails were stamped with times during which the rest of the world was sleeping. One night, she emailed me at 3:19 A.M. with an old high school photo she'd found online of a suspect I'd been looking at. It bore a strong resemblance to one of the composites of the East Area Rapist. "I know that at this point just about anyone can match one of the composites," she wrote, "but still thought that this was striking. This is what I do when I have insomnia, indulge in confirmation bias. . . ."

As I got to know her better, what impressed me was the way she digested information. She had never worked in law enforcement, never trained as an investigator, and hadn't worked a case with the depth necessary to make it a career. Yet she went about her work like a seasoned pro. She was very insightful, with the intellect to be able to take in mounds of information and process it—then keep an open mind so when new information came in, she was able to reevaluate and change direction. With her knowledge and her commitment to the case, she won over not just me but many of the other task force members and investigators. That in itself showed a level of investigative sophistication on her part. Mistrust of journalists is second nature to cops, yet I knew from the breadth of information she'd collected that she'd infiltrated the ranks. She knew more about the case than some of the investigators. I knew that revealing "just the facts" wasn't going to cut it for long. "Oh, come on," she said one day when she'd asked a sticky question and I hedged. "I know you know more than that."

My resolve to keep at least the most sensitive information confidential thawed one night in late summer of 2014 after I'd been working with Michelle for nearly a year. We'd fallen into a groove of mutual respect. We listened to each other's opinions and could agree to disagree. The discourse was refreshing. No ego involved. Just two people who were working together to do the right thing. I had started down a new path in my investigation that I hadn't confided to anyone. It was a hot August night, and I was pacing around my patio, debating whether I should tell her. *Should I tell her? . . . No. . . . But I trust her. . . . She's a journalist. . . . I have to share with someone . . . Why her? . . . She cares. Yes, I'm going to tell her.* Just before bed, I popped open my laptop and began to write, carefully choosing my words.

"All right, I'm making a bit of a calculated gamble here," I wrote. "It would hurt me professionally if it comes out that I shared investigative info with you prior to my fellow investigators. You're obviously exceptionally bright and trustworthy. I don't want to be seen as a tease or have you waste your time trying to figure out what I'm working on based on innuendo. Attached is a really rough compilation of what I am working on. It's a storyboard—a lot of the details are not present that I would normally fill in either in a narrative or a verbal presentation. Slides are out of order or incomplete. I'm still fleshing it out. However, I think you'll get the picture. Just keep this to yourself. . . . I think you will see why this suspect is somewhat sensitive. He also frequently leaves the country and could quickly take off and 'slip away into the dark of the night' if he needs to."

I attached my file and hit Send.

Michelle responded at 1:27 A.M. "Holy smokes, that's really interesting. I appreciate your sharing and you have my word it stays with me."

AFTER MY POTTS DISAPPOINTMENT, I'D TAKEN my search for EAR in a different direction. I'd focused on the map from the homework that Patty had found by the railroad tracks. I'd been studying it in my office one day, unable to make heads or tails of it. My first thought was that it was a planning map with EAR's targets. But I quickly backed away from that assessment. "Why is he drawing HVAC equipment on the roofs of the commercial buildings?" I asked myself. "Why draw the trees and bushes?" On the flipside was a series of scribbles with a larger, more predominant scrawl of letters at the center. I called out to our lab clerk, Lori. Sharp tongued with an even sharper wit, she appeared in my doorway, hands on hips. "What does this say?" I asked, pointing to the image. She came closer. "It says 'Punishment,'" she said matter-of-factly. The word was missing the "i," but she was clearly correct in her interpretation. "Punishment. You're right," I said. I felt my cheeks flush as Lori smirked and walked away. Studying the word, I saw that the pencil had been pressed harder with each successive letter. The writer was becoming increasingly angry as he wrote. It was completely consistent with EAR's psychology.

The map had become the focal point of my investigation. I thought it was unique enough that I might be able to use it to determine the Golden State Killer's profession. I'd consulted with multiple experts, a professor emeritus of landscape architecture at UC Davis, a professor of architecture at Cosumnes River College, and practitioners in the construction and development fields, including civil engineers, surveyors, and heavy equipment operators. The consensus was that the rough sketch was drawn by a developer in the process of laying out a master-planned community.

Whoever drew the sketch was skilled and bright. I was no longer looking for the troll under the bridge.

I'd begun compiling a list of real estate developers and eliminated most of them after cursory searches. After all the eliminations, one name still held promise. It was the name I'd shared with Michelle. Roger Murray (pseudonym) was a very successful developer. I discovered that the wife of the couple in EAR's March 18, 1978, attack in Stockton worked in the same field, which had put her in frequent contact with him. He had had some serious run-ins with the law involving potentially violent crimes, though no convictions. A geographic profile put Murray in the range of EAR's Northern California attacks. But it was his penis that put him at the top of my list. Murray's ex-wife had told a private investigator she'd hired during their divorce that his was so small that at first she thought "it was a birth defect." Enough victims had mentioned that EAR's penis was small that the detail caught my attention. I sent Michelle a summary of my meeting with the PI: "[The ex-wife] confided to [the PI] that Murray threatened her with death if she ever talked about his penis size. Murray was very sensitive about it. [The PI] said Murray is the kind of guy you could put a gun to his head and he wouldn't blink. He doesn't follow social norms and does whatever he wants. Back in the early 1980s as part of his role in the ongoing divorce proceedings, [the PI] remembers finding bondage-related porn in Murray's trash and that Murray was into 'S&M and bondage sex' with his various girlfriends."

I continued to drill down on Murray, sending Michelle updates as I got them. She pitched in with research, providing relevant property records, Facebook connections, and old, archived newspaper stories.

"Wow," she wrote in an email on October 14. "This guy gets more and more interesting. . . . I'm curious. . . . What are some things that make you question him as a suspect, or feel like they don't fit?"

I wrote back with a list. Murray was successful and wealthy, traits we'd never attributed to EAR. He was older than we'd estimated EAR to be. I couldn't place him in some of the attack locations.

"Yep. Makes sense," she replied. "Seems like no one could line up perfectly with all the contradictions in this case."

"Tell me about it," I said.

In my research, I discovered that Murray had been involved with a very attractive younger woman after his divorce. They had since split. I tracked her down, and she agreed to meet with me at a local restaurant. We had good chemistry, and after a long conversation, I broached the awkward subject of his penis.

"Um . . . the East Area Rapist was supposedly underendowed. What about your ex?" I asked.

She looked straight ahead, her forehead creased, as if she were visualizing something.

"No," she said finally. "He was normal."

Michelle was anxious to hear the outcome of the conversation. I texted her afterward. "So wife says small, girlfriend says normal. Go figure. Maybe the ex-wife put the information out there for revenge," I said.

In an attempt to settle the discrepancy, I undertook a study of EAR's penis size. I went through the case files and extracted the language his victims used to describe it. I cut and pasted each of their statements into an email to Michelle. The range provided by the victims was from three inches erect and very thin to five inches and average with various descriptions in between. To make matters more difficult, some victims used the descriptor "small" to indicate EAR was not fully erect, while others used it to mean he was small when erect. "So, if you are able to review the images, can you form an opinion on how big he is?" I asked Michelle.

She wrote back: "Was able to review the images. My opinion is definitely below average, around three to four inches, quarter or so diameter.

In a sexual attack, I think if anything you'd err on the side of describing something as bigger than it was, since it's violent and frightening; that so many victims make a point to describe him as small is significant to me."

Significant, yes. But I would not allow myself to commit another Potts-type mistake and use penis size in my evaluation of a suspect. "I have personally learned multiple times that what one intuitively thinks cannot be coincidence can in fact be coincidence," I said.

"I still think he's small," she responded.

By then, I had come to consider Michelle my unofficial detective partner. We didn't ride together, but we were in constant communication. She wanted information, but she could give as good as she got. We listened to each other's theories and hunches and shared our misgivings if we thought the other was headed on a wild goose chase. "I've already checked him out. No go," I'd say. "I'm not sure where you're going with that," she'd say. We shared the highs when one of us thought we'd found the guy, and the low lows when they were eliminated. We supported each other. In that way, Michelle had taken Sherrie's place in my life.

I SHARED WITH MICHELLE THE SENSITIVE information that an operation was in place to raid Murray's trash for possible DNA evidence.

On September 30, 2014, I emailed her. "Murray's trash is probably going to be picked up tomorrow."

"Will you know in a day or two?" she asked.

"Depends on what's in the trash," I said. "If there is a good source of DNA, it could be done within a couple of days. Trash is hit or miss. You could have DNA from many people or no DNA at all."

Enough similarities remained between my suspect and GSK that I needed his DNA to be able to eliminate him. An undercover team was dispatched to his neighborhood with orders to get a surreptitious sample. But in a community of million-dollar homes, narcs in beater cars stand out, and they did there. A neighbor hopped out of her BMW to peer through one of the smoked-out windows. The cop inside the car had to flash his badge to get rid of her. Mission aborted.

I went to plan B. The chief of police in Murray's town was someone I had gone to the academy with. I called her with my suspicion that he could be the East Area Rapist. She was aware of the sting gone bad and offered to help in any way she could. A few days later, she texted me. "Hey, Paul," she wrote. "I just ran into your suspect." I responded right away. "What do you mean?" Radio silence. I was squirming in my seat. Thirty minutes passed, and my phone rang. "The meeting was a complete coincidence," she said. She was in plain clothes and had gone to the city planning department on a routine matter and recognized Murray standing at the counter. He had blueprints in front of him. She hung around for a few minutes, trying to find out why he was there, when he recognized her. "You're the chief," he said. She nodded and asked, "Do I know you?" He introduced himself, and after a minute of small talk, she went out to her car to text me. As she was texting, she heard a knock on her window. The guy was a charmer with a gift of gab. "Hey, let's meet for lunch and talk about some ways I think I can help your department," he said. My friend is sharp. She seized the opportunity.

They choose a date and a restaurant on the bay overlooking the city-scape of San Francisco. The chief gets there early and, as planned, takes a table on the front side of the restaurant on the sidewalk. And so the undercover operation begins. An investigator poses as a busser. Detectives in street clothes and carrying cameras stand on the sidewalk, acting like tourists. An undercover car is parked across the street, a few feet from my own. I see the developer arrive. He greets the chief at the table, and they sit down. A moment later, another man walks up. He's dressed like a character in a spy movie: dark glasses, baseball cap, button-down shirt over a tee. I can't afford for him to see me, so I roll up my windows. It's sweltering in my car, and I'm in a suit. I don't want him knowing there's anyone in the car, so I can't start the engine to run the AC. I'm sitting on the passenger side, and he walks within ten feet of me. I think I might die from the heat. I take off my jacket and strip down to my T-shirt. The sweat is coming through my pants. I think I'm going to die here. He starts to move across the street, toward the restaurant. All that for nothing.

An hour passes, and I see the chief stand up from the table. Lunch is over. The suspect shakes her hand and walks away. The investigator who is acting as the busser grabs a spoon, a drinking glass, and a straw used by Murray. I take possession, thank the chief, and drive away with the goods. The radio is playing, and I'm on a high. *I've got him.*

It took two days to get the lab results back from the restaurant silverware. "Inconsistent" with EAR's DNA, it said.

I emailed Michelle with the news.

"Shit," she replied.

Michelle and I met again in early March 2016 in Las Vegas. A law enforcement conference was taking place, and she'd convinced Patton to be the entertainment. I'd gone with the sole purpose of meeting with her, and she and I used the time to sit together in their hotel suite to share information and theories about the case. Michelle told me she was pursuing a lead that she thought looked promising: a former football player at the University of the Pacific in Stockton who'd been eliminated after an EAR attack when law enforcement went to his door and saw that he had a leg injury. The rapist had a habit of jumping fences, so we wondered, "How could he do that with an injured leg?"

"Do you think this is a bona fide elimination?" Michelle asked. "How do they know that he still couldn't have attacked?" It was a great question. "You're right," I said. "He can't be eliminated." I wasn't big on the suspect, but I promised to contact the FBI to request that agents visit him and get his DNA.

Michelle had surreptitiously acquired files for some of the Southern California murders. She'd brought some of the crime scene photos and laid them out on a table. I'd been trying to get access to those photos for years but had always run into the competitive wall. She promised to send me the files when she got home.

It was the last time I saw her.

· · ·

THE FOLLOWING MONTH, ON APRIL 21, 2016, Michelle died in her sleep at home. The official cause of death was an accidental overdose from a lethal mix of Adderall, Xanax, and fentanyl. No one was aware that she was self-medicating. I've heard theories that she was taking the drugs to help her sleep and focus on her writing. I know Michelle was exhausted and worried about meeting her deadline, but I believe the reason is much more complex than that.

Few people know the pressures of the woeful world of homicide. It's a dreadful place, and not one to be entered lightly. No one leaves unscathed, not even the hardened professionals. Michelle was a wife and a mom by day and living among psychopaths and their victims in the dark of night. A writer on a mission to catch a serial killer may sound romantic, but it was a path that led to an obsession fraught with hidden minefields. I admired Michelle's keen criminal mind and her devotion to the undertaking of unmasking a serial killer. But four years of living in it was bound to take a toll. All that time the trauma was building. She may have recognized that she was tormented and turned to drugs to subdue the symptoms. I knew that feeling. Her drug cocktail was my bourbon, just more deadly.

I find myself wishing she had never embarked on the book. Wishing she had shared with me her struggles. I probably would have understood better than anyone. Had I known, I would have counseled her on the pitfalls of getting trapped in the case. The irony isn't lost on me. What attracted me to Michelle in the first place was her obsession. It validated my own.

Her last email to me was sent on Wednesday, April 20, 2016, just hours before she passed away. I opened it shortly after I got the news that she was gone. She ended the email with "Talk to you soon, Michelle." Attached were the files she'd promised me in Las Vegas. She was still helping me.

In the *Los Angeles* magazine story in 2013, Michelle had written: "In the past, when people have asked whether it worries me that the killer may still be out there, I've waved dismissively, pointing out that he'd be much older now—sixty-two, if I had to guess. 'He can't hurt me,' I say, not realizing that in every sleepless hour, in every minute spent hunting him and not cuddling my daughter, he already has."

In a way, she was the Golden State Killer's last victim.

Now I had more reason than ever to find him.

24

The Murders

The third murder attempt. That was his magnum opus. The time he got everything to go exactly the way he'd wanted. The first, in Goleta in October 1979—the one where he was psyching himself up, pacing and chanting *"Kill 'em"*—was aborted when the couple escaped. He'd learned his lesson and improved upon his method for the next attempt, two months later. That began a typical East Area Rapist attack. Dr. Robert Offerman, an osteopathic surgeon, and his companion, Dr. Debra Manning, a clinical psychologist, were sleeping when he broke into Offerman's upscale condominium on December 30 of that year. The couple were bound in their bed, but Offerman wriggled loose from his binding and charged. Now the budding serial killer was ready. He was carrying a gun. Offerman took a bullet to the chest. Manning was shot once in the back of the head while she lay bound and on her stomach. But there had been no satisfaction in the attack. Too clean. The third attack would be different. He wasn't going to let that one go bad. His rage needed a release.

It was because of Michelle and her gift of the homicide files that I was finally able to evaluate these murders. The Southern California contingent, even after the task force was formed, had continued to keep critical information close to the chest and not share. I didn't blame them. Everyone wanted to be the one to crack the Golden State Killer case—but not everyone was willing to jeopardize our collective chances of success by withholding information. A source in Orange County had finally given in to Michelle's "I'll scratch your back if you scratch mine" negotiations. For me, being able to finally read the CSI reports and pathologists' findings, and to see the crime scene photos and autopsy pictures, was like finding lost pieces to a puzzle. It was through those files that I got to know the Golden State Killer. Through thousands of pages of documents, I followed his evolution from the rapist I knew so well into the cold-blooded killer whose compulsion to kill was as strong as heroin to an addict.

Three months had elapsed since the last attack. In the last one, he had reportedly cried, and before his move south, the East Area Rapist was crying after his sexual assaults. I believed the tears were because he realized he wasn't getting what he needed anymore. I imagined he was unfulfilled by the sex act, the expression of fear he saw in her eyes, her begging him to stop. It wasn't enough anymore. He'd probably been fighting the urge to kill before he moved south and changed his mission. The couple in that first attack in Goleta would have been dead, except that he'd lost control. I was starting to appreciate how sophisticated he was. EAR had learned a lot from his experiences in our part of the state. He had polished his moves and developed new skills. In Southern California, he demonstrated his ability to resort to plan B if plan A didn't work. It was apparent to me in studying the cases that he was putting much more thought into his attacks. He was planning, surveilling, and developing tactics specific to each event. And with each attack that hadn't gone exactly as planned, he'd reassessed until, by the third attempt, he would finally succeed at getting a reprieve from the pressure of his craving. At least for a while.

• • •

LYMAN AND CHARLENE SMITH NEVER HAD a chance.

It was the middle of the night in March 1980 when the Golden State Killer slipped into their home in the upscale High Point neighborhood in Ventura and likely awakened them from their sleep. The Smiths were not your average couple. They socialized among elite and well-known Democratic circles. Lyman was forty-three and a former Ventura County deputy district attorney. He was poised to be appointed to a judgeship by Governor Jerry Brown. Charlene was ten years younger than her husband. She had been a secretary in his law firm before becoming his second wife. She was stunningly beautiful. That was the first thing everyone said when her name came up. Some speculated that's what brought the killer to the house that night. Perhaps he'd seen her on the beach or in the village and followed her home? Or had he had an encounter of some kind with Lyman, who could be aggressive in his work? We knew that EAR was vindictive. *I'll show you who I am.*

No one knows how the killer got into the house that night. There was no evidence of a break-in, no ripped screen or pried open doors. Surely they hadn't invited him in. In my analysis, he was feeling inadequate after his initial failures and needed to succeed this time to regain his feelings of power and control. Lyman and Charlene were bound at the wrists and ankles. But this time, the killer wasn't taking chances. He modified his MO to ensure his success. He pulled a blanket tightly across Lyman's chest and around his arms and back. A makeshift straitjacket. He couldn't afford another fiasco like the last time, when Dr. Offerman had taken a run at him. He had learned.

The killer proceeded with his plan. Lyman and Charlene were facedown on the bed. Lyman was nude. Charlene wore only a T-shirt. He carried in a log from a woodpile outside the house, a massive weapon. At some point after he'd sexually assaulted Charlene, he bludgeoned the couple with the log. The crime scene photos showed pieces of bark scattered on top of a pair of pants on the floor beside the bed. Had the log been intact when he was beating them, the bark would have been on the bed. Instead, it had been deposited on the pants beside the bed, evidence that while the couple lay there, helpless and terrified, he stood over them and peeled the bark off the murder weapon.

I put myself in the killer's head. Something in his life was making him mad. Had he lost a job? Was he going through a divorce? Fighting with his wife? Carrying out his hatred of his mother? His victims were proxies. The serial killer Roger Kibbe had a nagging wife. Every time she got on him, he went quiet, then left the house and spent the night trolling for victims. Whatever was causing GSK's anger, it was escalating. A simple shooting didn't do it for him anymore. But feeling the crushing of the Smiths' skulls as he bashed them in the head with the log? That's when the anger receded.

The Original Nightstalker had a longer refractory time between his attacks than the East Area Rapist, who could have four or five attacks in a week. ONS's postorgasmic time was between five and six months after the perfect outcome in the Smith attack. On August 19, 1980, he raped Patrice Harrington and killed her and her husband in Dana Point. On February 5, 1981, he raped and killed Manuela Witthuhn in her home in Irvine while her husband was away in the hospital. On July 27, 1981, he killed Cherri Domingo and her friend Greg Sanchez, who was visiting her in Goleta, where she was house-sitting. All were bludgeoning deaths.

My crime scene reconstruction showed Sanchez had put up a fierce defense. He fought back after being shot in the face. Blood smears told the story of an intense, prolonged battle. Sanchez had put up a hell of a defense, eventually succumbing from twenty-four blows to the back of his head. So much blood was shed that before the killer fled, he rummaged through the closet and took a pair of the owner's clean pants to wear home. I think Sanchez scared him and probably saved lives.

The killer went quiet for five years. But sometime during the night between May 4 and May 5, 1986, he returned to Irvine to rape and kill eighteen-year-old Janelle Cruz.

And then he disappeared.

25

Joseph James DeAngelo

By early 2017, I had exhausted all of my leads in the Golden State Killer case. The task force was running dry, and every suspect with any promise had been eliminated. I'd investigated two more in the ten months since Michelle had passed away. I kept swinging for the home run and falling short. Soon, I would retire from law enforcement and life as I knew it. I was staring down the end of my career and beginning to consider that twenty-three years of hunting GSK might wind up the way it had for every investigator before me: a dead end. I had a year to try to change that ending and not much to go on.

In February, I got a call from my friend Roxane Gruenheid, the seasoned investigator with the Sheriff's Office I'd worked closely with over the years. "I need you to come over," she said. I drove across town to Roxane's office. She was on speakerphone with Detective Peter Headley from the San Bernardino Sheriff's Office when I arrived. Headley was breathless. "We know who Lisa Jensen is," he told us. What? Headley had discovered the identity of a five-year-old who'd been abandoned in an RV park in the summer of 1996 by a transient claiming to be her father. The mystery of the girl's true identity had been the bane of many investigators over the years. Larry Vanner, the man who claimed to be the child's father, was tracked down and served less than two years in prison. Lisa was adopted, but only shadowy memories shed any light on her background. Vanner disappeared after jail and reemerged in our county in 2002 when the body of his girlfriend, Eunsoon Jun, was found under a pile of kitty litter in a crawl space under their house, and he was charged with her murder. DNA proved he was not Lisa's father. He died in prison in 2010 and took the secret of Lisa's identity to his grave. Now Headley had her name: Dawn Beaudin.

"How did you do it?" I asked Headley.

Headley said he'd used a website for adoptees searching for their biological parents. He'd been assisted by a genealogist named Barbara Rae Venter, who was experienced in helping adoptees find their roots. He couldn't explain exactly how the process worked, but he threw out the term "centimorgans." A centimorgan is a unit used to measure genetic linkage. I hadn't heard the word in a while. It was a totally different component from the ones I'd been using for my genealogy searches for GSK, and I wondered how it had made the difference in being able to finally give Dawn Beaudin her identity.

Driving back to my office, I felt a sense of excitement. My body was tingling with anticipation. I couldn't wait to get Venter on the phone to ask if the technique she'd used for Dawn might work to identify an unknown offender.

I called the minute I sat down at my desk. I told Venter I was working on a big case and was interested in learning about the technique used to identify Dawn Beaudin. "Can I identify a killer if all I have is his DNA sample?" I asked. "I see no reason why it wouldn't," she said. "Send me what you've got." I said I'd send a DNA "snapshot" of the offender that had been developed from semen evidence from the Golden State Killer's last known attack, the 1986 murder of eighteen-year-old Janelle Cruz in Irvine. The snapshot had been produced for Orange County by the DNA technology company Parabon for the purpose of developing a new composite of the serial killer. "Too bad you don't have a SNP profile," Venter said. I knew that SNPs (single nucleotide polymorphisms, pronounced "snip") were being used to identify disease-causing genes, and I'd seen presentations at forensic conferences over the years about researchers who were trying to figure out how to use them for human identification. But at this point, the standard in the forensic science community was STRs. I didn't know that genealogists were using SNP technology as a way to track ancestry. This was all new to me.

I sent off the Parabon profile and waited for Venter to let me know whether she could help. When a few weeks passed, I followed up our conversation with an email. No response. I assumed she'd thought better of working with me, since genealogists are often hesitant to collaborate with law enforcement for privacy reasons. Meanwhile, I submitted the Y-chromosome profile I'd done from one of the old Contra Costa County rape kits using the standard Y-STR technology and got a partial match on a free website called Ysearch.org. After the hit, I got a federal grand jury subpoena and cooperation from the FBI to get a DNA swab from the subject, a seventy-four-year-old man in a nursing home in Oregon, only to lead to the disappointing detail that he had not shared a relative with the Golden State Killer for nine hundred years. I realized then that the Y-STR technology was not going to pan out in this case. Back to square one. Again.

With no place left to go, and having not heard anything back from Venter, I began to study the link between SNPs and genealogy research to try to figure out how it all worked. I read everything I could find and spent endless hours watching YouTube videos about the process. The human genome is spread across twenty-three sets of chromosomes with twenty-two of them "normal" or autosomal chromosomes, and the last are X and Y chromosomes containing the DNA that differentiates males from females. The Y chromosome is passed down from fathers to sons relatively unchanged through the generations on the paternal side of a family. For years, I had used the DNA profile I'd generated for the Golden State Killer using Y-STR technology, which it turned out was limiting on the private ancestry sites. SNP profiles, however, were drawn from "autosomal" DNA, which went beyond the traditional search of chains of males and thus covered a much larger swath of the population. The genealogy companies were generating SNP profiles from the DNA samples their customers submitted, utilizing hundreds of thousands of SNPs across the entirety of the human genome. The power of what they were doing was staggering and all new to me. Law enforcement had been playing in the shallow end of the genealogy pool. I was ready to plunge into much deeper waters.

That spring of 2017 I got a call from Steve Kramer, FBI division counsel in the Los Angeles field office. I'd never met Steve, but we had a mutual contact at the bureau. Steve said he'd heard about my ongoing work on the Golden State Killer case. "Paul, I believe in the DNA and that the DNA is going to solve this case," he said. "How can I help?" I was happy to have the power of the FBI behind me.

We talked every day after that. Steve was a quick study and very intelligent. He had an advantage coming into the case of having interned in the mid-1990s with Woody Clarke, the attorney who handled DNA evidence for the prosecution at the O. J. Simpson trial. Steve is an extrovert and a type A personality. He's a bulldog. Once he latches onto something, he doesn't let go. This is someone I'm going to hitch my rope to, I thought.

As part of our process to move forward, I picked up the Parabon snapshot report I'd sent to Barbara Venter and read the section that explained their process for producing a DNA snapshot. Sometimes I believe in fate. Buried in the technobabble was a notation that they'd used a medical

DNA chip that looked at hundreds of thousands of SNPs from the DNA sample submitted by Orange County from the Cruz murder. Venter had seemed disappointed when I said we didn't have a SNP profile, but according to the report, Parabon had to generate a comprehensive SNP profile from the Orange County semen evidence in order to generate their snapshot. "Holy shit!" I said.

Law enforcement had been using genealogy to try to solve cases for years but had never been able to generate the type of DNA that could be used to search genealogy sites. Labs for places like Ancestry.com and 23andMe didn't know how to deal with degrading semen evidence. They worked with spit in a tube. The huge hurdle was always "How do we generate a compatible profile?" It looked to me like Parabon had solved the problem.

I called Kramer with the news. "This is how Ancestry and 23andMe are finding relatives of their customers," I said. "Parabon has 850,000 SNPs they've kept for themselves that we need." I had to have their entire analysis to be able to convert it to a new Golden State Killer DNA profile, one that worked on private genealogy sites.

For the next few weeks, we went back and forth on the advantages of using the SNP technology over the conventional law enforcement approach. We both concluded that SNP technology was the way to go—though it had never been used in a criminal investigation, and we were bound to hit obstacles along the way.

We hit the first one right out of the gate. Parabon claimed their report was "proprietary" and would not release it. "Bullshit," I said. Orange County had commissioned the report and provided the DNA sample, so that DNA profile belonged to them. After a discussion with the husband-and-wife team that owns Parabon, it was finally agreed that they would release it to me if they had verbal permission from the Orange County DA investigator they'd been working with. "No problem," I said.

My next call was to Erika Hutchcraft, the detective with the Orange

County DA's Office who was on the task force with me. Erika had been the one to employ Parabon to produce the snapshot for the purpose of developing a new composite of the Golden State Killer. "I need your permission," I said. She passed the request up to her sergeant, who called me. "Let me run it past my boss," he said. Kramer vetted the legality of law enforcement using private genealogy companies in criminal investigations. I was confident I could have a SNP profile generated for the Golden State Killer, but then we had to be able to legally search these private databases.

Once Kramer determined we were on solid ground, we began looking for a genealogical partner. We started with Ancestry.com, the largest. "What you have is not compatible with our technology," the privacy officer said. I wondered how many times they'd said the same thing to unknowing investigators who'd just accepted the response. I was ready. "We can generate a profile that is compatible with searching across your proprietary SNP profiles," I said. "I'll call you back," the privacy officer promised. A few weeks passed. Ancestry had an attorney present for the follow-up call with the privacy officer. Kramer is an attorney, and he and Ancestry's lawyer debated the legality of what we were trying to do. A federal grand jury subpoena could override the privacy issues, Kramer said. Not sufficient, Ancestry's attorney said. Maybe the courts would have to decide. "I'm game," Kramer responded.

We didn't need to find out. I discovered another website called GEDmatch where anyone can upload a profile and get search results. It's public domain. The beauty of it was that people from the private sites usually uploaded their profiles to GEDmatch as well, which would allow us to search a population from each proprietary database. GEDmatch was the Tower of Babel for genealogy DNA.

I emailed Kramer with the news on July 31: "I have a dummy Gmail account and have registered with GEDmatch—a public DNA matching site. Attached is a screenshot illustrating how GEDmatch can take raw

DNA data files from the various genealogy companies and upload them to search."

Finally, things were going our way. We still hadn't heard back from the Orange County DA's office, so Kramer arranged a conference call with Irvine PD to inform them about what we were doing and enlist their help. The chief and his detective were excited about our work and promised to cooperate with the investigation.

Investigations often have long lapses between developments, and this was no exception. It wasn't until October that I finally heard back from Orange County in an email from a former deputy district attorney, who had recently been brought out of retirement to work on the Golden State Killer case.

The Orange County District Attorney's Office had come late to the game. It was only after a meeting in the fall of 2016 that the district attorney Tony Rackauckas, at the urging of Sacramento County District Attorney Anne Marie Schubert, agreed to dedicate resources to the joint effort to solve the case, and Detective Erika Hutchcraft was assigned.

I agreed to a meeting date of November 1 with Rackauckas and drove the eight hours to Santa Ana with my presentation ready, excited to show him what we had going. Rackauckas stepped onto the elevator at the same time I did, and we exchanged pleasantries, but when I followed him to the conference room, I got stopped by two assistant DAs who were already in there. The attorneys went into a closed-door meeting with Rackauckas while I waited outside with Detective Hutchcraft. Forty minutes passed, and I was finally invited to join Rackauckas and his team. I took the seat at the conference table directly across from the district attorney. In the center of the table was a telephone. Rackauckas had two experts on a conference line. Okay, I thought, it would have been nice to know about this ahead of time, but . . . I was barely into my presentation when I mentioned Parabon, and the voice of one of the experts boomed over the speaker, interrupting me midsentence. Parabon is unethical, he said, ranting on. He was doing his best to try to shut me down from presenting anything further. I glanced at Rackauckas, who seemed to be smirking. This is a setup, I thought. This is why I was invited here. They want to discredit me. They want me and my investigation to go away. "Sir," I said, speaking to the expert. "Just hear me out. I am not suggesting we are using Parabon for anything. I'm saying they have already generated what I need, and I'm asking to get it." I attempted to continue. "Nah, I'm not keen on this," the expert said. He used a recent case in France to make a point that the way to go was still the STR route. The Golden State Killer had a rare type of STR marker. Cross-referencing that marker with a list of everyone in California's database was the way to narrow the pool of possible suspects, he said. "That's an interesting idea," I said. "Except when I did the calculations based on the size of California's DNA database, I estimated that twenty-four thousand people have that marker." I was even more convinced that the genealogy route was the way to go.

The meeting ended cordially enough. Rackauckas rushed out, and one attorney asked me to stay behind afterward. I thought she was going to ask follow-up questions, but her demeanor quickly turned from serious to furious. "You went behind our back," she seethed. Her hands shook with anger. "You went to Irvine." What? I went behind their backs? She was referring to the meeting that Kramer had arranged, and I had joined by phone. "Hold on," I said. "I didn't go behind anyone's back. Orange County had not responded to our inquiries, so Kramer and I did what any good investigators would do to move the investigation along. We went to Irvine, the source, to get them on board." In all my years on the job, I had never had a DA's office intercede. And to implicate us for doing our jobs? It was preposterous. Attorneys don't dictate investigations. They only get in the way. She didn't want to hear what I had to say. She became even more confrontational. The trip to Oregon to get DNA from the man in the nursing home was a complete waste of time and resources, she said, quaking. "Quite frankly, we need to do more," I said.

Walking away, I felt that I had been baited into a political firestorm and then ambushed. That Kramer had arranged a meeting with Irvine had so agitated Rackauckas he'd decided to exert his authority in the meeting with me. He was not about to allow a Contra Costa forensic investigator and some pompous FBI guy to solve his case.

I went from the debacle at the DA's office to the hotel bar. The following morning, as planned, I made the same presentation to the FBI, Irvine PD, and the Ocean County Sheriff's Office. At lunch I sat next to Irvine detective John Sanders. He was not pleased with the behavior of Rackauckas's team. Irvine had the authority to turn over what we needed, he said. "And we will give it to you."

A few days later, Kramer called me from his car. He was fuming. "You are not going to believe this," he said. "Rackauckas told the Irvine chief not to give us the sample."

I took a moment, trying to digest what Kramer had said.

"That's not his place to prevent an agency from investigating its own case," I said.

"What choice does Irvine have? The DA controls all cases they want to pursue."

"So much for the collaborative spirit of the working group," I said.

I was floored by the interference by Rackauckas. The DNA that the lab had gotten from Janelle Cruz's clothing was abundant. It was the best evidence we had. Now this guy who was supposed to represent truth and justice was shutting us down. I'm sure he thought his evidence was our only option, and I feared it was, too.

Kramer and I were in a scramble to find a new source of DNA, but was there another one out there that qualified? After evaluating all of the homicide cases, we decided that Lyman and Charlene Smith, the Ventura victims, were probably our best shot at getting enough DNA to convert it to a usable profile. We arranged to meet Steve Rhods, an investigator with the Ventura County DA, and Shanin Barrios, the supervisor of their crime lab. I gave them a rundown of what we had. Afterward, they sat there, incredulous. "Why wouldn't we do this?" Rhods asked. "The big questions are: do you have enough, and is it pure enough?" I asked. "Let me see what we have," Barrios said.

Time was of the essence. I worried that if Rackauckas learned about it, he'd try to stop it. Every minute counted as we waited impatiently for the DNA extract from the Ventura crime lab. Kramer assured me that once it was in the possession of the FBI, there was nothing Rackauckas could do. "I'm beginning to appreciate the authority the FBI brings to the table," I said.

Kramer alerted his contact at FBI Ventura to be ready to grab the DNA extract from the Ventura lab as soon as it was available. I had visions of the call coming in, and the agent rappelling out of a helicopter, grabbing the tube of DNA, and being retracted back up and in before flying off. It wasn't quite so dramatic. In mid-November, I received notice from the Ventura crime lab that they had been able to extract a wealth of DNA from the Smith evidence. The source was a pristine sample that had been stored in a freezer since the 1980 homicide. Claus Speth, Ventura's medical examiner at the time, had the unusual practice of producing duplicate rape kits, one to be used for the investigation and another for backup. Just in case.

Within days of the FBI agent picking up the sample from Ventura's lab, we were working with the genetic testing company FamilyTreeDNA to develop the new SNP profile from Charlene Smith's sexual assault swabs. The partnership was facilitated by Kramer and FamilyTreeDNA's founder Bennett Greenspan, who had gone out on a limb for us by allowing a computer comparison between our new profile with his company's 2 million customers. Kramer set up a FamilyTreeDNA account using a false identity, which enabled us to log in and see a ranked list of who in the company's database shared DNA with our killer and how much. I then took the profile and uploaded it into an undercover account in GED-match using log-in credentials provided by the FBI, which extended the scope of our search ability to 2.5 million profiles.

I met with Anne Marie Schubert and her staff at the Sacramento County DA's office to brief them about what Kramer and I were up to. She gave the nod for Lieutenant Kirk Campbell and Investigative Assistant Monica Czajkowski to assist with the genealogy work. Kramer brought in Melissa Parisot, an analyst from his office.

That same month, November 2017, Barbara Rae Venter emailed me. It had been nine months since our phone call. Venter said she was sorry for her silence, but she'd been dealing with a health issue. "Do you still need help on that case?" she asked. "Yes!" I said.

With Barbara's guidance, we took on the huge task of trying to find the Golden State Killer with genealogy. I was counting down to my retirement in four short months. Sherrie and I were planning a fresh start. Our house in Vacaville was on the market, and we were taking the kids, who were twelve and ten, to Colorado to live. Was I going to have to leave when we were so close to maybe solving the case? The sense of urgency I felt drove me even harder. I was working the case in my office by day and at home at night while everyone was sleeping. Old habits die hard.

Once we received the SNP profile from Charlene Smith's sexual assault kit, our team of six spent hundreds of hours building family trees for each of the potential matches. Barbara taught us a technique that genealogists had been using for years to find the birth families of adoptees. The triangulation technique, which had never been used to solve a homicide, involved utilizing distant relatives and triangulation back to a common ancestor. Evaluating family trees allowed us to narrow our focus. We filled out the branches using traditional genealogical research tools. We scoured birth records, newspaper clippings, and Facebook and other social media. The trees grew to be huge. At one point we were researching sixty possible distant relatives and tracing their family trees all the way back to the 1700s. The closest we came was third cousins, more than a dozen, which wouldn't bring us close enough for a manageable search. We were all getting frustrated. In February 2018, Barbara emailed Kramer and me. "We may have just caught a break." She had used her personal account on MyHeritage .com and found a second cousin to the Golden State Killer. We were one generation closer and a giant step further in the search.

Using the second cousin's name, we filled out branches. Through a process of elimination, we whittled down our list of possibilities to a small group of men who were roughly the right age and living in California during the time of the attacks. From there, we narrowed the search even further using physical descriptions from victims. Our suspect would be somewhere between sixty and seventy-five years old. A white male, of medium height, with a medium build, ice-blue eyes and a size 9 shoe (based on shoe prints left at some of the crime scenes). The most promising lead was a guy from Colorado. We were able to get his sister to submit a DNA sample. She wasn't the Golden State Killer's sister. The suspect was eliminated.

The next closest match was a man named Joseph James DeAngelo. The name had never been associated with the case. I began marching down on him on March 15. DeAngelo had a background in law enforcement. In his twenties and thirties, he'd worked stints at Exeter, Roseville, and Auburn PDs. Now wouldn't that be something, I thought, if our killer was a cop. He fell within the age range, and he lived in Citrus Heights in Sacramento County. He was married to a divorce attorney, but they hadn't lived at the same address for ten years. He had three daughters. Monica Czajkowski found a 1970 newspaper clipping announcing his engagement to a woman named Bonnie, but there was no record of a marriage.

After one of EAR's sexual assaults, he'd broken down, crying, "I hate you, Bonnie. I hate you, Bonnie."

DeAngelo became more interesting as I dug into him. His address history matched with the East Area Rapist's movements in the 1970s. Before buying his house in Citrus Heights, he was living in Rancho Cordova. In the early 1970s, when the Visalia Ransacker was breaking into and burglarizing houses in the San Joaquin Valley, he was living there. It had been long thought that the East Area Rapist began in his criminal career as the notorious Visalia burglar.

MY LAST OFFICIAL DAY WITH THE DA'S OFFICE was March 28, less than two weeks away. I need to start talking to people, I thought. I started by contacting the Auburn PD to ask for personnel records. That led me to former police chief Nick Willick, who had fired DeAngelo from the force in 1979 after he was caught shoplifting dog repellent and a hammer at a Sacramento drug store that July. Two months after his firing, the Golden State Killer was down in Goleta starting the killing phase of his series. I told Willick I was investigating a case that might involve a former cop in his department. Joseph DeAngelo. "He was a shitty cop," Willick said. What did he look like physically back then? I asked. "Five-ten, blond hair, athletic," he said. Just like EAR. Funny thing, Willick said, "I went to his house once, and his living arrangement was strange. He had his room, and she had her own, and if they wanted to get together, they had a room for that." What about his termination? I asked. "He got popped for shoplifting," Willick said. "We searched his house. There was so much stolen property in there you wouldn't believe it." After he was fired, Willick got word that DeAngelo had threatened he would kill him. The same vindictive nature as GSK, I thought. Then the weirdest thing happened, the former chief said. "My daughter comes to me one night and says, 'Dad, there is a man outside my bedroom window with a flashlight.'" Willick rushed outside and found fresh shoe impressions around the entire perimeter of his house. "I know that was DeAngelo," he said. I could feel the goose bumps rise on my arms. That was EAR at work, I thought.

I called Kramer next to brief him. We agreed we had to get DeAngelo's DNA.

My retirement was a day away.

I left Martinez and headed to Citrus Heights. I had to at least see where he lived before heading to Colorado with Sherrie to buy a house.

26

Operation Golden State Killer

The surveillance of Joseph DeAngelo began in mid-April 2018. Tactical undercover teams from the FBI and the Sacramento County Sheriff's Office watched the house on Canyon Oak Drive around the clock. Driving borrowed used cars so as not to stand out, they sat inconspicuously at strategic locations around the perimeter of the Citrus Heights neighborhood. An FBI plane made regular passes overhead. DeAngelo lived with his oldest daughter and teenage granddaughter. All eyes were on him as he went about his daily routine of yard work and tinkering with his Volvo. Ken Clark from the Sacramento DA's office was in charge of the surveillance operation. My retirement became official at the end of March, so I was traveling back and forth and was house hunting in Colorado when Ken called to say the secret op to collect DeAngelo's DNA had begun. On Wednesday, April 18, a team of investigators followed the suspect to a Hobby Lobby store in town, and while he was inside shopping, they'd swabbed his car handle.

Over the next two days, as we waited for the lab results, my phone buzzed constantly with calls from Ken, Kramer, and Kirk Campbell, the lead investigator for the Sacramento County DA's office, keeping me appraised of the planning. On Friday, April 20, Sherrie and I had just put in an offer on a house—one with a fully equipped sewing room. We were having dinner at PF Chang's when I saw Kirk Campbell's name on my phone. I walked outside to take his call. There were no greetings, just the sound of his breathless voice. "You cannot tell a soul!" he said. "I'm not sure what this means, but the lab seems really excited." He read me the DNA report. It's him, I said.

Oh my God, it's him.

We had a genetic map with a direct route to the door of the seventy-two-year-old former cop. Evil finally had a name. The vicious serial rapist and killer was a father and grandfather with a fishing boat in the driveway and a Volvo in the garage; a "regular guy" who passed the time building model airplanes; a proud homeowner who liked his grass nice and short. When he was finished mowing, he got on his hands and knees to clip all around the decorative rocks he had scattered around. I'd passed his neighborhood countless times during the twenty-four years I worked this case. The whole time I'd been looking for him, he was hiding in plain sight.

It was dusk in Colorado, and a light snow had begun to fall. I looked up at the stars and breathed in the moment. I'd been on this journey for twenty-four years. Twenty-four years of the highest highs and desperately low lows. I'd chased the East Area Rapist through my first marriage and hunted the Golden State Killer during my second. The case had come before everything, and just a few weeks into retirement, I'd started to recognize the toll it had taken. Sherrie and I had been in marriage counseling for a few months, but now she refused to continue until I got help for myself. I'd continued to drink bourbon, often to excess. I was hoping that my retirement and the move to Colorado might give me some peace of mind. But I couldn't imagine that anything would feel like this moment, standing under the stars and staring out at the mountain range, knowing that the Golden State Killer was about to get his due, and the people whose lives he'd destroyed might finally get some rest.

I walked back into the restaurant, where Sherrie was excited to read me the message in her fortune cookie: *You will find your dream home.* "Open yours!" she said. I stared at her without speaking. A few seconds passed. "What did Kirk want? . . . Did the DNA come back already?" she asked. I continued to stare at her. "No!" she said. I nodded once. "It's him?" she asked. I nodded again, knowing that if I began to speak neither of us would be able to stay calm. We paid the bill, and Sherrie pushed me out of the restaurant. "Tell me. Tell me. Tell me." Driving back to the hotel, she expressed how relieved she was that this was over. She'd always worried that one day he'd come looking for the person who'd been pursuing him for so long. Neither of us slept well that night. We flew back on Saturday after our offer on the house was accepted, and we signed all of the papers. I was told to report to the Sacramento County Sheriff's Office on Monday.

Out of an abundance of caution, Sacramento DA Anne Marie Schubert had ordered that a second sample be collected. Surveillance teams watched and waited for an opportunity to carry out the order. On Monday evening, DeAngelo put his garbage out for the next day's collection. After dark, agents grabbed the bags of trash from the receptacle and pulled out everything that could have his DNA—Dr Pepper cans, water bottles, anything he might have eaten from. Eleven items were collected, and at the last second, a twelfth was grabbed. A piece of tissue that had been an afterthought. A rush was put on the order to the lab. While we waited for the results, Ken Clark and I wrote the forty-four-page arrest warrant for a judge's signature and the tactical team planned their strike. It was a super-secret operation. Only Ventura, the agency that had provided the evidence that led to DeAngelo, was notified.

The secondary DNA results came back on Tuesday, April 24. DNA from the tissue was a perfect match. The Black Bag Operation went into action. The plan was to wait until DeAngelo left his house and then follow him. When he got to a public place, the agents would swarm him and pull him into an unmarked van. DeAngelo's habit was to straighten up the house in the early evening, and he hadn't left to go anywhere on Wednesday. The consensus of the team was that it was too risky to wait another day. The sun was just starting to set when DeAngelo finally made an appearance in his side yard, a place with no gate, no fence, and no door to escape back into the house. A group of us at Sacramento Homicide listened to the new plan play out on a secure police radio. "Green light," the op commander said. "Go!" The team swooped in. We were on the edge of our seats. DeAngelo was a dangerous serial killer. We knew he'd collected an arsenal of guns over the years. He could shoot a cop. Take his family hostage. Kill himself. Everything went quiet. Moments passed. I felt a drop of sweat trickle down my back.

The op commander finally spoke. "Suspect in custody."

Sacramento Homicide erupted. Hooting, hollering, and high fives all around.

DeAngelo, dressed in black shorts and a white T-shirt, his wrists cuffed behind him, was led out of his house and into the police van. "I have a roast in the oven," he said in a high-pitched squeaky voice. "Cooking."

THAT EVENING, ALL OF THE AGENCIES with cases were notified that the killer was in custody. DeAngelo was brought to Sacramento Sheriff's Homicide. A crowd of us watched as he was escorted by three armed officers to the interrogation room. Some took pictures. The monster who had savaged so many lives was old and overweight. Except for his evil scowl, he looked like your average Joe. I'd always thought he would. He was cuffed to the table in the interrogation room, a small room with gray walls and a two-way mirror. I couldn't take my eyes off of him. For the next hour, he never moved. Not even a twitch. "This is what he did when he was attacking," I said to Kramer as we watched. I thought about all of the times victims of the East Area Rapist recalled him standing silently beside their beds—so still that they didn't know he was there.

For the next several hours, interrogators took their turn with him. He had nothing to say. He just stared at the wall. The only time he turned was when a female detective walked in to ask if he wanted something to drink. A bottle of water? Perhaps a Dr Pepper? Watching his reaction through the glass, I felt a chill rise up my spine. He turned toward her, an evil scowl on his face, slowly looked her up and down, then turned back to the wall.

After hours of attempts to get him to say anything, DeAngelo was left alone when it became clear that he wasn't going to speak. I left my headphones on and watched as he began muttering to himself. I couldn't make out most of what he was saying, but what I did hear was clear. "I should have been stronger," he said, in the low guttural whisper so many of his victims had described. "He made me do it."

27

Is It Him?

After three hours of sleep, I returned to Sacramento to attend a press conference called by Anne Marie Schubert. But first, a few of us were invited to take a walk through DeAngelo's house. It was unremarkable: three bedrooms, a living room with a TV, and a kitchen with counters piled high with junk food. Open boxes of chocolates, crackers, chips, soda cans. I wondered where he'd hidden the trinkets he'd taken from the crime scenes. I imagined him back in the '70s leaving his wife and daughters in the middle of the night to search for prey. What had they thought? What had he told them? DeAngelo's bedroom was the last stop. As soon as I stepped inside, my eyes locked on a computer monitor. It sat on a desk inside the bedroom door, an open jar of peanut butter with a spoon next to it. I walked closer. The flat screen monitor was covered with a towel. *Oh my God,* I thought. *That's what he did as EAR.* Just before he raped a woman, he put a towel over the TV screen or the lamp to get that soft glow. The voices of the victims flooded back. *He blindfolded me and then put a towel over the light before he raped me. . . . He tore off my blouse and put it over the lamp, then asked me if I'd fucked that night. . . . He turned me on my stomach and tied my hands and feet; then he went to the bathroom and got a towel to put over the light.* I turned to Kramer, who was standing behind me. "This is him reliving his attacks."

THE SACRAMENTO DA'S OFFICE WAS SWARMING with media from all over the United States and overseas. Contingents from each of the jurisdictions were arriving just as I pulled up. Orange County's contingent included District Attorney Tony Rackauckas and the attorney who'd read me the riot act at our meeting. Rackauckas swept by me without so much as a hello. His associate stiffened when I attempted to greet her. It was clear to me, watching them posture over who would speak first, that the poignant end of a forty-year tragedy was going to turn political.

True to form, Rackauckas walked to the podium with an attitude of entitlement. Watching him, I imagined the buttons on his starched white shirt straining against his puffed-up chest as he boasted about Orange County this and Orange County that. "Finally, after all these years, the haunting question of who committed these terrible crimes has been put to rest," he said, as the cameras clicked and whirred. *And no thanks to you,* I thought.

I turned to Kramer, who looked at me knowingly. I'd had enough of the arrogance of politics. "I have to go," I said. "I have victims I need to call." He nodded.

As if on cue, my cell phone rang. The name on the screen was one I hadn't seen in years. I'd given her my number, as I did all of the victims in the case. I tucked myself behind my car and answered.

"Mary?"

Mary was one of DeAngelo's last rape victims and one of the youngest.

She was headed into the eighth grade in that summer of 1979 when the creep broke into her home at 4 A.M. and raped her in the pretty pink bedroom with unicorns painted on the walls. The girl who believed her father died three years later from a broken heart because he hadn't been able to help her.

Now she was calling, desperately wanting to hear that what she was seeing on TV was true.

"Mary, is that you?" I asked.

She spoke in a trembling voice. "Is it really him?"

"Mary, I'm one hundred percent confident," I said. "And he is never going to see the light of day again."

Nearly forty years of heartache and fear spilled out all at once. All of the memories had come flooding back. "I'm sorry," Mary finally said, speaking through her sobs. "I'm sorry! I'm sorry! I'm sorry! I'm not upset. I'm just so happy."

28

A Sense of Purpose

I t was the end of May before I sat with myself to reflect on the Golden State Killer case. The weeks after the press conference were packed with media requests and calls from agents and television producers asking if I'd be interested in talking about the case. I was getting more than a hundred calls a day from journalists all over the world. That spring afternoon I was home at the new house in Colorado for the first time in two weeks. Sherrie and the kids were out, and it was quiet. I poured myself a bourbon and pulled up a photo of DeAngelo that I'd taken on the night he was arrested. He's sitting in the interrogation room, hunched over and alone, looking dejected. "Got you," I said out loud.

The case had brought me a kind of celebrity. For two years following the arrest, I was on the road for all but a few days assisting agencies across the country with cold cases. Sherrie had been left alone to settle herself and the kids into our new life, while I pursued cases for a crime show on TV. That was how I was introduced to the Carla Walker case in Fort Worth, Texas. Meeting Carla's brother, Jim, in December 2019 had an emotional effect on me that I hadn't expected. Hearing him recount how, as a boy, he'd returned time after time to the lonely culvert where Carla's body had been found, something inside of me broke.

Jim was a seventh grader with freckles and tousled strawberry blond hair when Carla was killed. He was with his parents when, three days after Carla didn't come home, sheriff's officers came to the Walkers' front door to give his mom and dad the news that her body had been found. He had gone with his parents to the hospital morgue to identify Carla's body and stood by helplessly when they collapsed with grief. More than four decades later, his mother's scream still rang in his ears.

"It was that . . . death scream," he told me, choking back tears.

I clenched my teeth, trying to keep my composure. "It's such a hard way—to have to identify a loved one like that," I said, fumbling for words, as if any words were appropriate at that moment.

"As a twelve-year-old kid, that's what angered me. I saw the devastation—on the family and our community," Jim said. "Fear escalated. There's a killer out there among us."

"You saw where she was found?" I asked.

Jim said when he was old enough to drive, he took a ride out to the culvert where Carla's body had been dumped. "I wanted to see it," he said haltingly. "I wanted to know . . . if my sister was still alive when she went into that . . . place . . . what she saw, what she smelled, how it felt. I sat out there for six hours one night. It was cold. I just wanted to experience that." He said it was the first of many nights he spent there, waiting and hoping that Carla's killer would return to the scene of the crime, as killers sometimes do.

My words caught in my throat. I was looking at a tormented man who, as a boy the age of my youngest son, had been sentenced to a life tied to that cow culvert. How can that be justified? How could I not do whatever it took to help quiet his troubled mind and bring him the peace that only justice might? How could I not make Carla's case a priority over everything else in my life when there was a chance I could help to ease his suffering?

When a cold case is reevaluated, the people closest to the victim are assessed. That means meeting with their relatives and friends. When so many years have passed, there are bound to be people in that circle who have passed away, which Carla's parents had. But her siblings were still living—Jim and older sister, Cindy—as was Carla's boyfriend, Rodney, who had been with her at the time of her abduction and still lived under a cloud of suspicion forty-five years later. When it happened, Rodney told police that he and Carla had been parked at the local bowling alley after the prom when a man with a gun pulled open the passenger-side door, struck him in the head with the butt of a gun, and dragged Carla out of the car. The last thing he heard was Carla say, "Go get my dad!" When he regained consciousness, Carla was gone.

I visited Rodney during my time in Fort Worth, where he still lives. He's in his early sixties now and divorced. When we met, he was in the process of getting over a hurtful breakup with a longtime girlfriend, and I sensed an underlying sadness. Other than that, life seemed to have treated Rodney pretty well. He'd had a successful white-collar career and was still a good-looking guy in top physical shape. He told me he did a hundred push-ups a day. Rodney came off as a genuinely likeable guy. Here I was, coming in to drudge up the worst night of his life, to ask him pointed questions, yet he was gracious and welcoming. It wouldn't take long for me to see that 1974 was as close as the tears waiting to spill down his cheeks.

"She was stolen," he said, his obliging smile suddenly quivering. He bit his lip and looked off into the distance, trying to compose himself. "I was part of what happened," he said, his words fraught with remorse. Watching him try to hold it together, I thought, *If he has nothing to do with Carla's murder, how unjust it is that he has had to live under a cloud of suspicion for his entire adult life.* I was pretty sure the residual sorrow and guilt over losing Carla, and the way he lost her, had tainted many moments over the decades.

"You were a victim," I said, assuming that his story about what happened that night was true.

"We are all victims," he said looking away, fighting for composure. "There are so many victims."

It was such a poignant trip. The collateral damage of Carla's murder was vast and unrelenting. From her parents to her siblings to her boyfriend and the entire Fort Worth community, so many had suffered. So many were trapped in that sad past, yet the person who had taken so much had just walked away.

I was flooded by feelings leaving Fort Worth. Grief over the tragic loss of a young girl's life. Horror over what she'd experienced during her last moments. Desperation to solve her case so I wouldn't let her family down. Sitting behind the steering wheel of my car, I sobbed. I'd always been able to tuck my feelings away after each case. When they did escape, it was usually in the form of a middle-of-the-night panic attack. The last one had been so severe I fainted on the bedroom floor. Now my emotions spilled over. I buried my face in my hands. I wondered if I would ever stop crying. I was scared and confused.

After Fort Worth, and my experience at Jumbo's Clown Room when I returned to California to film the TV series, I went home to Colorado to spend the holidays with Sherrie and the kids. In the evenings, while she sewed, I continued to work on Carla's case. Forensic testing had been underway as we were filming. During my consultations with Fort Worth investigators, I'd suggested we send Carla's clothing to the lab for testing. The DNA analyst had given us good news. She'd gotten a semen sample off of Carla's bra strap. It was a perfect sample for retrieving DNA, and we were certain we would soon have a match we could cross-reference with genealogy. But heartbreak soon followed. The genealogy lab sent a cursory email saying they'd consumed the entire sample and couldn't get results. We were all crushed. I went back to the beginning. The DNA analyst had found a second source of DNA, although it was a fraction of the first, degraded and not nearly as promising. In May 2020, I consulted with my friend David Mittelman, who in 2018 founded a new technology company, Othram, with a state-of-the-art forensic DNA sequencing laboratory. "They used the wrong technology," he said when I explained what had happened with the first lab. "We use genome sequencing." Could our less-than-pristine sample possibly be converted in a way that would be compatible with searching proprietary genealogy databases? I asked. "We've got to try," I said. Yes, he agreed, we had to try. At least there was hope, but I'd been down this road so many times before. Now all I could do was wait on the sidelines while the Fort Worth investigators worked with Othram on the next steps.

ONE NIGHT SOON AFTER I RETURNED from the California trip, Sherrie and I were in the kitchen alone when she turned around from the kitchen sink and looked at me with tears in her eyes. "You need to see someone," she said. That night I learned that Sherrie had come to see me as someone who could leave her and the kids and be perfectly happy living with my cases. She thought the Golden State Killer case would be the end of it, but now I was obsessed with solving the case in Texas. It was all I talked about. All I thought about.

"Do you even care about us?" she asked. If only I could have expressed my desire to reconnect with Sherrie and the kids. But I couldn't find the words. I wanted my marriage to work. I loved Sherrie. I loved my children. "I understand why you think that," I said, crying. "But I know how I feel. I'll try to be better."

Sherrie found a therapist who specialized in treating PTSD, and I made an appointment. While the therapist listened, I outlined my career and described some of the cases I'd worked. "Every time you are confronted with something like that, you get a bleeding injury," she explained. "It's a cut that never heals. You've never addressed it, and now you're bleeding out." The emotional trauma of my cases had built and built over the years, and my solution was to lock my feelings in individual boxes in my head. Now the boxes were full and seeping sadness. Bourbon was a Band-Aid. If I didn't deal with the sorrow, eventually the Band-Aids wouldn't stick.

I left the therapist's office determined to face my feelings. I *would* try to be a better husband and father. I just wasn't sure that I could ever be enough. For Sherrie. For anyone. I struggled with the thought that my inability to give love the way most people need it might mean I would have to navigate my life alone. I felt all of the emotions I thought I was supposed to feel, felt them deeply, but what good was it if it wasn't enough? What I know without any uncertainty is that I can solve cases that others can't, and my commitment to victims is genuine and real. My work is not just something I do. It is my mission, I believe, my reason for being. My sense of purpose is rooted in my engagement with cases. I feel worthy when I am helping others. There were so many Jims—good people whose lives had been tragically put on hold because they didn't have the answers they needed to finish the grieving process and move forward. I had the will to help them get those answers. Was that enough? I don't know.

IN THE SUMMER OF 2020, the process of genetic genealogy in the Carla Walker case began. The second sample had done its job and produced a usable profile. Investigators couldn't afford any leaks, so the progress reports as the small team worked through GEDmatch and proprietary sites was kept confidential. In August, during the same week that the Golden State

Killer was sentenced to the rest of his life in prison, Jeff Bennett, one of the investigators on the Walker team called me. "Paul," he said, "I so want to tell you what's going on, but I just can't." He didn't have to when he explained why he was calling. Bennett needed an expert opinion on the legalities of obtaining a surreptitious DNA sample, the way we had done with DeAngelo's car and garbage. The question told me that with genealogy they'd narrowed their search to someone they needed to test.

THE TEXT LANDED ON MY PHONE at 5:54 on the morning of September 22, 2020. "Good morning, Paul. This is Jim Walker in Fort Worth, Texas. When you have a chance, if you could give me a call. I would like to share some exciting news with you, my friend. God bless you, Paul, and I look forward to talking to you soon!" It had been nine months since I'd been invited into the Carla Walker case. Now the forty-five-year-old cold case was solved.

Carla's killer was a seventy-seven-year-old man named Glen McCurley. He was still living in Fort Worth. The team had found distant relatives and used public records to reconstruct family trees, then narrowed the search to investigative leads. McCurley had been one of several suspects at the time of the murder, but the evidence had never been there. He would later be sentenced to life in prison after pleading guilty to kidnapping, rape, and murder shortly after his trial began.

I called Jim as soon as I received his message.

Jim is devoutly religious. "God bless you, Paul. This case would never have been solved without your involvement. I thank you from the bottom of my heart."

After forty-five years of not knowing, Jim Walker finally had an answer. It wouldn't bring Carla back, but it would give her brother a sense of resolution that he'd been searching for since he was twelve years old and sitting in the culvert where her body lay. I had helped a good man find some peace, and I had kept my promise to Carla by doing all that I could to help identify her killer.

Hanging up the phone, I sat back in my home office chair wondering how I would juggle the future. I had so many requests for help from families and law enforcement around the country that I wasn't even able to respond to them all, but we were still struggling at home, and I'd resolved to enjoy life and devote more time to family. With the kids heading into their teenage years, Sherrie decided to resume her career. She took a part-time job as a serologist at a local police crime lab. Our relationship had begun with our common interest in science and homicide and now Sherrie came home from work talking about her cases. Like those early days, we were reconnecting with long conversations about work. Hers and mine. Those long talks had gotten us through tough times before. But, as Sherrie said, there was more to living than work and I still needed to focus more on family and our home life. I promised I'd try. I'd practice guitar and learn woodworking. I'd take my son mountain biking with me. When I was home, I would work on just "being." Maybe I could even get used to the board games Sherrie and the kids liked to play.

As I stood up to go tell Sherrie about my conversation with Jim Walker, my eye caught the black binder on the shelf next to my desk. I had kept it in sight at my office in the county and brought it with me when I retired. It was the cold case of Cosette Ellison, a fifteen-year-old girl with a crooked little smile who'd been abducted and killed on March 3, 1970, on her way home from school in Moraga. Her broken body was found ten months later in a creek a few miles away. The monster who raped her and took her life was likely still out there somewhere, and all I had to go on was a composite sketch of a man with a cap and an easy smile. The case haunted me.

I pulled the binder off the shelf and opened it.

Acknowledgments

First and foremost, thank you to my wife, Sherrie, for putting up with me through all of those times I should have been there and wasn't. Like any obsession, my career has consumed me, often to the detriment of our family. To my four kids, you bring infinite joy to my life, though I know that physical and emotional distance has not always made it easy for you to see me as "Dad."

Thanks to my parents for your unconditional support. My professional admiration for my friend John Conaty is only exceeded by my gratitude for our friendship. Professionally so many people have contributed to my career. A special shout-out to my East Area Rapist Task Force partners: Anne Marie Schubert, whose friendship, vision, and unwavering support will always be appreciated; Ken Clark and Larry Pool, buddies who I so enjoyed talking shop with and so respect for their contributions to the investigation; and Kirk Campbell, Monica Czajkowski, and Melissa Parisot, whose diligent attention to detail and believing in the genealogy tool were critical to our success. In particular, I would not be writing this book, nor would Joseph DeAngelo have been caught, without the partnership with my friend Steve Kramer. And thanks to Barbara Rae Venter, who played a vital role by providing the expertise and guidance that allowed the genealogy team to identify DeAngelo as the Golden State Killer.

Michelle McNamara, the brief time we spent together inspired me. I wish it could have been longer.

Robin Gaby Fisher, let's keep this partnership going. Your ability to turn my thoughts into such eloquent prose is absolutely amazing.

Meredith Miller, my agent at UTA, I am so grateful for your support and commitment to my story. Thank you for finding the right home for it.

Ryan Doherty and Cecily van Buren-Freedman of Celadon Books, your keen interest and guidance helped take this story to the next level. Thank you for your belief in the project and your dedication to making it the best it could be.

Lastly, so many victims, so much pain—if I have played even a minor role in helping to bring resolution, it has all been worth it.

About the Authors

In 2018, Paul Holes retired as a cold case investigator after spending more than twenty-seven years working in Contra Costa County, in San Francisco's Bay Area. Paul specialized in cold case and serial predator crimes, lending his expertise to notable cases, including the murder of Laci Peterson and the kidnapping of Jaycee Dugard. Most prominently, Paul's career culminated with his identification of the Golden State Killer, Joseph DeAngelo, the most notorious and cunning serial predator in U.S. history.

Since the arrest of DeAngelo, Holes has been very involved on the media side, continuing to assist law enforcement and victims' families with their unsolved cases through the television shows *The DNA of Murder with Paul Holes* and *America's Most Wanted* and the podcast *Jensen & Holes: The Murder Squad*.

Robin Gaby Fisher is a *New York Times* bestselling author. She shares a Pulitzer Prize in news reporting and has been a finalist twice for the Pulitzer Prize in feature writing.

CELADON
BOOKS

Founded in 2017, Celadon Books, a division of
Macmillan Publishers, publishes a highly curated list
of twenty to twenty-five new titles a year. The list of
both fiction and nonfiction is eclectic and focuses
on publishing commercial and literary books and
discovering and nurturing talent.